Woolf
Studies
Annual

Volume 13, 2007

PACE UNIVERSITY PRESS • NEW YORK

Copyright © 2007 by
Pace University Press
41 Park Row, Rm. 1510
New York, NY 10038

All rights reserved
Printed in the United States of America

ISSN 1080-9317
ISBN 0-944473-80-6 (pbk: alk.ppr.)

Member

Council of Editors of Learned Journals

Paper used in this publication meets the minimum requirements
of American National Standard for Information
Sciences–Permanence of Paper for Printed Library Materials,
ANSI Z39.48–1984

Editor

Mark Hussey   *Pace University*

Editorial Board

Tuzyline Jita Allan	*Baruch College, CUNY*
Eileen Barrett	*California State University, Hayward*
Kathryn N. Benzel	*University of Nebraska-Kearney*
Pamela L. Caughie	*Loyola University Chicago*
Wayne K. Chapman	*Clemson University*
Patricia Cramer	*University of Connecticut, Stamford*
Beth Rigel Daugherty	*Otterbein College*
Anne Fernald *(Book Review Editor)*	*Fordham University*
Sally Greene	*Independent Scholar*
Leslie Kathleen Hankins	*Cornell College*
Karen Kaivola	*Stetson University*
Jane Lilienfeld	*Lincoln University*
Toni A. H. McNaron	*University of Minnesota*
Patricia Moran	*University of California, Davis*
Vara Neverow	*Southern Connecticut State University*
Annette Oxindine	*Wright State University*
Beth Carole Rosenberg	*University of Nevada-Las Vegas*
Bonnie Kime Scott	*San Diego State University*

Consulting Editors

Nancy Topping Bazin	*Old Dominion University*
Morris Beja	*Ohio State University*
Louise DeSalvo	*Hunter College, CUNY*
Jane Marcus	*Distinguished Professor CCNY and CUNY Graduate Center*
Brenda R. Silver	*Dartmouth College*
Susan Squier	*Pennsylvania State University*
Peter Stansky	*Stanford University*
J. J. Wilson	*Sonoma State University*
Alex Zwerdling	*University of California, Berkeley*

Many thanks to readers for volume 13: Judith Allen (U of Pennsylvania), Jessica Berman (U of Maryland Baltimore County), Kristin Czarnecki (U of Louisville), Emily Dalgarno (Boston U), Penny Farfan (U of Calgary), Christine Froula (Northwestern U), Diane Gillespie (Washington S U, Emerita), Evelyn Haller (Doane C), Molly Hite (Cornell U), Georgia Johnston (St Louis U), Michael Lackey (Wellesley C), Barbara Lounsberry (U of N Iowa), Krista Ratcliffe (Marquette U), Diana Royer (Miami U), Janet Winston (Humboldt S U).

Woolf Studies Annual is indexed in the *American Humanities Index*, *ABELL* and the *MLA Bibliography*.

The Society of Authors has been appointed to act for the Virginia Woolf Estate. Inquiries concerning permissions should be addressed to:

Mr. Jeremy Crow
The Society of Authors
84 Drayton Gardens
London SW10 9SB

Phone: 020 7373 6642
Fax: 020 7373 5768

Email:
info@societyofauthors.org

URL:
www.societyofauthors.org

Contents

Woolf Studies Annual

Volume 13, 2007

	x	Abbreviations
Emily Hinnov	1	"Each is part of the whole: we act different parts but are the same": From Fragment to Choran Community in the Late Work of Virginia Woolf
Renée Dickinson	25	Exposure and Development: Re-Imagining Narrative and Nation in the Interludes of *The Waves*
Jane Goldman	49	"Ce chien est à moi": Virginia Woolf and the Signifying Dog
Erica Delsandro	87	"'Myself'—it was impossible": Queering History in *Between the Acts*
Jennie-Rebecca Falcetta	111	Geometries of Time and Space: The Cubist London of *Mrs. Dalloway*
Eve Sorum	137	Taking Note: Text and Context in Virginia Woolf's "Mr. Bennet and Mrs. Brown"
David Sherman	159	A Plot Unraveling Into Ethics: Woolf, Levinas, and "Time Passes"
Beth Rigel Daugherty	181	"Letters from Readers": Corrections

GUIDE

183 Guide to Library Special Collections

REVIEWS

Jane Garrity	201	*Virginia Woolf and the Bloomsbury Avant-Garde: War, Civilization, Modernity* by Christine Froula
Emily Dalgarno	205	*Virginia Woolf's Novels and the Literary Past* by Jane De Gay
Mark Hussey	208	*"My Madness Saved Me": The Madness and Marriage of Virginia Woolf* by Thomas Szasz; *Our Culture, What's Left of It: The Mandarins and the Masses* by Theodore Dalrymple
Vara Neverow	213	*British Modernism and Censorship* by Celia Marshik
Beth Carole Rosenberg	220	*Virginia Woolf: Feminism and the Reader* by Anne E. Fernald
Jay Dickson	225	*Virginia Woolf's Nose: Essays on Biography* by Hermione Lee; *Bombay to Bloomsbury: A Biography of the Strachey Family* by Barbara Caine
Nick Smart	229	*Radio Modernism: Literature, Ethics and the BBC* by Todd Avery
Jane De Gay	234	*Women's Vision in Western Literature: The Empathic Community* by Laurence Porter
Beth Rigel Daugherty	238	*Recovering Your Story: Proust, Joyce, Woolf, Faulkner, Morrison* by Arnold Weinstein
June Elizabeth Dunn	244	*To the Boathouse: A Memoir* by Mary Ann Caws; *Letters to Virginia Woolf* by Lisa Williams

Notes on Contributors 250

Policy 252

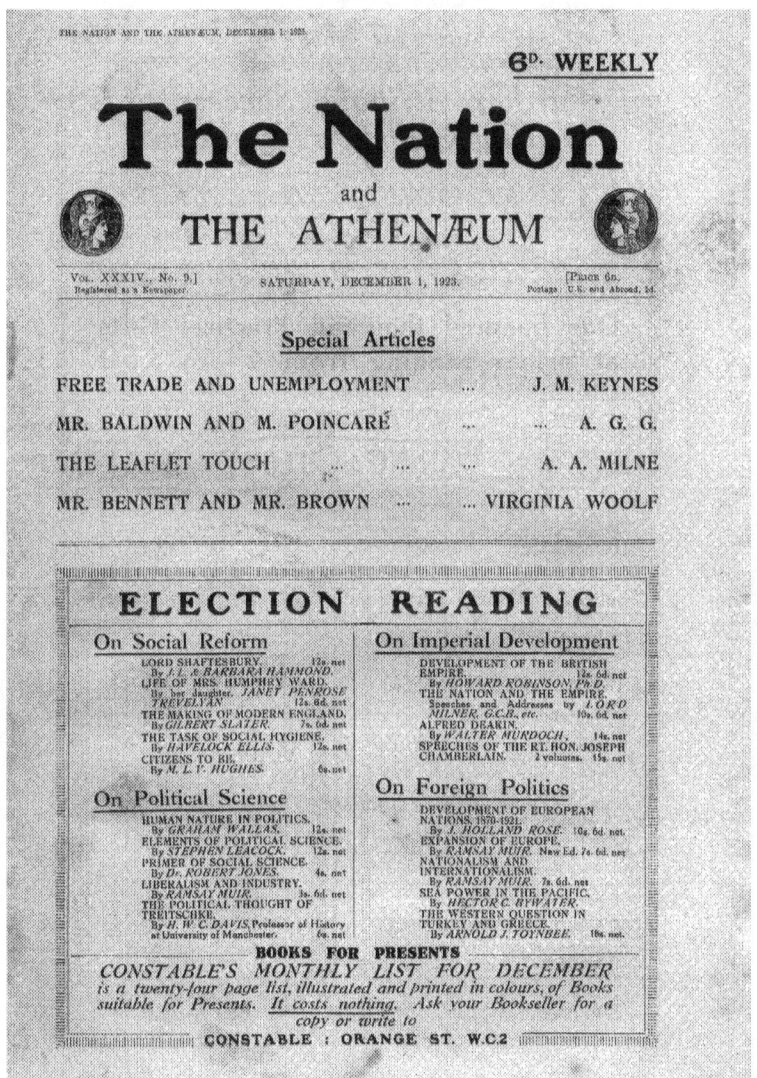

The Nation and The Athenaeum. Dec. 1, 1923 containing Woolf's "Mr. Bennett and Mrs. Brown." The typo is not repeated inside.

Abbreviations

AHH	*A Haunted House*
AROO	*A Room of One's Own*
BP	*Books and Portraits*
BTA	*Between the Acts*
CDB	*The Captain's Death Bed and Other Essays*
CE	*Collected Essays (4 vols.)*
CR1	*The Common Reader*
CR2	*The Common Reader, Second Series*
CSF	*The Complete Shorter Fiction*
D	*The Diary of Virginia Woolf (5 vols.)*
DM	*The Death of the Moth and Other Essays*
E	*The Essays of Virginia Woolf (6 Vols.)*
F	*Flush*
FR	*Freshwater*
GR	*Granite & Rainbow: Essays*
JR	*Jacob's Room*
L	*The Letters of Virginia Woolf (6 Vols.)*
M	*The Moment and Other Essays*
MEL	*Melymbrosia*
MOB	*Moments of Being*
MT	*Monday or Tuesday*
MD	*Mrs. Dalloway*
ND	*Night and Day*
O	*Orlando*
PA	*A Passionate Apprentice*
RF	*Roger Fry: A Biography*
TG	*Three Guineas*
TTL	*To the Lighthouse*
TW	*The Waves*
TY	*The Years*
VO	*The Voyage Out*

"Each is part of the whole: We act different parts; but are the same": From Fragment to Choran Community in the Late Work of Virginia Woolf

Emily M. Hinnov

In a familiar passage from "A Sketch of the Past," Virginia Woolf speaks to the organic, matrixial linkage between all of humanity, accessible through our participation in art: "we—I mean all human beings—are connected with this; that the whole world is a work of art; that we are parts of the work of art . . we are the words; we are the music; we are the thing itself" (72). Woolf sees beauty in sacred "moments of being" that transcend modes of living death with fullness of mind and spirit, all within the mesh of a wider web of humanity. As this passage and the line in my title from *Between the Acts* suggest, Woolf's art opens up the possibility for illuminated moments of communal awareness based upon convergence in spite of difference—what I term choran community. Further, Woolf's comparison of the world to art calls us to witness the redemptive power of the world. My argument here will be concerned with fragments, or isolated individuals, vs. choran community in Woolf's late work.

As Melba Cuddy-Keane comments, "Woolf's acceptance of difference and discord is closely related to her sense of the multiplicity of reality" (282), and, I would add, choran community. By choran community I mean textual instances that communicate the possibility of a genuine interface between self and other which also implies an awareness of the larger, interconnective community. My term draws upon Julia Kristeva's concept of "the semiotic chora," a prelinguistic state of consciousness of connection with the maternal body that leads to an integrated understanding of self and, by extension, other.[1] For, rather than ending her discussion of the semiotic chora with the individual psyche, Kristeva uses psychoanalysis as a model for accepting otherness within in order to, in turn, develop an ethics that will embrace peoples of different nations and ethnic backgrounds. She writes, "I love the other, who is not necessarily me, and who gives

---

[1] See Julia Kristeva, "A Question of Subjectivity—An Interview." *Women's Review* 12 (1986) 19-21; Phillip Rice and Patricia Waugh, eds., *Modern Literary Theory: A Reader* (New York: Arnold, 1996) 131-7. For a comprehensive collection of Kristeva's work, see Kelly Oliver, ed., *The Portable Kristeva* (New York: Columbia University Press, 1997). My discussion of Kristeva's chora also stems from Jacques Lacan, "The Mirror Stage as Formative of the Function of the I as revealed in Psychoanalytic Experience." Alan Sheridan, trans., *Ecrits, A Selection* (1949): 1-7.

me the possibility of opening myself to something other than myself; what I call love is openness to the other, and it is what gives me my human dimension, my symbolic dimension, my cultural and historic dimension" (*New Maladies of the Soul* 379). As Kristeva's work suggests, choran community can be found in the late work of Virginia Woolf in descriptions of encounters *between* characters, denoting an expansion that also includes the wider interconnective community. Expanding upon Kristeva's work, I argue that the desire to create such an aesthetic moment allows Woolf (and her reading audience) to represent a wholeness of self—the first step toward finding intersubjectivity—and finally, to create choran community.[2] Hence, unlike the Joycean epiphanic moment, Woolf's choran moments happen not just for the sake of the solipsistic individual, but instead for the greater—yet still diverse—community. For Woolf, an acceptance of difference defines not only consciousness of self and other but also the human community itself.[3] Further, then, I contend that Woolf's choran moments evince a form of sacred, even redemptive modernity, as represented by interconnective encounters between her characters which promise renewal and wholeness.

What follows in this essay is an exposition of my concept of choran community in *The Waves* (1931), *Three Guineas* (1938), and *Between the Acts* (1941). In her late work, Woolf utilizes the ideal of choran community in order to give her characters and her readers a vital moment to think, to then reinvigorate a wholeness of self, and finally to rebuild a sense of communal unity. Carrying us through oscillations between fragment and wholeness, Woolf depicts and practices choran community throughout her later work. This essay is structured by this movement from fragment to wholeness as represented through a chronological picture of Woolf's developing theories and practices of choran community in response to "history," which was predominantly present for Woolf and her contemporaries in the form of fascism. Woolf draws fascism, patriarchy, and militarism together under the category of a "history" defined as master narrative and tool of oppression whose form relies upon notions of progress and teleology. Her understanding of a counter-history to fascism, as represented most

---

[2] Jessica Berman, in her article on ethics and aesthetics in Woolf's work, "Ethical Folds: Ethics, Aesthetics, Woolf" *Modern Fiction Studies* 50.1 (Spring 2004): 151-172, comments most relevantly that "using aesthetics to make an ethical realm, or a fold, between the potentially universal and the personal" (159) invents a "radically new ethical encounter" (160). Berman's notion of an ethical fold speaks to Woolf's project of creating a literary art that might illuminate the connections between selves.

[3] See also the work of Jean-Luc Nancy in *Being Singular Plural* Trans. Robert D. Richardson and Anne E. O'Byrne. (Stanford: Stanford UP, 2000). Her assertion that "the essence of Being is only as co-essence" (30) which in turn forms community, is closely related to Woolf's representation of choran community in her art.

explicitly in her later work through textual choran community, advocates for more personal, creative, and eventually communal narratives rather than authorized versions of history as told by fascist and/or patriarchal institutions of power. Authorized histories have great and often tragic effects upon marginalized members of society, and Woolf's belief is that art allows audiences to contemplate human choices and find instances of human agency in the real world.

I acknowledge here that "wholeness" and "unity" are themes historically consistent with fascism. As Simonetta Falasca-Zamponi observes, "The possibility of unifying around national symbols ensured the cohesion of otherwise inchoate 'masses,' their shaping into a homogeneous political body" into a "unitary hierarchically structured whole" (5; 189). Falasca-Zamponi attempts to "distinguish totalitarianism's homogenized wholes from democratic models of social unity, totalitarianism's aesthetics from a democratic radical one" (193). The only idea of kinship allowed under fascism was the "feeling of community" that "would presumably produce a disciplined fascist citizen who would subordinate his or her self to the organism of the state" (Berezin 249). A comprehensive explanation of fascism itself is beyond the scope of this essay. However, following Falasca-Zamponi, my definition of choran unity allows and respects difference. The choran moment and its consequential interconnective community do not absorb individual desire in order to advocate worship of an ideologue ruler; nor does it depend upon mechanistic or war-mongering notions of a regenerative collective. To repeat Falasca-Zamponi's phrase, choran community instead enacts a "democratic radical" aesthetic.

Finally, my intent here is to outline two forms of activism presented in Woolf's work: the first being the author's, and the second, the readers I would hope to create through teaching and reading Woolf's texts with attention to choran community. Woolf's representation of choran community is significant for understanding her oeuvre as simultaneously aesthetic and political. More precisely, this essay seeks to make a contribution to the ongoing conversation concerning Woolf's politico-aesthetic by tracing her representation of choran community in later works, allowing a fuller understanding of the ways in which Woolf campaigned against fascism in the decade preceding World War II. As an activist writer of both novels and polemical essays, Woolf produced these illuminated moments and other radical uses of narrative time with the purpose of telling stories that might reveal in the present, or generate in the future, Woolfian choran community.

Woolf and Her Contemporaries Against the Shaken Fabric of Fascism

A brief tracing of Woolf's ideas about fragments and community from the late '20s—against the developing ideology of fascism—will place my discussion of her later works in context. In the aftershock of World War I, Virginia Woolf countenances the modernist point of view, writing in her essay, "How It Strikes a Contemporary" (published in *The Common Reader* in 1925) that, "It is an age of fragments" (324) for those artists who, like Woolf herself, were concerned with expressing and critiquing contemporary culture through their art. Woolf is an artist engaged in political and aesthetic projects that might change the shape of a history promulgated by the increasingly fascistic powers of the patriarchy. Expressing the shattering effect of World War I on the consciousness of all communities, but particularly the writing community, she warns, "We are sharply cut off from our predecessors. A shift in the scale—the war, the sudden slip of masses held in position for ages—has shaken the fabric from top to bottom, alienated us from the past and made us perhaps too vividly conscious of the present" (326). As a political artist, Woolf's view of history as shaken fabric—utterly disrupted, displaced, overcome by violence—shows us that the First World War had blinded her contemporary society to anything redemptive, or any way of being beyond the "here and now" of utter destruction. Here she suggests that if one is "too vividly" conscious of the shocking present moment, without an understanding of the ever-present underpinnings of past and future, one might become stagnant and thus unable to promote positive social change.

Woolf is consistently concerned with hegemonic constructions of history that seduce us into reiterating patriarchal and fascistic institutions of power in which we become complicit. She recognized fascist art as destructive early on in *A Room of One's Own*: "Poetry ought to have a mother as well as a father. The Fascist poem, one may fear, will be a horrid little abortion such as one sees in a glass jar in the museum of some country town" (103). Merry Pawlowski and the scholars in her edited collection on Woolf and fascism offer astute perspectives on "Woolf's voice against tyranny and her resistance to fascist seduction" (Pawlowski 2). Instead of becoming seduced by master narratives of fascism, Woolf as author of the 1920s offers an alternative in her contention that the power of art to transform the present society to choran community is a gradual process in which artists of her present day can only play a small yet significant role. She advises modern novelists in particular to:

> take a wider, a less personal view of modern literature, and look indeed upon the writers as if they were engaged upon some vast building which being built by common effort, the separate workmen may well remain anonymous ... scan the horizon; see the past in relation to the future; and so prepare the way for the masterpieces to come. ("How It Strikes a Contemporary" 332)

This need to scan the horizon for positive prospects reveals Woolf's desire to form a collective that will use art to "create afresh" and anew a modernist vision of community, while still remaining cognizant of the interweaving strands of present, past and future narratives. The anonymous, communal, and common effort of artists and audiences will realize the expansive horizon of possibility. Furthermore, Woolf's call for communities extends beyond writers or spectator-protagonists toward those reading modernist texts.

For Woolf, modern artists must participate in creating a kind of collective counter-history through their art, one that opposes the tremendous tyrannical narratives of war or fascism. In response to these increasingly destructive forces, Woolf invites collaborative meaning-making when it comes to possible social outcomes of art in future generations. Coming of age as an activist writer along with the Bloomsbury avant-garde, as Christine Froula tells us, Woolf and her contemporaries "integrate[d] political and suprapolitical thinking with aesthetics and everyday praxis . . . where the work of art calls people to see as one but to see differently and seek . . . arduous negotiation of an always changing *sensus communis*, or common understanding" (3). Even at this early, perhaps more optimistic stage of her continuing project to imagine alternative communities that struggle against the current age of uncertainty through common understanding, she admits, "our contemporaries afflict us because they have ceased to believe" ("How" 329). Woolf's statement suggests that a positive, politically-engaged aesthetic project can only begin in the present moment of belief and in the context of community, even in the midst of a terrifying and ultimately debilitating mode of fascism that will later be recalled as a horrific time in "history."

Woolf made a sharp distinction between art and propaganda, both theoretically and practically, in her critical response to the state's use of art for their own fascistic purposes. The British government promoted war through censorship and propaganda, and her fiction, as well as her essays, show how Woolf resists such manipulations of consciousness. However, many High Modernist writers of the '20s have been accused of being complicit with fascism because their art was considered too highbrow and socially aloof; the common reaction to literary modernism was that it was remote from politics and "real" life.[4] Woolf was often concerned that her work would be too didactic and too propagandist to be considered art; she was apprehensive about whether propaganda is necessarily

---

[4] For more on the modernist split between art and politics, see Levenback, where she argues that although there was a great "chasm between the 'artist and politics'" for many of Woolf's contemporaries, Woolf herself shows us that "no one enjoys immunity from war" (5).

incompatible with art, as well as with the use of art for direct teaching.[5] Instead, Woolf sought to "criticise the social system, and to show it at work, at its most intense" (*D2* 248) in order to "reveal the social patterns that sketched such personalities [in her fiction] to re-create the social world" (Phillips xxi). Woolf's work asks her audience to collaboratively discover—through personal and coequal interaction—the socially redemptive value of art.

Other modernist intellectuals, such as Walter Benjamin, valued the notion of personal perception in the construction of a more humanist history as well. For both Woolf and Benjamin, "history" should be written as counternarrative to canonical or authorized versions of history, but always with full awareness of the events that undergird our personal perceptions.[6] It is important to note here that Woolf's flashes of insight reveal what Benjamin would call "the true picture of

---

[5] Woolf's diary entry in 1935 warily states of *The Years* that "this fiction is dangerously near propaganda" (*D4* 300). Her essay "The Leaning Tower" (read to the Workers' Educational Association in May 1940) states, "The novel of the classless and towerless world should be a better novel . . . there might be a common belief which he could accept, and thus shift from his shoulders the burden of didacticism, or propaganda" (151).

[6] Through common engagement in what Woolf's contemporary, cultural theorist Walter Benjamin calls the "redemptive optics" available in the newly democratized role of art, Woolf contends that audiences might collaborate and participate with a new version of living aesthetics. Benjamin famously argued that in the age of mechanical reproduction, art has lost its original aura. For Benjamin, the dialectical image afforded by the lately egalitarian place of art in modern society offers a veritable constellation of interpretations. Moreover, the reproduced photographic work of art produces flashes of insight about what history as the story of the past might mean, which, with the benefit of communal interaction, will lead to social transformation for both artist and viewer. Through collective response and interpretation by its "readers," art might rebuild genuine wholeness and a sense of community, revealing a counternarrative to any despotic narratives of dominance perpetuated throughout history by those in power. Woolf's vision of the world as a living work of art in which the wider audience must play an integral part speaks to Benjamin's concept of redemptive optics; both modernist philosophers provide relevant context for the choran moment as a narrative aesthetic (found both in the novel and the photograph) which creates the opportunity, through cooperative (re)action, to rebuild community.

See also Karen Jacobs, *The Eye's Mind: Literary Modernism and Visual Culture* (Ithaca and London: Cornell UP, 2001). For further discussion of Woolf and Benjamin's relationship to each other and with fighting fascism, see Leslie Kathleen Hankins's chapter, "Virginia Woolf and Walter Benjamin Selling Out(Siders)" in *Virginia Woolf and the Age of Mechanical Reproduction*. Ed. Pamela L. Caughie (New York: Garland Publishers, 2000): 3-35; and Marilyn L. Brownstein's "Silver Spoons and Knives: Virginia Woolf and Walter Benjamin (Some Notes on a Practical Approach to Cultural Studies)" in *Virginia Woolf: Emerging Perspectives*. Eds. Mark Hussey and Vara Neverow (New York: Pace UP, 1994): 204-9.

the past ... The past can be seized only as an image which flashes up at the instant when it can be recognized and never seen again" (Benjamin, *Theses* 255). The seemingly small, lived, personal moments are actually what make up the larger (antifascist) narrative of human history. Incidentally, the alternate title of her novel *The Years* (1937), "Here and Now," points to Woolf's common concern with living balanced between illuminated moments and the knowledge of time passing. Woolf and Benjamin were both concerned with artwork composed of fragmentary materials as a response to the seeming whole of the fascist threat.

In the 1930s, Woolf's work suggests a stronger resistance to fascism than what we read in "How it Strikes a Contemporary" or *A Room of One's Own*. Her later work evinces a politico-aesthetics particularly concerned with the threat posed by fascism as a totalitarian ideology stemming from patriarchal notions and the success of imperialism, dependent upon militarism, and implicit in British public and private life as well as abroad. Woolf focuses instead on the cosmic pattern that transcends distinctions between the past, present, and future and its connection with the everyday interfaces between selves. Her later novels and essays illustrate counternarratives of community in action against fascism; she uses her poetics of prose to engage with the central political issue of her day—the rise of fascism—in imagining how they might play out in the future for a still-to-be-redeemed humankind.

Woolf's works of the 1930s, the novel *The Waves* (1931) and the phototext *Three Guineas* (1938), show us that hegemonic, fascistic notions of history can be resisted by both writer and reader through engagement with choran community. In *The Waves* Woolf creates a narrative structure of soliloquies as possible meditations of a character's deeper motivations. This narrative device further complicates her representation of selfhood within a militarized and increasingly fascist society. The seven "characters" of the novel are not whole in themselves, but they do experience brief moments of harmony and congruity. They create a composite character in that their multiplicity of perspectives offers a whole, complete vision, even in difference: "A single sided flower as we sat here waiting, but now a seven-sided flower, many-petalled, red, puce, purple-shaded, stiff with silver-tinted leaves—a whole flower to which every eye brings its contribution" (*TW* 127). In *Three Guineas*, Woolf argues that the origins of fascism are not to be found in nationalism but within the patriarchal family, while the connection between male supremacy and war are rarely overt in her fiction. *The Waves* and *Three Guineas* brilliantly illustrate the sense of waxing and waning inherent in the creation of choran communities that welcome outcasts and outsiders into the fold, from an individual consciousness revealed as necessarily a fragment, to a coherent and unified world (one that will be rediscovered once again in *Between the Acts*). In the following section, I will show how Woolf uses the metaphor of vacillation between fragment and wholeness—from passive models of consciousness in *The Waves* to participating activism in *Three Guineas*—in order to represent and produce choran community.

Reading Against Fascism in *The Waves*

The symbol of the wave itself suggests chaotic unity, fluidity of identity where the self merges back, and a cyclical view of the universe. In the movement from collision to separation in *The Waves*, there is a process of psychological growth. *The Waves* predominantly asks how we can form a somewhat coherent identity or self in light of the pressures of modernity. Each character's painful process of individuation—"We suffered terribly as we became separate bodies" (241)—necessitates a fragmenting; disunity from the whole is required for eventual unity. The wavelike movement is both a break and a merge. Personal epiphanies are often examples of separation that reveal disconnection from the whole in order to reform the self. Bernard, whose behavior functions like a wave, becomes the ultimate individual at the end of the novel when he absorbs all their characteristics in an attempt to create coherence through flashes of insight: "The illusion is upon me that something adheres for a moment, has roundness, weight, depth, is completed. This, for the moment, seems to be my life" (238). Yet even in Bernard's absorption of the other characters, we are reminded of the fleeting quality of individual identity, especially when considered against the larger cosmic whole of time and nature.

The wave-like movement between self and unity is reflected not only in the characters' lives but also structures the narrative itself. The structures of the interludes suggest progression in age, opposites of sunrise/sunset, childhood/old age, rise/fall and break, spring/winter, movement through history, the rhythm of life, and most prominently the cosmology of time and human history vs. nature in cyclical, repetitive images. These interludes evoke a Darwinian aesthetic—rot, fear of death and decay—yet they also give life and renewal: "Down there among the roots where the flowers decayed, gusts of dead smells were wafted . . . The skin of rotten fruit broke . . . Now and then [the "gold-eyed birds"] plunged the tips of their beaks savagely into the sticky mixture" (75). The imagery of natural decay and survival of the fittest simultaneously suggests life, as these birds will be nurtured by the spoils of the earth. Ultimately, however, we are all of momentary importance in this cosmos of chaos over which we have no control. The invocation of Indian mysticism, the emphasis on astronomy, and the randomness of life in the interludes contrasts with the death of white Western culture. According to Jane Marcus, "By making the sun set in the British Empire in her novel . . . Woolf surrounds the text of the decline and fall of the West (the transcendental self striving and struggling against death) with the text of the East, random natural recurrence" ("Britannia" 155). The lack of traditional plot structure offers more of a rhythmic history of these English lives, revealing the rise and fall of empire and its internalized constructs of whiteness and patriarchal supremacy, which of course all lead to fascism.

Woolf utilizes the character of Percival to represent fascism's inheritance of imperialism. Percival is utterly fragmented by death, and he never quite finds a sense of unified community like the other characters in the novel. Ironically though, Percival's death is futile, yet it creates stability, order and unity. At the same time his role as supreme imperialist is bitterly satirized:

> Behold, Percival advances; Percival rides a flea-bitten mare, and wears a sun-helmet. By applying the standards of the West, by using the violent language that is natural to him, the bullock-cart is righted in less than five minutes. The Oriental problem is solved. He rides on; the multitude cluster round him, regarding him as if he were—what indeed he is—a God. (*TW* 136)

Each character idealizes him because as a colonial administrator, he is in a position of power in modern British culture. Percival appears like a knight in Arthurian legend who finds the grail—he is an imperialist god and a colonizer central to India's rising. Percival does not speak; as an icon of British imperial identity, he is a blank slate allowing for the other characters' projection. His high stature in this community contributes to his role as a would-be fascist. If Percival is to represent, in part, imperial power and its ties to fascism, then Woolf's solution to the problem of an individual's fascistic potential is to dispense with it. As a potential fascist figure, he has too much power, but, furthermore, his untimely, rather unheroic fall from his imperial glory on a flea-bitten mare reminds the rest of the community that there is no hierarchy—we are all equal specks in the universe. The death of a fascist character such as Percival reveals the redemptive power of *The Waves* because his necessarily more limited power must subside. Once again, in a waning back toward fragmentation, characters and readers are reminded that without recognition of the place of self within the larger cosmic scheme, we are relatively insignificant as individuals.[7]

Woolf's attention to characters inhabiting the outer edges of her novel—outcast figures such as the broken and alienated Rhoda and the class-conscious

---

[7] Although Jessica Berman finds Woolf's creation of community as represented in a modern cosmopolitan perspective, her discussion of communal forms informs mine: "Woolf develops an expanded notion of personal identity, one that constitutes subjectivity as coming into being always in fluctuating relation to a small group of affiliated yet singular others" (*Modernist Fiction, Cosmopolitanism and the Politics of Community* 121).

Louis—helps us to connect the role of colonialism and fascism to constructions of difference and division within potential communities. Woolf intended to restore community with her writing, because the outsider must "in no way hinder any other human being, whether man or woman, black or white" (*Three Guineas* 66). If we attend to those outsiders present on the fringes of Woolf's narratives because of gender, class, or race, then we can become more aware of the interdependence of black and white (or the relationships between Woolf's fragmented characters), therefore reifying our understanding of choran interconnectivity.[8] In the recurring images of India, Africa, unexplored territories, and the representation of Percival as cardboard hero projection of those who don't speak, Woolf bitterly tackles the problem of colonialism and its relationship to fascism. Many of the characters see themselves in reference to the exotic or primitive Other. For instance, Susan and Bernard appear as adventurers in an undiscovered country while the gardeners are imagined as hostile natives: "Let us take possession of our secret territory" (*TW* 22). In the English school child's imagination, imperialism is a significant part of nationhood and selfhood, revealing the psychology of Empire and, by extension, fascism.[9] Yet at the same time the meandering narrative of *The Waves* itself is one of Woolf's prime examples of the literary representation of unity among humanity *not* based upon the hierarchical, mechanistic collective of fascism that would surely obliterate those designated as other. Instead, this anti-"history" is a retelling of choran

---

[8] Toni Morrison reminds us that modern American literature is constructed by the encounter between blackness and whiteness, and that that interchange enriches the text. For Morrison, the notion of the white self always depends upon the black other: "The subject of the dream is the dreamer" (17). Her project offers important insight into the dynamic of primitivism as a fundamental part of modernism. The focus, then, becomes the face behind the projective mask, a site from where we might uncover a deeper understanding of how modernist texts re-envisioned the self and the larger community.

More recent work on the interplay between whiteness and blackness in modernist literature includes Robin Hackett's study of *Sapphic Primitivism: Productions of Race, Class, and Sexuality in Key Works of Modern Fiction* (New Brunswick: Rutgers UP, 2004). Hackett demonstrates the connections between modernist white women's texts by such authors as Woolf, Warner, Cather, and Olive Schreiner, and their use of the trope of "sapphic primitivism," a literary device whereby blackness and working-class culture are seen as representing sexual autonomy, including lesbianism, for white women in their portrayals of race, class, and sexuality. Also of note is Jane Marcus's *Hearts of Darkness*, where she observes the ways that Woolf, Djuna Barnes, Nancy Cunard, and Mulk Raj Anand contend with the end of empire and the rise of fascism before the Second World War in their work.

[9] For further discussion of Woolf's critique and representation of the elements of fascism in *The Waves*, see Pawlowski, Froula, Berman's *Modernist Fiction* and Phillips.

communal awareness that resists boundaries of fascism and includes everyone in its story.

A case in point appears at the conclusion of *The Waves*. In an ultimate moment of choran unity, the symphonic imagery at the end of the novel suggests the possibility of rebuilding community out of the metaphor of art. By novel's end, the community of Neville, Susan, Louis, Jinny, Rhoda, Bernard "and a thousand others" creates a "symphony, with its concord and its discord and its tunes on top and its complicated bass beneath . . . Each played his own tune, fiddle, flute, trumpet, drum or whatever the instrument might be" (256). In the choran moment of total intersubjectivity—"I am not one person; I am many people; I do not altogether know who I am . . . or how to distinguish my life from theirs" (276)—Bernard, perhaps not unlike Woolf herself, defies the viciousness of colonialist or fascist history that seeks to pull us apart and away from our collective unconscious. The "unborn selves" (289) and the abjected "brute, too, the savage, the hairy man" (289) are all "contained" (290) and presumably continually restored. The colonialist's "primitive" hairy man is tossed and combined with the would-be white imperialist in the fluid composition of community. The multitudes of selves which become one in "the eternal renewal, the incessant rise and fall and fall and rise again" (297) embody the dance and the wavelike interplay between personal and cosmic time. The waxing of communal identity and the waning of fragmentation finally cease and the seven characters, refracted through the common consciousness of Bernard, come home to a coherent and unified world. As we shall also see in *Three Guineas*, fragments become whole once again through the power of choran community.

Antifascism in a Phototext: Woolf's Choran Community of Outsiders in *Three Guineas*

In the pacifist essay *Three Guineas*, Woolf's argument with fascist forms of history is perhaps more potent than in her fiction before the late 1930s. As demonstrated in *The Waves* and here in *Three Guineas*, Woolf's symbols of choran community—the symphonic seven-sided flower and the extranational Outsider's Society—allow for a look forward "to a postpatriarchal community of 'Outsiders'[,] reaffirm[ing] the vital relevance of Woolf for those who work for peace in any sphere" (Hussey 12). Woolf's pacifism contributes to her ideas about community because she wanted to destroy the war mindset with her work, which is most often connected with fascist powers seeking to conquer the fragments of society in the form of woman, nonwhite, and non-Westerner. The merging of those othered by fascistic modes of consciousness creates an alternative community. The present space of the home front will reveal the origins of the fascist's brutal mode of action and, finally, transcend it. In the novel form of *The Waves*, Woolf reveals the transcendent power of choran community through the final intricate, even discordant, symphony of choran community; in the essay form of *Three Guineas*, Woolf creates an ideal mode of unity against patriarchal/fascistic forces in the society of outsiders. For Woolf, the community's continuance depends upon the implied community of readers as well. In the future, through the invention of a communal awareness that allows men and women of all races and classes to acknowledge the fundamentally coequal nature of humanity, we, as readers or daughters of educated men, can finally rebuild the web of community, and, once again, find a sense of home in a unified and coherent world.

Three Guineas was primarily written for Woolf's own class and sex because for Woolf, women could not accurately be called bourgeois in a repressive patriarchal society. According to Woolf, fascism is analogous with patriarchy and oppression; all lead to dictatorship: "Dictator as we call him when he is Italian or German, who believes that he has the right, whether given by God, Nature, sex or race is immaterial, to dictate to other human beings how they shall live; what they shall do . . . Nature has done well to entrust the man with the care of his family and the nation" (53). Her argument is that oppression and war begin within the family and on the level of personal human relationships, especially those which are patriarchally-bound. Therefore, with an attitude of "complete indifference" (107), membership in the Outsider's Society necessitates a refusal to participate in the public sphere of war because the nature of male-dominated institutions that perpetuate war is fascistic. In response, Woolf writes a satire on the academic document in an embittered tone, including endless footnotes and a seemingly convoluted argument. She understood that when facing the encroachment of fascism in women's daily lives, anger is both reasonable and even liberating because the patriarch's "fear and anger prevent freedom in the private house . . . [which] may prevent real freedom in the public world" (131). Yet if women, as outsiders, react to fascism with similar anger they may also play a part in perpetuating war: ". . .they may have a positive share in causing war" just like the men in power. Woolf was adamantly against war in the name of patriotism or jingoist nationalism because, "as a woman, I have no country. As a woman I want no country. As a woman my country is the whole world" (109). The pattern of alienation (and even fear) that encompasses those members of the Outsider's Society, instead of reenacting fascism, actually creates productive community. As Erica Johnson has recently argued,[10] the extranational space of "the whole

---

[10] Johnson's presentation was entitled "The Legacy of the 'Outsider's Society': Woolf and Postcolonial Nationhood" (MLA Convention. 28 December 2004,

world" is an alternative place of belonging for those disenfranchised by reason of gender, class, and race. I would add as well that this dynamic is created out of the communal space in between, embodied in Woolf's art by choran community. For Woolf, men and women must reform themselves first, and then urge those of their own class to join in the revolution. It is the recognition of a renewed and whole self, a reunion with one's inner spirit, which precedes and even allows the restoration of greater society.

Three Guineas surveys British social institutions like the crown, the law, education, the church, the military, and the family and their complicity in war and imperialism—all within the form of a phototext.[11] Most importantly here, the photographs represent fragments used to create a new wholeness, a unity between viewer and subject. Woolf envisioned photographs as an integral part of the argument from early on; their later absence in some editions "diminish[es] connections" Woolf makes "between fascism and patriarchy, foreign and domestic politics, and dominance and hierarchy in the public and private spheres" (128).[12] The photographs are vital to her argument. Their exclusion assumes that they are "subsidiary" and "dependent" upon the written word, while Woolf actually uses them to parody institutions of empire, as well as to reveal their connection with fascism (129). Her text and the accompanying images provide—by inciting an activist viewing—counter-readings to the icons of British tradition and power, providing resistance to the ideology that their power is absolute. Woolf's choice to combine the photo and the text in *Three Guineas* exemplifies this objective.

Philadelphia, PA). She discussed a postcolonial point of view on the nation as an exclusive sociopolitical space in the work of Woolf, Adrienne Rich, and Diane Brand.

[11] Jane Marcus's *Three Guineas* (San Diego: Harcourt, 2006), with her annotation and introduction, is the first new edition to be published in the US and the only one that restores the photographs, which were long unavailable in any American edition. In her Introduction, which includes an enlightening argument of the "subversive role played by the photographs" (lxiii), Marcus discusses the radical nature of Woolf's feminist-pacifist polemic that serves as "the Communist Manifesto for women" (lii). See as well Gualtieri, for more on the "causal link between war, Fascist ideology and the psychological and institutional make-up of patriarchal society" (165). Additional pertinent discussions of *Three Guineas* include: Diane Gillespie, "'Her Kodak Pointed at His Head': Virginia Woolf and Photography." Diane Gillespie, ed. *The Multiple Muses of Virginia Woolf* (Columbia: U of Missouri Press, 1993): 113-147; Patricia Laurence, "The Facts and Fugue of War: *Three Guineas* to *Between the Acts*" in Hussey, 225-45; and Brenda Silver, "The Authority of Anger: *Three Guineas* as Case-Study." *Signs* 16.2 (1991): 340-70.

[12] Julia Duffy and Lloyd Davis skillfully assess the ways in which Woolf's phototext critiques the dominant culture by revealing it to itself in images and allusions to male authority figures.

Woolf substitutes images of dead children with Englishmen dressed in uniforms associated with the Church, the State, and Academia in order to show that there is an implicit connection between death and what she perceives as fascist institutions of power. By omitting the photographs of bombed homes and people, she avoids exploiting their destruction and instead turns our focus to the patriarchal institutions responsible for these outcomes of war. She also disrupts the idea of facts and evidence so relied upon by regimes of imperialism and realistic photography in general. The photos, both seen and unseen, challenge the idea of objectivity and embody a mockery of political discourse, undercutting and satirizing the pomposity of those men in power. Here there is a subversive interaction between the visual and verbal texts that allows the reader/viewer to contemplate the message inherent in both. For, as Woolf detects, "Photographs . . . send [their] messages in a flash through every past memory and present feeling. When we look at these photographs some fusion takes place within us" (*Three Guineas* 11). This optic shock or flash of recognition brings about a visceral reaction, but it is one that might cause us to think more clearly. Our "horror and disgust" (11) become a point of unity against the explicitly fascist father, whose "eyes are glazed; his eyes glare. His body, which is braced in an unnatural position, is tightly cased in a uniform . . . he is called in German and Italian Führer or Duce; in our own language tyrant or dictator. And behind him lie ruined houses and dead bodies—men, women, and children" (142). Our common reaction to the juxtaposed images of oblivion and leader suggests that we might be able to fight the "fact" of their "evil" (143).

If Woolf thinks of photography as embodying optic shocks, then images hold within them the expressive power to enact political and social change by virtue of the viewer's recognition.[13] Those illuminated fragments, those flashes of insight engendered by the photographs, are what compel us reader-viewers and

---

[13] Susan Sontag problematically concludes that the photographs cannot ultimately be read as redemptive. She finds Woolf presumptuous when she states in *Three Guineas* that the photographs of dead children "are not an argument" but instead represent an instance of collapse between spectatorship and identification which might then give rise to ethical action. Although she finds her "brave" (3), Sontag claims that Woolf does not succeed in using photographs to imagine an ethical stance on preventing war because photographs can only bear witness to the impossibility of our bearing witness to atrocity. Yet Woolf is not simply assuming that "generic" images of war will engender an activist response. Woolf is making the choice not to be cynical and therefore stagnant in her desire to view the redemptive possibility inherent in photography, both art and document. Woolf dares to assert that the encounter with otherness is not utterly futile. She does not, as Sontag contends, view photographs as positive documentary proof. As an alternative, photographs offer the possibility of evoking empathy and the potential for self-positioning. The interaction between viewer, image and photographer can create productive unity.

implied communal Outsiders to take action. Those arrested moments, such as those Woolf includes as images equating patriarchal institutions with the fascist outcome of dead children, allow readers and viewers what Gloria Anzaldúa calls "the space in-between from which to think" (172), offering personal (and possibly communal) transformation. Photographs, like all narrative art, ideally create energetic space that helps us to better understand our interconnectedness, and that acknowledgement is a political act in itself:[14] "A common interest unites us; it is one world, one life . . . if we in the intensity of our private emotions forget the public world [,] [b]oth houses will be ruined, the public and the private, and material and the spiritual, for they are inseparably connected" (*TG* 142-143). In a moment of revolutionary repose, Woolf ventures that we, as part of the newly defined Society of Outsiders, can resist from inside forces of destructive dominance and instead view the photographs as redemptive in forming community.

The Society of Outsiders, then, located in the extranational borderland, might disrupt and deny, through their engagement with the fragments of these photographs, the patriarchal and fascist assumptions of patriotic identity that lead to oppression and war. Woolf's goal in *Three Guineas* is to undermine those social systems which continually militarize the lives of women and the lower classes. She views discourse as political action and censorship as oppression; the discourse represented by this polemical essay incites, in the minds of its readers, recognition of communal action against fascism. Indeed, Woolf's polemical writing was a necessary endeavor, enabling her to fight fascism with potent words that could transcend historical rituals of death and destruction. Yet again, she does not want to preach or convert or create propaganda, because "if we use art to propagate political opinions . . . literature will suffer the same mutilation that the mule has suffered; and there will be no more horses" (qtd. in Carlston 162; *Three Guineas* 155n30; 170n39). Instead, Woolf argues that the invigorating power of art depends upon our common, open interaction in a collective project to create counternarratives to fascism through the emergence of choran community. What follows is Woolf's most precise representation of choran community and its ability to resist fascism, her final novel *Between the Acts*.

---

[14] For more on photographs, aesthetics, and politics, see Strauss. As Strauss reminds us, photographs must evoke a sense of tension in order to be compelling to the viewer, so that viewers can respond with appropriate awareness of the complexity inherent in the interaction between image and any pre-existing condition in the viewer: "Aestheticization is one of the ways that disparate peoples recognize themselves in one another" (10). Even when a photograph documents the suffering of another, it must "persistently . . . register the relation of photographer to subject. . . . and this understanding is a profoundly important political process."

"Orts and Scraps" of Choran Redemption in *Between the Acts*

In Woolf's novel *Between the Acts* (1941), I find a modernist model for effective social activism through the practice of art. This novel adds to our understanding of choran community because not only does Woolf portray a community here, she also (as she suggests in *Three Guineas*) necessitates her readers' participation in that community's interpretive process and thence in that community. Melba Cuddy-Keane argues that Woolf uses a comic mode in such novels as *Between the Acts* to create a community with a "collective voice" (276). However, my conception of choran community differs with Cuddy-Keane's belief that Woolf's use of comedy "celebrates an irreversible dismantling of order and . . . advocates a permanent instability" (280). Rather, I hope to show that Woolf's deployment of choran community reveals interconnectedness and even a sense of permanence (for both protagonist and reader) as stabilizing modes of consciousness that can be taken with us when we need solace, even in future times of despair. The annual pageant, interspersed with villagers' strolling, taking tea, and talking, represents the collaborative nature of art; both audience and artist must participate in mutual meaning-making as the text of the play comes alive through the performance of both actor and spectator. The effect of a play depends upon its reverberation with the present moment, the audience, and their relationship with what has come before it.[15] For Woolf, art transforms our behavior in the world by reconfiguring our relations to both the artwork and its audience; art is a shared experience, and its resonance releases the possibility of positive change in the future. In her final novel, Woolf ventures a hopeful resistance against any view of hegemonic history as dominant or overpowering to the masses (most clearly represented by the late '30s in the rise of Hitler's power), even if only for fleeting yet sacred moments.

In *Between the Acts*, pageant director Miss La Trobe is trying to give people this kind of transformative art, from fragmented moment to moment. As onlooker Lucy murmurs, "We've only the present" moment to try to resist the encroachment of fascism, or, "The future disturbing our present" (82), evoking the larger threat that Hitler represents. Once again, the optic shock created by the performance might draw the audience into positive action. However, Miss La Trobe cannot control the play or the reactions of the audience, but her efforts do at times create seized moments of time, a gathering in that might make the audience stop to think: "Hadn't she, for twenty-five minutes, made them see? A

---

[15] For more on the conception of a literary legacy based upon resonance, see Wai Chee Dimock's "Toward a Theory of Resonance." *PMLA* (1997 October 112): 1060-1071.

vision imparted was relief from agony . . . for one moment . . . one moment" (98). Even if she feels she has failed in the next breath, the play has opened the possibility, through its varied imaginings of history, that the audience has agency in choosing what to remember, what to live by, what to discard or recreate. They all search for some kind of pattern or coherence or order, "some inner harmony?" (119) that might explain the whole of existence. But it is really only Nature, that uncontrollable, celestial force, that establishes unity against the fragments of war: "And the trees with their many-tongued much syllabling, their green and yellow leaves hustle and shuffle us, and bid us, like the starlings, and the rooks, come together, crowd together, to chatter and make merry while the red cow moves forward and the black cow stands still" (120). As in *The Waves*, nature's influence possibly reveals some cosmic good that is broader than the human universe, as well as human connectedness and a yearning for lost unity.[16] The background itself is the splintered, fragmented conversation about the play about British history, which encompasses accounts of "Dictators" and the present of "the papers" and "the Jews? The refugees . . . People like ourselves, beginning life again" (121). There is definitely an atmosphere of renewal among fragmentation afoot here. The wisps and murmurs and the syllabling of nature evoke the babblings of infant and mother in those past moments of jubilant wholeness, suggesting that a reconnection with organic sound could somehow restore us.

In *Between the Acts*, Woolf most explicitly extends the play's effect on its fictional viewer to the larger scope of the novel's readers. At instances such as this representation of the seemingly disjointed present moment in the play, and at the end of the novel, Woolf suggests the possibility of writing a new history if you examine the old one while also maintaining a faint hope for rebuilding civilization. There may be a possible unity formed out of the disruption of having to truly see ourselves, even in its "distorting and upsetting and utterly unfair" reflection in "the looking glasses [as they] dart . . . flash . . . expose" (184). If the audience can rest upon this moment for an instant that allows repose, they can reveal the momentary truth about themselves: "And the audience saw themselves, not whole by any means, but at any rate sitting still" (185). They will learn to break from history by looking within to a sense of personal, inner time, as opposed to the machination of fascist controlled order: "The hands of the clock had stopped at the present moment. It was now. Ourselves" (186). The audience begins to realize that British civilization is not so mighty or totalizing

---

[16] See Carlston, where she shows how Woolf's "love of country, like the fascist's, is rooted in the semiotic seductiveness of archaic orality and the oceanic maternal embrace. . .[yet] for her, any particular motherland is at most the specific source of a nonspecific, undifferentiated love of humanity" (157).

as they thought—"*Look at ourselves, ladies and gentlemen! Then at the wall; and ask how's this wall, the great wall, which we call, perhaps miscall, civilization, to be built by* (here the mirrors flicked and flashed) *orts, scraps, and fragments like ourselves?*" (Woolf's italics, 188). If history is just orts and scraps, then what have we to do but gather them up and create our own narratives of restoration rather than war?[17] I use "we" here to denote the community of readers since I have pointed out how Woolf demonstrates her consciousness of audience as a plurality of readers with the potential for radical action—if we will only look at "ourselves."

Between the Acts is a test case in the performance of choran community, and that performance, through the shared experience of audience and actor in the text, contemporary readers, and our own current scholarly community, holds within it the prospect of reconstructing a redemptive mode of human history. Even her plot demonstrates Woolf's despair at their ability to overcome history long enough to change its practices, and hence its oppressive power as practiced by patriarchal/fascist society. Woolf was concerned with the connection between personal and universal understandings of time throughout her life and work. In *Between the Acts* she finally and deftly deconstructs both as not necessarily ameliorative or progressive. By the time she was writing this novel, Woolf was struggling to maintain some optimism within the current political situation.[18] Nonetheless Woolf finds the possibility of unity, both through the illuminated present moment and in the recuperative future, in the midst of fragmented scraps that might represent the destructive outcomes of fascist history, leading to social transformation through Benjaminian redemptive optics. Given the direction of the play and its attention to its own audience in its continuous making, it helps its audience and its readership to envision an alternative choran community.

Indeed the ending of *Between the Acts*, with the curtain that rises on Isa and Giles, suggests a possibility for communal renewal. The couple and the crowd, through their newly democratic participation in art, may be able to recast history's fascist implications. As the play closes, the audience becomes "united" in

---

[17] Karen Phillips, in *Virginia Woolf Against Empire*, argues as well that "*Between the Acts* sweepingly examines historical events and attitudes that have led to England's present role in fascism and disaster" (202). However, she concludes that Woolf suggests that no "true community ever existed" because all of society has been implicated in the crime of war. I argue conversely that Woolf continues to hope that community can be rebuilt and recreated through recognition of choran interconnectivity.

[18] As Nancy Topping Bazin notes, Woolf's later work "reflect[s] . . . not only [her] increased sense of the meaninglessness of life but also her horror as she observed supposedly sane individuals and nations preparing for another world war . . . a normal state of psychological wholeness was by 1941 no longer possible for Virginia Woolf" (17).

the spectacle, and in their "flower gathering" they are "crashed; solved; united" (189) through their mutual response to art. In "raising their eyes" and truly seeing themselves and each other in this common experience of art, "Each is part of the whole . . . We act different parts; but are the same" (192), much like the unity of characters in *The Waves* through the image of a seven-sided flower. The collaborative art of this play initiates a movement from fragmentation to wholeness through the newly created dialogic community "to which real differences, as Arendt says, are so much less dangerous than indifference; a community of spectators who enact a public 'form of being together' where 'no one rules and no one obeys,'. . . against the Nazis' scapegoating version of community" (*Froula* 314). Each player/observer—in spite of any differences—rediscovers and recreates the wholeness of choran community in response to fascism.

As in *Three Guineas*, this profound level of correlation extends back home to intimate relationships. Once the play has finished and Isa ruminates on "orts, scraps, and fragments" (215), she observes her husband Giles and their troubled marriage: "'The father of my children, whom I love and hate.' Surely it was time someone invented a new plot." As Isa reads about prehistoric man rising out of the ashes of history and prepares to make love to her husband, we glimpse, although the view is complicated by "enmity" and "love" as well as the urges to "fight" and "embrace" (219), a new way of thinking that might not repeat the mistakes of the past. In a conclusion that anticipates postmodernism, Woolf leaves her reading audience with the end of a novel that presupposes a beginning: "Then the curtain rose. They spoke." This couple is about to engage in embracing conversation, as Woolf would argue we must also do as we "invent a new plot." As in *The Waves* and *Three Guineas*, fragments of individuals come to wholeness in their combined vision of choran community. As Natania Rosenfeld states, "We must all, [Woolf] says, become the authors of a new, truly intersubjective plot, a plot that excludes no one and accounts for the complexities of the human soul" (15). Woolf's final novel reveals that she had not completely lost faith in humanity's ability to form a communal ethos; that task resides in her reader's participation in choran community.

The Future of Woolf's Choran Community

Woolf continued her quest for peace to resist the brutality of war until the end of her life. Ultimately, for Woolf it is vital that we excavate the darkness within, the potential power-monger in all of us. We might then recreate a purity and authenticity of the self, which has been mired by historics of war and fascism most potently connected with World War II, in order to find an outlet of healthy, productive, even ethical community. In her essay "Thoughts on Peace in an Air Raid" (1940), she writes: "Unless we can think peace into existence we—not this one body in the one bed but millions of bodies yet to be born—will lie in the same darkness and hear the same death rattle overhead" (243). Peace, for present or future generations, depends upon the synergy of intellect and social activism. As in *Three Guineas*, Woolf again places the blame on patriarchal institutions of power: "The defenders are men. The attackers are men. Arms are not given to the Englishwoman to fight the enemy or to defend herself. She must lie weaponless tonight." Critiquing the cult of the mother who happily sends her sons off to be sacrificed for the love of country, she notes that some would say that, "The maternal instinct is a woman's glory" (246), while for men that glory lies in fighting.[19] Rather than allowing ourselves to be overcome by patriarchy or maternal militarism, Woolf instead insists that our intellects undo the impulse to fight. She has hope that we will overcome the utterly nonsensical nature of the fascistic powers that be: "There is another way of fighting for freedom without arms; we can fight with the mind. We can make ideas that help the young Englishman who is fighting up in the sky to defeat the enemy . . . Mental fight means thinking against the current, not with it" (244). She insists that our minds can create communal counternarratives that will free us from militaristic oppression.

More importantly, Woolf argues that we must consciously eradicate any domineering, fascistic hostility we might harbor in the relationship between self and other. She pointedly asks, "Who is Hitler? What is he?" and answers, "Aggressiveness, tyranny, the insane love of power made manifest, they reply. Destroy that, and you will be free" (245). Her response to this vital question once again points to the individual awareness which will flower into communal action. Woolf's sage words—"Let us try to drag up into consciousness the subconscious Hitlerism that holds us down. It is the desire for aggression; the desire to dominate and enslave . . . They are slaves who are trying to enslave"—speak to this necessity to rediscover ourselves as well as those in our wider community in order to make real progress in preventing war. She still hopes that our cooperative creativity will make a positive difference: "They would give them other openings for their creative power. That too must make part of our fight for freedom . . . We must create more honourable activities for those who try to conquer

---

[19] The image of Mother England was especially potent during the First World War. See Jane Marcus's brilliant Afterword to Evadne Price's *Not So Quiet. . .Stepdaughters of War* (1930), "Corpus/Corps/Corpse: Writing the Body In/At War" (New York: The Feminist Press, 1989): "The fearful huge matriarch who points the way to the Front . . . She is the Home Front, the Mother Country, the one who gives birth and also kills. It would never do to blame the old men who make war, the kings and Kaisers and their counselors" (160). In *Three Guineas*, Woolf points the finger directly at those men in power.

in themselves their fighting instinct, their subconscious Hitlerism" (247). Woolf's collective intellectual project resists internalizations of a naturalized perception of self-superiority, a subconscious fascism. The only fighting Virginia Woolf affirms is the fight for common emancipation from tyrannies of authorized history.

Woolf writes of our common emancipation from tyranny through our recognition and creation of choran community. Studying Woolf's formations of choran community in her later work illuminates the important tension between self and community so that we might fully understand her resistance to fascism. Moreover, examining Woolf's creation of choran community on the page is necessary to our understanding of what community can be, and so may determine a future in which we do not repeat the mistakes of the past. For Woolf, it is the creative mind, body, and soul that will finally redeem humanity, and these vital elements of human life can only be excavated in our new understanding of communal wholeness. We, as present and future literary critics and teachers, are the scholars who can benefit from Woolf's potentially transformative aesthetic of choran community.

Works Cited

Anzaldúa, Gloria. *Borderlands/La Frontera: The New Mestiza.* San Francisco: Aunt Lute Books, 1987.

Bazin, Nancy Topping. *Virginia Woolf and the Androgynous Vision.* New Brunswick, NJ: Rutgers UP, 1973.

Bell, Anne Olivier, Ed. with asst. Andrew McNeillie. *The Diary of Virginia Woolf.* 5 vols. New York: Harcourt Brace Jovanovich, 1978-84.

Benjamin, Walter. "The Work of Art in the Age of Mechanical Reproduction." [1936]. *Selected Writings: Walter Benjamin.* Eds. Marcus Bullock and Michael W. Jennings. Cambridge, MA: Cambridge UP, 1996.

——. "Theses on the Philosophy of History." *Illuminations: Walter Benjamin, Essays and Reflections.* Ed. and Intro. Hannah Arendt. New York: Harcourt, Brace, Jovanovich, Inc., 1986.

Berezin, Mabel. *Making the Fascist Self: A Political Culture of Interwar Italy.* Ithaca and London: Cornell UP, 1997.

Berman, Jessica. "Ethical Folds: Ethics, Aesthetics, Woolf." *Modern Fiction Studies.* 50.1 (Spring 2004): 151-172.

———. *Modernist Fiction, Cosmopolitanism and the Politics of Community*. New York: Cambridge UP, 2001.

Carlston, Erin G. *Thinking Fascism: Sapphic Modernism and Fascist Modernity*. Stanford, CA: Stanford UP, 1998.

Cuddy-Keane, Melba. "The Politics of Comic Modes in Virginia Woolf's *Between the Acts*." *PMLA* 105.2 (March 1990): 273-285.

Duffy, Julia and Lloyd Davis. "Demythologizing Facts and Photographs in *Three Guineas*." *Photo-textualities: Reading Photographs and Literature*. Ed. Marsha Bryant. Wilmington: U of Delaware Press, 1996: 128-139.

Froula, Christine. "*Three Guineas* and the Photograph: The Art of Propaganda." *Virginia Woolf and the Bloomsbury Avant-Garde: War, Civilization, and Modernity*. New York: Columbia UP, 2004.

Gualtieri, Elena. *Women Writers of the 1930s: Gender, Politics and History*. Ed. Maroula Joannou. Edinburgh: Edinburgh UP, 1999.

Hackett, Robin. *Sapphic Primitivism: Productions of Race, Class and Sexuality in Key Works of Modern Fiction*. New Brunswick: Rutgers UP, 2004.

Hussey, Mark, ed. *Virginia Woolf and War: Fiction, Reality, and Myth*. Syracuse, NY: Syracuse UP, 1991.

Johnson, Erica. "The Legacy of the 'Outsider's Society': Woolf and Postcolonial Nationhood." MLA Convention, 28 December 2004, Philadelphia, PA.

Kristeva, Julia. "A Question of Subjectivity: An Interview." *Modern Literary Theory: A Reader*. Eds. Phillip Rice and Patricia Waugh. New York: Arnold, 1996.

———. *New Maladies of the Soul*. Trans. Ross Guberman. New York: Columbia UP, 1995.

Levenback, Karen L. *Virginia Woolf and the Great War*. Syracuse, NY: Syracuse UP, 1999.

Marcus, Jane. "Britannia Rules *The Waves*." Ed. Karen R. Lawrence. *Decolonizing Tradition: New Views of Twentieth-Century Literary Canons*. Urbana & Chicago: U of IL Press, 1992.

———. *Hearts of Darkness: White Women Write Race*. New Brunswick, NJ and London: Rutgers UP, 2004.

Morrison, Toni. *Playing in the Dark: Whiteness and the Literary Imagination*. Cambridge: Harvard UP, 1992.

Nancy, Jean-Luc. *Being Singular Plural*. Trans. Robert D. Richardson and Anne E. O'Byrne. Stanford: Stanford UP, 2000.

Pawlowski, Merry, ed. *Virginia Woolf and Fascism: Resisting the Dictator's Seduction*. New York: Palgrave, 2001.

Phillips, Kathy J. *Virginia Woolf Against Empire*. Knoxville, TN: U of Tennessee Press, 1994.

Rosenfeld, Natania. *Outsiders Together: Virginia and Leonard Woolf*. Princeton, NJ: Princeton UP, 2001.

Sontag, Susan. *Regarding the Pain of Others*. New York: Farrar, Straus and Giroux, 2003.

Strauss, David Levi. *Between the Eyes: Essays on Photography and Politics*. New York: Aperture, 2003.

Woolf, Virginia. "'Anon' and 'The Reader': Virginia Woolf's Last Essays." Ed. Brenda Silver. *Twentieth-Century Literature* 25, 3-4 (Fall/Winter 1979): 356-437.

——. *A Room of One's Own*. 1929. New York: Harcourt Brace, 1989.

——. *Between the Acts*. 1941. New York: Harcourt Brace, 1969.

——. *Moments of Being: Unpublished Autobiographical Writings*. Ed. and Intro. Jeanne Schulkind. Sussex: The University Press, 1976.

——. *The Moment, and Other Essays*. 1947. New York: Harcourt, Brace and Co., 1974.

——. *The Common Reader*: First and Second Series Combined in One Volume. 1925; 1932. New York: Harcourt, Brace, & Co., 1948.

——. *The Waves*. 1931. New York: Harcourt Brace Jovanovich, 1959.

——. *Three Guineas*. 1938. New York: Harcourt, Brace, & Jovanovich, 1965.

Exposure and Development: Re-Imagining Narrative and Nation in the Interludes of *The Waves*[1]

Renée Dickinson

The popular 19th century expression, "the sun never sets on the British Empire" (Wilson), encapsulates the established association of the sun with the reach of empire and with the mission of British imperialism. This mission included "images that show the natives being freed from despotic rule, raised from their ignorance, and saved from cruel and barbarous practices. These vignettes tell of the civilizing mission, which is primarily a story about the colonizing culture as an emissary of light" (Sharpe 100). The story of imperialism thus tells the story of "the colonizing culture" representing and bringing "civilizing" light to the "natives." As Gayatri Spivak reminds us, "imperialism, understood as England's social mission, was a crucial part of the cultural representation of England to the English. The role of literature in the production of cultural representation should not be ignored" (Spivak 269). This story of British imperialism, then, not only instructs the colonized but also instructs the English, justifying imperialism and contributing to the shape of English national identity and narrative formation.[2]

---

[1] A longer version of this article appeared as a chapter under the same name in my dissertation, "The Corporeum: Re-imagining Body, Land, Nation and Text in Virginia Woolf and Olive Moore." U of Colorado at Boulder. 2006.

[2] I refer to imperialism and colonialism according to the following definitions: "'*Imperialism*' is the concept that comprises all forces and activities contributing to the construction and the maintenance of *transcolonial empires*. Imperialism presupposes the will and the ability of an imperial center to *define* as imperial its own national interests and enforce them worldwide in the anarchy of the international system" (21); "'*Colonialism*' is a relationship of domination between an indigenous (or forcibly imported) majority and a minority of foreign invaders. The fundamental decisions affecting the lives of the colonized people are made and implemented by the colonial rulers in pursuit of interests that are often defined in a distant metropolis" (16 –17) from Jürgen Osterhammel's *Colonialism: A Theoretical Overview*. Trans. Shelley Frisch. Princeton: Markus Wiener, 1997. Thus, colonialism implicitly requires domination of one group over another whereas the ideologies and materialities of imperialism, which may result in colonialism, do not. Imperialism does, however, involve "an incursion, or an attempted incursion, into the sovereignty of another state . . . . one power has the will, and, if it is to succeed, the capacity to shape the affairs of another by imposing upon it. The relations established by imperialism are therefore based upon inequality and not upon mutual com-

The Waves, widely regarded as one of Virginia Woolf's most experimental texts, attends to national identity as well as textual experimentation. Specifically, the nine interludes, often neglected in criticism on *The Waves*, are deeply concerned with the politics of empire which "resonate through the interludes . . . . their images replay[ing] ruling-class expectations of mastery and fears of turbaned, armed warriors assaulting their shores" (Scott 31).

In their essential function, the interludes of *The Waves* show the movement of the sun from rising in the east to setting in the west, fixing and moving the reader's gaze from the east, a site of expansion and empire-making, to the west, the site of the British homeland.[3] Here I refute Jane Marcus's germinal argument that *The Waves* "emphatically dramatizes the very historical moment in which the sun does set" (155). In fact, the light of empire is not extinguished by any means.[4] Instead, the interludes reveal how, like their ongoing solar and oceanic cycles, the imperial impulse continues—and, at this moment of anxiety about the future of the empire, specifically continues in the homeland as well as in the colonies.[5]

Imperial colonization enacts violence ideologically by reducing its subject to an object and by placing it within the realm of the Other. Imperial colonization enacts violence materially by subjecting that subject/object to the position of

---

promises of the kind which characterize states of independence" (54). See this and an extensive discussion of British imperialism in Cain and Hopkins.

[3] See also Garrity 286.

[4] See various historians' arguments, such as those of Cain and Hopkins who argue that "the growth of the formal empire was a product of Britain's relative decline as a great power: the extension of sovereignty in Africa as only a poor recompense for the shrinkage of the informal economic empire elsewhere" (27), but that "imperialist enterprise was enfolded in a grand development strategy designed by Britain to reshape the world in her own image. It was spearheaded, not by manufacturing interests, but by gentlemanly elites who saw in empire a means of generating income flows in ways that were compatible with the high ideals of honour and duty, and it remained a dynamic, expanding force long after decline, as measured by British comparative industrial performance, is conventionally thought to have set in" (57), as well as Jennifer Mooney, who, on her University of Vermont website, cites that the British Empire was actually at its height in the 1930s. India and Pakistan did not become independent nations until 1947, remained "Dominions" for some time thereafter, and are still considered "Protectorates."

[5] For the purposes of this project, and in accordance with the focus of the interludes themselves on England, my analysis focuses on the effects of the imperial gaze on the homeland, not on the colonies and the colonized. For criticism on *The Waves* analyzing the effects of empire in the interludes and elsewhere in the text, see Phillips; Marcus; Heidi Stalla, "Empire and Elveden: New Light on *The Waves*." *Virginia Woolf Bulletin*. Vol 12, (Jan. 2003): 20–29; and Patrick McGee, "The Politics of Modernist Form: Or, Who Rules *The Waves*?" *Modern Fiction Studies* 38.3 (Fall 1992), 631-50.

the Other through physical and political domination (see footnote two). Considering these effects of objectification, the colonized space and the feminized space operate comparably, then, in the ideology of imperialism which requires that each occupies the place of the Other in opposition to the dominant (colonizing and/or patriarchal) force of empire. Thus, in *The Waves*, it is not surprising to find the incorporation of feminine images in the representation of the colonized. What is surprising is the use of feminine images to also represent the imperial project itself. It is these two intertwined depictions of the feminine within imperialism—the subjugation of the feminine as it is relegated to the status of the colonized and the utilization of the feminine to further the cause of imperialism—that I propose to unravel in this essay and that I argue the interludes of *The Waves* also seek to expose and resolve.

As I explore at length in the first section of this essay, *The Waves* utilizes the imagery of the sun to demonstrate the effects on representations of the feminine, here used to denote the companion to the monolithic term "patriarchy," in both the imperial project in general (in its use of images and bodies of women to promote and extend the empire) and colonization in particular (in its inhabitation of feminized spaces). As the sun of the interludes, at first metaphorized as a lamp borne aloft by a woman, comes to invade feminized spaces in the novel, the feminized subjects, be they women's bodies or the domestic space of the home, become objectified through the aggression of the sun which, I argue, essentially operates as an imperialistic and patriarchal figure in the interludes.[6]

As if in response to patriarchy's employment of images and bodies of women, *The Waves* also concerns itself with creating a new kind of textual space or "cultural project" that "consists . . . in offering the possibility of *different* modes of subjective positionings in language beyond the pretty fictions of the patriarchal order" (Paccaud-Huguet 230). These "subjective positionings" include identity formation at both the national and textual levels: the text challenges empire as a basis for national identity and challenges patriarchy as a basis for narrative. To that end, *The Waves* disrupts patterns of narrative and form to create not only new stories but new ways of telling stories through its imagery of light and shadow and through its structure of cycle and disruption.

Critics and historians have already delineated how identity configurations of British female subjects, both produced by and performed for patriarchal imperialism, are critical to national identity and, therefore, to imperial ideology. As

---

[6] The episodes also depict both the ideology and activities of imperialism in the homeland as they dramatize how, as Patrick McGee states, "there are obvious and subtle differences of gender and class among the six characters, but all of them are shaped by the imperialist ideology into which they are fitted and into which they fit" (ibid. 645).

Kathy Phillips has argued in her detailed analyses of Woolf's work, "The attitudes that determine the pecking order at home also fix the hierarchical oppressions of the Empire" (182). The equation also works in reverse: the same attitudes, hierarchies, and, one could say, stories, are repeated at home as they have been played out in the colonies. Historians Cain and Hopkins claim that "elite women acted as influential adjuncts to the masculine empire, whether as missionaries, doctors, managers of emigration societies, founders of the Girl Guides, or as propagandists," and that "[t]he gentlemanly elite was to this extent strengthened by its lady-like complement; both had their roles shaped by the empire they were trying to civilize" (13). They, thus, tell the story of women's role in empire building as being "adjuncts" and "complement[s]" to the patriarchal powers of imperialism. These stories of empire, as retold in the interludes of *The Waves*, reveal the "hierarchical oppressions of the Empire" (Phillips 182) and their effects on women, the domestic space of the home, and on narrative construction.[7]

I propose, therefore, that *The Waves* attempts to reverse the objectification of women in the service of empire in its "reshaping" (Katz 232) of imperial and modernist tropes of enlightenment and textual experimentation. *The Waves'* portrayal of the imperial project and its effects on the homeland in its use of gendered bodies of women and domestic spaces does not preclude all possibility of locating a new shape of identity subjectivity for women. Instead, I concur with Tamar Katz's reading of modernist textual experimentation:

> Modernist experiments in narrative form often take as their goal the reshaping of narrative to a newly-envisioned subjectivity. Stream-of-consciousness, impressionism, point-of-view narration—a range of narrative strategies offer the perceptual processes of the subject as the real story, and in doing so raise the question of just what shape subjectivity might possess. (232)

I argue that Woolf's textual experimentation not only questions "what shape subjectivity might possess," but also attempts to propose a new shape of female subjectivity through a new textual form that re-imagines narrative construction and, with it, national identity and the feminine inscriptions upon which it relies.

The tension between these two impulses of exposing and proposing emerges early in the first interlude in the image of the sun as a woman shining a lamp: "*as if the arm of a woman couched beneath the horizon had raised a lamp*" (*TW* 7). Although tempting to suggest that Woolf illuminates a feminist presence in the

---

[7] In addition, see Goldman, in which she claims that "Rhoda imagines becoming the ultimate female imperial subject, a counterpart to Percival" (194), and demonstrates the ways in which women saw themselves as active participants in the imperial project.

novel through this imagery of a female sun, I argue that the lady with the lamp *does not* operate as a feminist figure, controlling the solar cycle, but is instead a figurehead for the sun and a tool of imperialism.[8] Viewed this way, the lamp may be interpreted as the light of empire extending from the horizon back to the homeland. As I will argue, this imagery of the light becomes increasingly violent and militaristic throughout the interludes, extending the effects of empire and its violence onto the domestic spaces of England. Through both the narrative's reclamation of the imagery of enlightenment and shadow, and through the form of the text's experimentation in the interludes, Woolf attempts to extinguish imperialism's domestic gaze and reclaim language which has been in the service of empire. I, therefore, take the paradoxical position that *The Waves* creates at once an alliance between the feminine and nature through the imagery of the sun and a simultaneous critique of that alliance. This position proves productive because of the way Woolf reveals how the feminine, through this solar imagery, is portrayed as complicit in the work of empire and thus paves the way for Woolf's re-imagining of the feminine through imagery of shadow.

This essay, then, proceeds to argue for *The Waves*' exposure of imperialism's annexing of female imagery and its subsequent development of alternative feminine representations. I do so by considering, first, how the feminine is inherent in the work of empire and how the interludes of *The Waves* both expose and undermine that relationship and, second, how the textual experimentation of the interludes contributes to both the revelation and disruption of this relationship.[9] To that end, I argue that Woolf deploys her experiments with narrative and form to recover the image of the feminine from its uses by imperialism and to simul-

---

[8] See Madeline Moore's proposal that "Looked at in strictly biographical terms, the cosmological woman-as-sun, who dominates the poetic prologues of *The Waves*, resembles Julia Stephen, who was both nurturing and arbitrary, and was possibly a model of a deified sun goddess for her adoring daughter" (27) in *The Short Season Between Two Silences: The Mystical and the Political in the Novels of Virginia Woolf* (Winchester: Allen & Unwin, 1984), as well as Jane Marcus' argument in "Britannia Rules the Waves" regarding the sun in the interludes comprising an invocation of the sun as in Sanskrit poems, creating "a discourse for an alienated Western woman like Rhoda to have a 'heroic death,' like Indian widows in sati" (137).

[9] The narrative of the episodes, while important, useful and necessary to extend the connections between women, empire, and modernist form that I suggest, have already accrued much critical attention and thus are, here, supplemental to the primary focus of this argument on the more neglected developments of narrative and nation in the interludes. In this reading, then, the episodes become the text *between* the interludes, rather than the typical reading the other way around. To that end, my attention to the episodes is minimal, often footnoted, and discussed in their connection to and in their tension with the interludes.

taneously create a space in which that feminine can thrive outside of the reach of empire and its violence.

Gendered Imperialications: Women's Bodies & The Light of Empire

During the interwar period, the imperial project utilized women in its efforts to both produce citizens and represent national ideologies. Historian Susan Kent's research on images of women during World War I reveals that:

> metaphors utilized to explain and justify the war drew upon images of women in a variety of ways. Women were depicted variously as the terrain of war in representations that decried the rape of Belgium and France; as the objects of war in propaganda and recruiting posters; as the victims of war in reports of German atrocities; as the parasitic beneficiaries of war in *Punch* cartoons or irate letters to newspaper columns; as the wagers of war in tributes to women's wartime service, particularly that of munitions workers; even as the cause of the war in some accounts of prewar suffrage militancy. (9–10)

Kent's descriptions of images of women during the war illustrate the various manipulations of these images and their apparent transformative quality from "victims" to "the cause of war" as best suited the need of the wartime propagandists. After the war, women's bodies facilitated establishing definitions of self and other as well as (re)produced national subjects when they were "cultural[ly] appropriat[ed]"(Moran 149) by and for patriarchy and imperialism through their "corporeal identification" which marked them as "implicitly incompatible with the spiritual aims of citizenship" (Garrity 245). Through the machinations of patriarchy and imperialism, then, women's bodies, marked as pure and as purely bodies, became vessels for the production of citizens and for the symbolic representation of imperial ideology. In the colonies, the role of women was to provide an "attachment to the mother country" by making colonies which were "peopled with loyal British women as well as British men. . . . Without that home-life settlers will bring with them none of [their] peaceful influence" (Thane 31). Women were both essential and essentialized in the project of empire by representing and recreating the homeland in the colonies. For women to provide this "attachment to the mother country," they must already embody and portray an established representation of the mother country. Their identity, as Jane Garrity argues, "arises from the ability to reproduce conventional models of British womanhood—models which, whether generative or purely sexual, are dependent on some valorization of an essentialized female body" (260). Both physical and national identitifications, then, mark women's bodies and demarcate women as signifiers of nation and empire.

In *The Waves*, the light of imperialism fixes its gaze on the bodies and identities of women as a site of tenuous national identity and imperial domination. As *The Waves* also criticizes imperialism's use and determination of female identity, it reveals deeply established inscriptions of the feminine in the work of empire. I argue that in the interludes of *The Waves* the image of the sun as the lady with the lamp exposes these implications of imperialistic demarcations for women.[10] Through the lady with the lamp, the woman's body heralds not only the sun and the light of empire, it also calls forth other symbolic representations which inscribed women's bodies, namely the re-emergence during the inter-war period of the emphasis on woman's maternity, purity, and domesticity.[11] From the first interlude, the body of the lady with the lamp is employed in the work of imperial enlightenment as the bearer of the light which spreads from the horizon to the home:

> *Behind [the horizon], too, the sky cleared as if the white sediment there had sunk, or as if the arm of a woman couched beneath the horizon had raised a lamp and flat bars of white, green and yellow, spread across the sky like the blades of a fan.*[12] *(7)*

[10] The phrase "the lady with the lamp" denotes popular depictions of Florence Nightingale which showed Nightingale holding up an oil lamp over the soldiers at Scutari. Woolf would have been familiar with these images and with Lytton Strachey's critical account of Nightingale's life and work in *Eminent Victorians*. Woolf's depiction of the sun as a lady holding a lamp above the horizon summons these images and their depictions of Nightingale as a ministering angel as well as Strachey's subsequent criticism. See Lytton Strachey, *Eminent Victorians* (Middlesex: Penguin, 1948), as well as Renée Dickinson, "The Lady with the Lamp: Florence Nightingale and *The Waves*." *The Art of Exploration: Selected Papers from the Fifteenth Annual Conference on Virginia Woolf*. Ed. Helen Southworth and Elisa Kay Sparks (Clemson: Clemson U Digital Press, 2006).

[11] Susan Kent writes on the role of maternity and motherhood for the "new" feminists after WWI: "Britons sought a return to the 'traditional' order of the prewar world, an order based on natural biological categories of which imagined sexual differences were a familiar and readily available expression . . . . A gender system of separate spheres for men and women based upon scientific theories of sexual difference, a new emphasis upon motherhood, and an urgent insistence upon mutual sexual pleasure within marriage provided parameters within which 'normal' activity was to be carried out and a return to normalcy effected . . . . As Riley has argued, 'women's' thorough implication in 'the social'—especially, as it became, in the interwar years, obsessively focused on maternity and motherhood—limited feminism's ability to exist and operate effectively" (140-141). See also, Denise Riley, *War in the Nursery: Theories of the Child and Mother* (London: Virago, 1983), and Jane Lewis, *The Politics of Motherhood: Child and Maternal Welfare in England, 1900 – 1939* (London: Croom Helm, 1980).

[12] The fans of colors and later of waves further the feminine imagery. The description of this imagery as feminine is confirmed through association in the penultimate

Demonstrating both agency and complicity, this passage shows how the woman is both powerful in her ability to raise the lamp of the sun, changing the colors and texture of the air, sea and sky, but is also an agent of a power outside herself (i.e. the lamp). Her body, specifically her arm, is used to hold up the lamp whose light shines on the waves, the beach, the garden, and the house, and thus extends the light from the horizon to the home.

Jane Marcus persuasively refers to this arm as "the mighty white arm of empire and civilization" (159), placing the agency of empire in the body of the woman itself and extending the symbolism of geographical enlightenment specifically to imperial activity. Although I agree with Marcus's correlation between the lady/sun and empire, I argue that the lamp itself, not the woman's arm, contains the light and thus represents imperial enlightenment. The woman's arm, only a tool for holding the lamp, situates the body of the woman as a manipulated figurehead lacking agency of her own.[13] In the interludes, broadly, I suggest the woman's body becomes the tool for spreading the light of empire, and her status as imperial instrument indicates that *The Waves* perceives women in an inextricable and subordinate relation to imperialism.

Some critics characterize the feminized sun as a herald of a new, feminist space. For example, Madeline Moore sees that "[i]n the first prologue prior to the children's birth, the creative force of nature is anthropomorphized as a great mythic woman who is the source of all creation. She is the symbolic figure out of which Woolf establishes a cosmogony in *The Waves*" (228-9). For Moore, the lady with the lamp becomes a powerful protofeminist and the basis for the entire "cosmogony" of *The Waves*. Moore's analysis ultimately essentializes women as earth mothers and as producers (and reproducers) of nature, platonically reducing them to a lesser status than the thinking man. Specifically, by associating women with nature, Moore's reading reduces women to a less-civilized, utilitarian and/or iconographic status rather than proposing equality or alterity for women, and therefore falls short of locating an alternative to patriarchal forms and stories, including mythic ones.

I instead align this argument with Jane Goldman's which states that the sun in *The Waves* is "predominantly patriarchal," demonstrating women as the "enslaved functionary of the patriarchal order" and as "appropriating the icon of masculine subjectivity (the sun)" (189). To this I add that Woolf preserves the

---

interlude when the "girls, sitting on verandahs, look up at the snow, shading their faces with their fans" (237).

[13] See Jane Garrity's further discussion of women and women's bodies' collaboration in the work of empire in which she states that "In *The Waves*, perhaps more than in any other of her works, Woolf acknowledges that women's quest for linguistic inclusion is legitimized by and embedded in the doctrine of expansion and rule" (271).

essence of the sun's patriarchal position in order to criticize the use of women as figureheads of patriarchy and imperialism.[14] As the sun's gender transforms throughout the interludes, its "patriarchal" position is ultimately revealed.

Throughout my argument in this section, I trace three progressions in the interludes: the progression of the sun's gender from feminine to neutral, the progression of the sun's characterization from feminine to primitive, and the progression of the imagery of the sun from feminine light to feminine darkness. First, the sun's gendered physicality, first seen in the image of the lady with the lamp, devolves by interlude three into that of a girl. Eventually, the metaphor of *"The girl who had shaken her head and made all the jewels, the topaz, the aquamarine, the water-coloured jewels with sparks of fire in them dance"* (73) in the third interlude regresses further into a neutered *"it,"* staging the continued evolution of the sun into an ungendered and violent entity. The fourth interlude abandons the feminine imagery of the sun so that it no longer *"couch[es] on a green mattress"* or *"dart[s] a fitful glance through watery jewels."* Instead, the sun, now directly *"bare[s] its face"* and *"look[s] straight over the waves."* Although Woolf actively promotes androgyny in other texts, namely *A Room of One's Own*, in the interludes of *The Waves*, I argue that the seemingly androgynous "it" enacts violence when associated with imperialism and is therefore a place holder for patriarchy.[15] This, then, is not the kind of idealized social and/or authorial androgyny Woolf advocates in *AROO* but a gradual unveiling of the patriarchal forces behind the feminine figurehead of imperialistic enlightenment.

Paralleling this progression to gender neutrality is a simultaneous devolution of the light from feminine to primitive, in both the text's use of *"lances"* (108) in the fourth interlude and its conversion of the lady with the lamp into *"turbaned men with poisoned assegais"* in the third and fourth interludes (75, 109). The sun thus moves from a feminine icon of enlightenment to a now specifically masculine stereotype of the primitive warrior. Mariana Torgovnick asserts that "the primitive was coded metaphorically as feminine, collective, and ecstatic, and civilization was coded as masculine, individualistic, and devoted to the quotidian

---

[14] See also Eileen B. Sypher's commentary in Ginsberg and Gottlieb's *Virginia Woolf: Centennial Essays* (New York: Whitston Publishing Company, 1983) in which she states that "the image of the female sun is tentative. (Often the sun's 'femaleness' is imaged in a simile and after the sun becomes hot, 'uncompromising' (*TW* 148), Woolf drops the metaphor/simile altogether and the sun becomes 'it')" (195).

[15] In *A Room of One's Own*, Virginia Woolf writes that "[p]erhaps to think, as I had been thinking these two days, of one sex as distinct from the other is an effort . . . . Coleridge perhaps meant this when he said that a great mind is androgynous . . . . Perhaps a mind that is purely masculine cannot create, any more than a mind that is purely feminine" (*AROO* [Harvest, 1957] 97-8).

business of the family, city, or state" (14). In this definition, the masculine governs the civilized state and empire, each inhabited by the primitive feminine. Torgovnick further argues that this "fascination with the primitive . . . can express itself in a variety of ways: negatively—for example, as fear of the primitive or as a detour into violence; and positively—as admiration for the primitive, conceived to be the conduit of spiritual emotions" (7). The association of woman with the negative expression of the primitive—with violence—is exactly the kind of progression or "detour" at play in the interludes of *The Waves*. Although the solar imagery abandons the mask of the female figurehead, the evolution of the imagery as well as the common association of women with the primitive as outlined by Torgovnick, suggest a continued interchange between the feminine—which is at once both the pure English rose and the primitive savage—and the imperial project. This association reveals not only the appropriation of women's bodies for the spread of imperialism through the lady with the lamp, but also the inherent violence involved in this act.[16] Significantly, the etymology of "couch" used in conjunction with the lady with the lamp in the interludes reveals additional violence. Although in *The Waves* it denotes to "lie or lay down," it also connotes its other definitions—"to lie in ambush" and "to lower a lance into position for an attack"—further suggesting the ambiguity of women's involvement in empire and war in the interludes.

The devolution into the primitive also reveals the paradoxical position of women in empire as passive symbols rather than active agents in empire making, conveniently manipulating and adapting the images of women to advance the cause of empire.[17] In the fifth interlude, the solar imagery is more explicitly connected to the work of empire:

> *It was no longer half seen and guessed at, from hints and gleams, as if a girl couched on her green-sea mattress tired her brows with water-globed jewels*

---

[16] At the same time, in the episodes, Percival's work in India represents the work of the empire in the colonies (see pages 116, 123, 126, 136, 137, 145, 147, 151 and 153). The narrative of the episodes adds a double valence to the primitivism of the sun by extending its militaristic violence to the colonies. The primitive, then, as seen in the colonial subject and in the bodies of women, both comes under attack by the empire and figures as an image of the attacking empire.

[17] See Kathy Phillips's argument that "[i]n trying to recreate an unspoiled land in England, Jinny further forgets that she has portrayed the jungle not only as a refuge of beautiful license but also as a place of death" (175). Jinny here actively participates in the creation of nation and imperial identity through her portrayal of the jungle in contrast to England, yet, Phillips claims, she does so unwittingly, "forget[ting]" the consequences of her rhetoric.

that sent lances of opal-tinted light falling and flashing in the uncertain air like
the flanks of a dolphin leaping, or the flash of a falling blade. (148)

The *"water-globed jewels"* in this passage connect the sun to sea exploration, empire building and the booty of each, decorating the female figurehead with imperial activities which she then carries and carries out. By the end of the description, these *"jewels"* are connected further to violence as well as they *"sent lances"* like *"the flash of a falling blade."* Through the solar imagery, the interludes of *The Waves* reveal how the ideology of empire creates a false alliance between the feminine and nature and uses that alliance to further its imperial goals. The imagery of the sun also exposes patriarchy as hidden behind feminine representations, making the image of the lady with the lamp a kind of Trojan horse, appearing at first a benign girl but eventually revealed to be accompanied with the violent *"lances"* and *"blades"* of warfare. The conversion is complete as what once were the lady with the lamp's "blades of a fan" (7) in the first interlude become in the fifth interlude *"a falling blade"* (148) of the warrior's lances.

Although the increasing gender neutrality of the sun may appear to create an androgynous space in the interludes, the association of that space with primitive and violent, militaristic imagery proves destructive for women and the images of them used to advance the light of empire. The disturbing depiction of the woman's body as a tool for spreading the light of empire takes on not only the activity of empire per se, of enlightenment, but also its violent attitudes and patriarchal behaviors through the imagery of the sun's military acts of stereotypical savages with spears and assegais and of the war machine of cavalry. Thus, the images and bodies of women are implicated through the imagery of the sun to be complicit agents of empire and its violence, albeit unwitting ones. In contrast to the episodes, where the characters are working to distinguish themselves in their gendered, national, and vocational identities, the interludes develop a dissolution of these same identities as the sun becomes gendered neutral and then masculine, for example. The violence of the waves, at its height in the fourth interlude, preceding Percival's departure for India, continues in the fifth and sixth interludes, after Percival's death. In this way, the violence of the waves replicates the activities of empire, continuing its crashing upon and through the colonies even after the dream of imperialism has died.[18] Kathy Phillips suggests that "[r]eferences

---

[18] For further discussion of military violence in the episodes, see Phillips' discussion of Percival, Louis and British education where she argues that "Percival epitomizes . . . two of the most dangerous qualities inculcated by the schools—regimentation and militarism" (155), culminating in Woolf "expos[ing] the totalizing impulse of Empire as totalitarian, and, in fact, Louis resembles the fascists coming to power in Europe in the decade before *The Waves*" (161).

to imperialism and militarism often occur together because, once a country accepts the need for colonies, it must rely on force to put down local rebellions and fend off other European nations" (225), asserting the inexplicability of colonialism, read here as an extension of imperialism, and violence.

In addition, as the solar imagery becomes gender neutral, and the façade of the feminine is abandoned, the light of the sun increasingly penetrates the domestically coded home and homeland. From the first interlude, as the light touches the house, it "*sharpen[s] the walls of the house, and rest[s] like the tip of a fan upon a white blind and ma[kes] a blue fingerprint of shadow under the leaf by the bedroom window*" (8). Here, the light is figured as necessary as the house and "*all within*" is still "*dim and unsubstantial*" and in need of enlightenment. In the second interlude, as the sun lays "*broader blades upon the house*" (29), the sharpness of the light in the first interlude becomes "*blades*" so that what in the first interlude seems like a neutral clarity, here becomes a tool of violence. In the fourth interlude, where the light has devolved from feminine to neutrality, it now "*[falls] in sharp wedges inside the room*," reasserting the violence of the light's imagery—"*A knife looked like a dagger of ice*" (110)—and conjuring the imagery of the warriors' "*lances*" and "*assegais*." The imagery of the sun, as "*sharp*," "*blades*," "*a knife*," and "*a dagger*," thus appears to invade and attack the house, revealing how imperial violence comes to bear on the home of the homeland. Nearly every interlude's description moves from the horizon to the house, moving the imagery of violence from the distant sites of colonization into the supposed havens of domesticity in the homeland and enacting the effects of imperialism on the colonizing country as well as on the colonized.

The third progression follows the transformation of the imagery of the sun from feminine light to feminine shadow. As the light strengthens, it contributes to the creation of its opposite, darkness, and with it creates a greater distinction between light and dark, self and other, masculine and feminine. In the fourth interlude, "*as the light increased, flocks of shadow were driven before it and conglomerated and hung in many-pleated folds in the background*" (110). Here, the shadows become cloth-like, and are gendered feminine, as the light drives it/them out of view. With this feminizing of the shadows, the unmasking of the sun as masculine is complete. Furthermore, the sun's striking "*straight upon the house*" with "*sharp-edged wedges of light*" in the fifth interlude is even more of an attack on the "*dark windows*" "*of impenetrable darkness*" (150) of the feminized home. The light of empire is locked out of the house, unable to penetrate the feminine, domestic sphere still described here as "*darkness*." The inscription of the feminine as uncivilized or savage, evidenced earlier in the imagery of the sun, here becomes displaced in and converted into the shadows of the domestic sphere. These feminized shadows now become the target of the imperial light's pursuit and violence, a threat that must be extinguished although created by that selfsame light. Ultimately, in the sixth interlude, as the "*[l]ight driving darkness before it split itself profusely upon the corners and bosses; and yet heaped up darkness in mounds of unmoulded shape*" (166), the light pursues but cannot eradicate the darkness or shadows.[19] The transformation of the activities of the sun from bearing the feminine light to attacking the feminine darkness exposes both the masculinist basis of imperial activity and the effects of that activity on the feminine, be that representations of women's bodies or the feminized space of the home.

All three progressions—from feminine to androgyny, from feminine to savage, and from feminine light to feminine darkness—work to expose the violence inherent in imperialism. Through the use of feminine imagery, the interludes also expose how this violence first utilizes a feminine façade and then abandons it when attacking the feminized, domestic spaces of the homeland.

As if in response to the invasion of the light, the imagery in the interludes of *The Waves*, having exposed these representations of women as both light and shadow, reverses itself and reclaims the image of feminized darkness. In the closing interludes, the image of the lady with the lamp, tainted with imperialist ideology and practice, is revealed as no longer useful for women. Woolf instead reclaims the ideology of women as dark or unenlightened (primitive) by here refiguring the imagery of shadow in the interludes as a space of alterity for female subjectivity. The description of shadow and darkness, used throughout the interludes, by the eighth interlude encompasses all of the landscape of the interludes:

> *As if there were waves of darkness in the air, darkness moved on, covering houses, hills, trees, as waves of water wash round the sides of some sunken ship. Darkness washed down streets eddying round single figures, engulfing them; blotting out couples clasped under the showery darkness of elm trees in full summer foliage. Darkness rolled its waves along grassy rides and over the wrinkled skin of the turf, enveloping the solitary thorn tree and the empty snail shells at its foot. Mounting higher, darkness blew along the bare upland slopes, and met the fretted and abraded pinnacles of the mountain where the snow lodges for ever on the hard rock even when the valleys are full of running streams and yellow vine leaves, and girls, sitting on verandahs, look up at the snow, shading their faces with their fans. Them, too, darkness covered.* (237)

---

[19] This progression of increased violence demonstrates the anxiety of the feminine in the homeland during peacetime. To review a specific example, Alison Light argues that "[s]ince war, whatever its horrors, is manly, there is something both lower-class and effeminate about peacetime" (7). Alison Light, *Forever England: Femininity, Literature and Conservatism Between the Wars* (London: Routledge, 1991).

Here, the antithesis to the lady with the lamp, the "girls, sitting on verandahs . . . shading their faces with their fans" (237), emerges as an alternative to embracing the light and work of empire. Instead of being invaded by the militaristic sun, the girls are protected by darkness and shield themselves from the imperial solar gaze; instead of being light bearers, emanating or carrying the light themselves, the girls are shadow seekers, refusing to participate in the work of enlightenment. The language of darkness with its implied femininity and subjection of the feminine, inherent in the ideology of empire, changes in the interludes to a language of possibility and freedom, defying the trope of darkness as savagery or ignorance and converting it instead into a means of protection from the light of empire. Unlike the house in the interludes which is shuttered away from the light—containing "*still denser depths of darkness*" (150)—the girls, rather than cloistered from incorporation into the imperial project, are posed to see a world without the harsh light of empire and free from the violence and inhabitation of the imperial sun.

With the setting of the sun, Woolf temporarily extinguishes the light of empire and its co-opting of the imagery and labor of women. In doing so, she proposes the darkness as a place of possibility for a new female subjectivity to emerge. Just as Woolf proposed removing the Angel in the House, described in *The Pargiters* as "the woman that men wished women to be" (qtd. by Hussey 219), she here proposes removing the woman as bearer of imperial enlightenment, the Lady with the Lamp. As the cyclical nature of the sun promises that it will return, Woolf prepares for a new image of woman, resistant to the light of empire and its violence, to replace the iconic lady with the lamp. In the face of the oncoming darkness, the imagery of the girls shading themselves from the light, rather than triggering ignorance or danger, presents a conscious refusal to be touched by or to be bearers of the light of empire. Through these girls the text suggests that future generations may not embrace the light of imperialism, may not engage in the work of empire. Additionally, the girls "*look up at the snow*," focusing on an element that resists the potency of the imperial sun and directing their own gaze upon a symbol of resistance. Whereas the lady with the lamp, the "*woman couched*," conducted light, these girls refuse to look at it, and in turning from it, turn also from the inscriptions of imperial enlightenment on female subjectivity that accompany it.[20]

---

[20] For further discussion of the implications of Woolf's use of light and shadow see Patrick McGee's argument that in the episodes,"[t]he collective identity of all these individualized characters depends on the ethnocentric mapping of the world into areas of light and areas of darkness" (645). In addition, though, he claims that "[Marcus'] reading still would have Woolf dividing the world along ethnocentric lines into a zone of light associated with culture (the West) and a zone of darkness associated with nature (the East)"

Textual Occupation: Pushing Words to the Margins

The textual experimentation of *The Waves* likewise exposes similar concerns about empire as those witnessed through the solar imagery of the interludes. Just as the imagery of the sun exposes the strategic use of images of women in the imperial project and the violent ramifications of this practice on the feminine, *The Waves* employs a linguistic practice that has a penetrating presence, demonstrates a two-way movement of hybridity,[21] and reveals an anxiety about ending and continuing, further exposing the text's concerns about the practices and effects of imperialism through its narrative construction.[22] *The Waves* as a visual text tries to fill its entire world by filling all the blank spaces on the page. Its dense, blocky form, found most clearly in the later episodic chapters, extends the textual experimentation of Woolf and others beyond that seen in Woolf's earlier works. This attempt to fill the page can be seen to represent the imperial impulse to fill the blank spaces on the map. The increased occupation of the margins of the text as the narrative progresses parallels and pictures the heightened imperial activities in the 1930s (see footnote nine) as well as the heightened anxiety about

---

(646). Thus, McGee asks us to consider the ways in which we read light and darkness and suggests, too, that Woolf attempts to question and undermine these associations with culture and nature.

[21] Homi Bhabha describes hybridity in detail as "the sign of the productivity of colonial power, its shifting forces and fixities; it is the name for the strategic reversal of the process of domination through disavowal . . . . the revaluation of the assumption of colonial identity through the repetition of discriminatory identity effects. It displays the necessary deformation and displacement of all sites of discrimination and domination. It unsettles the mimetic or narcissistic demands of colonial power but reimplicates its identifications in strategies of subversion that turn the gaze of the discriminated back upon the eye of power" (34-5) "Signs Taken for Wonders." *The Post-Colonial Studies Reader.* Bill Ashcroft, Gareth Griffiths and Helen Tiffin, eds. (London: Routledge, 1995), and: "The paranoid threat from the hybrid is finally uncontainable because it breaks down the symmetry and the duality of self/other, inside/outside. In the productivity of power, the boundaries of authority—its reality effects—are always besieged by 'the other scene' of fixations and phantoms" (116) in "Signs Taken for Wonders: Questions of ambivalence and authority under a tree outside Delhi, May 1817." *The Location of Culture* (London: Routledge, 1994). Bhabha's analysis of the breakdown of inside/outside boundaries contributes to this argument as I suggest below that *The Waves* embodies both the dissolution of inside/outside narratives and the subsequent anxieties produced.

[22] In the last episode, Bernard asks, "Should this be the end of the story? a kind of sigh? a last ripple of the wave? a trickle of the water to some gutter where, burbling, it dies away? . . . . But if there are no stories, what end can there be, or what beginning? . . . . our waters can only just surround feebly that spike of sea-holly; we cannot reach that further pebble so as to wet it. It is over, we are ended" (267), fusing both anxieties about narrative and imperial activities and closure in his concerns about telling and ending stories in the metaphor of accessing other lands.

the continuation of empire. In addition, as I argue in detail below, the incorporation of interludic language into the episodes, depicts an impulse toward "literary hegemony" on the part of Bernard in particular and the episodic narrative in general.[23] If, as Simon Gikandi has argued, "the imperial map of the world was to thread its way into the cultural products of the West and become a vital part of its 'texture of linguistic and cultural practice'" (5), *The Waves* reflects the violence of its cultural practice, a practice which attempts to push out all other voices and into all other spaces. In this way, *The Waves* can be seen as a text which exposes the practices of imperialism in its physical construction of a visual monopoly of the words on the page.

The Waves betrays its deep anxiety not only about the empire's dominance but also about its future. National cultures, as Anthony Easthope claims, "are . . . reproduced through narratives and discourses" (12), and so the national culture reproduced through *The Waves* is one of intense anxiety about its position in the world, both nationally and textually, demonstrated most clearly through the imperialist "hero" (123), Percival, who dies from being thrown from his horse or because "[h]is horse tripped" (151), turning the activities of imperialism into a farce. In the interludes of *The Waves*, this anxiety emerges through concerns about hybridity and conclusion, both concerns of this later stage of imperialism as well.

The hybridity of the text is evidenced in the cross-pollination of interludic and episodic languages. In the fifth interlude we hear the echo of Louis' beast from the episodes: "*The waves fell; withdrew and fell again, like the thud of a great beast stamping*" (150). The language of the interludes is in turn taken up by the episodes. At Percival's dinner, Rhoda's remarks incorporate interludic imagery of "birds' wings," a "white arm," and "the sea" (139). Rhoda alludes to several of the tropes of the interludes, but in many sites of the episodes, the exact language of the interludes mingles with the narrative. Bernard's soliloquy in the last episode serves as the most striking example: "Day rises; the girl lifts the watery fire-hearted jewels to her brow; the sun levels his beams straight at the sleeping house . . . the house is whitened; the sleeper stretches; gradually all is astir. Light floods the room and drives shadow beyond shadow to where they hang in folds inscrutable" (291-92). The specific interludic language of the girl's watery jewels and the house's folds of shadow suggest a violation of the bound-

---

[23] Jane Marcus argues that not only are "[t]he fragmented selves of the 'civilized' characters in *The Waves* . . . directly related to the politics of British imperialism" (144), Bernard's character specifically enacts these imperial politics as in "an act of literary hegemony; he absorbs the voices of his marginalized peers into his own voice" (142). Bernard's "literary hegemony" then narratizes the visual production of the text in its own encroachment on the margins.

aries of the established form and create a hybrid discourse between the episodes and interludes. In addition, the specific gendering of the sun as "his beams" creates a further hybridity with the previous phrase's depiction of the sun as "the girl." In Bernard's final monologue, as Patrick McGee states, "the voice of the interludes," "[n]o longer italicized, no longer safely confined to the margins . . . erupts from within the discourse of the imperialist subject" (638). The narrative of *The Waves* moves beyond the textual borders demarcating interlude and episode and threatens the purity of narrative with hybridity. As McGee continues, "if Bernard's final monologue is *explicitly* contaminated by the voice of the interludes that are supposed to frame it, then the entire set of monologues, by virtue of the abstractness of Woolf's style is *implicitly* contaminated by such a frame" and "this instability of the frame is also an instability of the center" (639). McGee's analysis utilizes the language of hybridity in its concern about contamination and the resulting unsettling of identity, in his analysis of narrative identity, and, in post-colonial theory such as Bhabha's, of national and imperial identity. Thus, again, the two activities of narrative construction and national and imperial identity construction and maintenance intertwine in the novel and prove their co-reliance. It is at this moment of greatest textual hybridity that the narrative of the text becomes the most resistant, demonstrating in Bernard's final cry of defiance—"Against you will I fling myself, unvanquished and unyielding, O Death!" (297)—all of the anxiety about the return of the empire to the homeland, the encroaching contact with the other (narrative), and the desire for continuance.[24]

The interludes develop these concerns about continuance and hybridity when the light, upon invading the domestic space of the house in the fourth interlude, creates ambiguity and monstrosity: "*A jar was so green that the eye seemed sucked up through a funnel by its intensity and stuck to it like a limpet*" (110). In this example, the sun of empire does not enlighten or civilize the domestic, it creates freakish hybrids and monsters, its violence proving destructive to the purity of the domestic and indicating the anxiety of imperial decline and of contamina-

---

[24] See also *The Interrupted Moment* by Lucio Ruotolo where he argues that in the latter interludes "[t]he rhythm of the interludes is now marked by Bernard's unyielding rhetoric. As if in a final act of proud transcendence, Bernard's art stamps its image on the surrounding emptiness. The last aspect of the external world is reduced to a vestige of his own rhetoric, and the world, as it were, dies with him" (170). Here, Ruotolo demarcates the interludic space as "surrounding emptiness" and that with the death of Bernard as author, the narrative dies as well. Lucio P. Ruotolo, *The Interrupted Moment: A View of Virginia Woolf's Novels* (Stanford: Stanford UP, 1986).

tion.²⁵ Once the light enters the house in the sixth interlude, the language becomes inundated with violent military imagery: "*The blind hung red at the window's edge and within the room daggers of light fell upon chairs and tables making cracks across their lacquer and polish. The green pot bulged enormously, with its white window elongated in its side*" (165-6).²⁶ The red of the blind conjures the blood and violence of war, but also the "*daggers of light*" that "fall" upon the symbols of domesticity—chairs and tables—and cause cracks in their polish. Here, I further propose that the "*lacquer and polish*" and "*green pot*" imply the spoils of empire brought home from the colonies, merging the feminine and the colonized in the same space and representing the presence of the colonies in the homeland. The translation of the imperial impulse onto homeland domesticity is secured through the symbols of the colonies, exposing the anxieties about bringing the empire into the home and its potential contamination.

Yet, *The Waves* reverses or answers this position of anxiety through its textual form which, as the interludes break up the chronicle of the chapters, demonstrates the possible disruption of the traditional patterns and stories of nar-

---

²⁵ An alternative reading here, by looking at the episodes, would consider the following episode's dinner with Percival as a moment of unification. Rather than creating monstrous, hybridized identities that merge one character into another, this moment creates a unifying identity around Percival which the characters relish. Jinny, in fact, says: "Let us hold it for one moment, . . . love, hatred, by whatever name we call it, this globe whose walls are made of Percival, of youth and beauty, and something so deep sunk within us that we shall perhaps never make this moment out of one man again" (145).

²⁶ The violent entry of the sun in the domestic sphere of the house precedes the characters' remembrance of the colonist, Percival, during their everyday living of the sixth episode. Louis considers his death as one of many ("all deaths are one death" [170]) and then exhorts himself to "out of the many men in me make one" (170), echoing the unifying effect of Percival. Susan imagines Percival "com[ing] home, bringing me trophies to be laid at my feet. He will increase my possessions" (172), echoing the booty of imperialism in this interlude. Jinny briefly alludes to Percival as "[i]n one way or another we make this day . . . . Some take the train for France; others ship for India. Some will never come into this room again. One may die tonight" (176), but, like Louis, couches this in a discussion of unification as "[t]he common fund of experience is very deep" (175). Neville compares himself to Percival and finds that he "could not ride about India in a sun-helmet and return to a bungalow," and compares his lover to Percival who consoles Louis "for the lack of many things—I am ugly, I am weak—and the depravity of the world, and the flight of youth and Percival's death, and bitterness and rancour and envies innumerable" (181). In all, the characters of the episodes recall the unity brought by the imperialist, Percival, a unity that the imperial sun here, in the preceding interlude, disfigures and destroys. In this comparison, then, the ideals of imperialism as represented by Percival in the episodes, are shown to be false compared to the realities of its consequences as shown by the activities of the sun in the interludes.

rative and nation. The episodes of *The Waves*, while enacting a break from traditional narrative form, still progress systematically from childhood to old age and death. With the addition of the interludes, *The Waves* strays further from traditional narrative form by breaking the pattern of beginning, middle and ending, and interspersing the stories of the lives of the characters with a separate narrative of the ongoing solar and oceanic cycles. Although the lives of the characters continue to play out the sequence of traditional narratives (albeit in a very nontraditional narrative form), this narrative is interrupted by a static, continuous story of the sun, "arrest[ing] the linear sequence of writing by using the techniques of simultaneity through the use of spaces of silence like the interludes of nature" (Laurence 180).[27]

The use of both "poetic language and experimental structure" in the interludes enacts what Jane Marcus terms "anti-imperialist" "radical politics" that liberate the image of woman from the confines of collaboration with the imperial project (Marcus 155). By re-imagining women's affiliations with nature through the shadows of possibility rather than through the light of empire, the interludes "suggest the end of writing and the end of a certain kind of culture" (Marcus 155) based on the hierarchies of patriarchy and imperialism as reinscribed through narrative. The interruption of traditional patterns of narrative in *The Waves* "resist[s] not only authoritative narratives that use words to define and communicate thoughts and feelings but also the very hierarchically structured patriarchal culture that relies upon and uses these words to dictate to, define and dominate women" (Burford 269). The interludes, then, despite revealing the power of patriarchy and empire through its imagery of the sun and its violence, paradoxically serve to disrupt the patriarchal and imperialistic episodes, creating a textual alternative that resists conventional narrative progression and creates a place in the text that exists outside of traditional forms and their hierarchies.

Woolf's experimentation with textual form, then, is also an experiment with spaces of personal and national identity, an attempt to find a place where different kinds of stories and nations may be created and enacted without the threat of dissolution or destruction. Woolf accomplishes this by creating not only an experimental narrative form, but by interspersing the narrative of the episodes with an alternate story of the interludes. In this alternate space, the cycle of the sun promises that the story of the interludes will continue and can, in fact, continue free of humanity's imperialism and language of violence, domination, and

---

[27] Miriam Wallace also argues that "Even the interstices of italicized text are contiguous: to each other visually, to the voices sequentially, and through shared images" (299). Miriam L. Wallace, "Theorizing Relational Subjects: Metonymic Narrative in *The Waves*." *Narrative*. 8.3 (Oct. 2000): 294-323.

inhabitation. In this alternate space, too, not only can the imperialistic language be reclaimed and reworked, but the imperial ideology, too, can be refigured.

Exposure and Development: The Old Empire and the New Woman

Throughout my explorations of the solar imagery and the textual experimentation in *The Waves*, I illustrate how the interludes expose the machinations of imperialism through the unveiling of the sun as masculine, imperial, and violent and also imperialism's effects on women and the feminine through the confiscation of the female figure as a representation of imperial ideology and practice and the extension of the inherent violence involved in these practices upon the feminine other of the colonized as well as on the feminine sites of the homeland. Eventually and simultaneously, as the shadow imagery replaces the attempted enlightenment of the imperial sun, the textual experimentation also refigures imperial ideology through its practices of hybridity and disruption, experimentation and alterity. Thus, the exposure of imperialism's ideological and practical apparatuses lays juxtaposed with the development of future subjectivities of the feminine and of narrative as a kind of post-occupation reconstruction of the text.

In the third interlude, as the light of the sun enters the house, the furnishings appear to meld into one another so that they are both "*separate*" and "*inextricably involved*" (75). Likewise, the text of *The Waves*, comprising two separate but connected narratives and narrative strategies in the interludes and episodes which operate independently and interconnectedly, replicates the text's ideological tensions through its material form. Woolf's positioning of these two textual formats of the episodes and interludes in juxtaposition and dialogue with each other foregrounds the tension between the imperial impulse to colonize and the possibility of a new story beyond imperialism. With the conclusion of the interludes, as the shadows encroach upon the girls on the verandah, the interludes present a scene with the potential for the playing out of new narratives. If, as Torgovnick has argued, "In its most generalized sense, 'primitive' refers to a posited but ultimately unknowable original state" (4), then I propose that Woolf deliberately points back to a supposedly primitive or dark place outside the light of imperialism, a place with other and undiscovered alternatives for the stories of women and nation. In order to develop feminine subjectivity and narrative, Woolf seeks to begin in an imagined prehistory, in a time and place that exists prior to or outside the inscriptions of the feminine developed by patriarchy and imperialism.[28]

---

[28] See also Gillian Beer's discussion of "Virginia Woolf and Prehistory" in *Virginia Woolf: The Common Ground*, (Ann Arbor: U of Michigan P, 1996) in which she writes that "prehistory is seen not simply as part of a remote past, but as contiguous, continuous,

In this way, the interludes act as preludes, preparing the scene and creating anticipation for a new woman to speak on this stage still set in darkness.[29]

The final line of the novel, "*The waves broke on the shore*," could be read as a continuation of the language of imperialism in its reference to the imperial and militaristic activities of the sun and with that the promise of imperialism's continuation. As part of the interludes, though, it can also be read as a *break* with the tradition, ideology and language of empire. Just as Woolf reclaims and refigures the language of darkness, she in this final interlude refigures imperialistic language of violence by turning it upon itself. Thus, *The Waves* concludes with the newly-redefined darkness which offers new possibilities for women and the text to develop away from the light of empire.[30]

---

a part of ordinary present-day life" (9) and that "in Woolf" there is an "emphasis upon lost and unreclaimable origins" as well as "a counter-insistence on perpetuity and on the survival of what precedes consciousness, precedes history" (11). Both movements, of a lost origin and of a survival of prehistory, are at work here in the interludes of *The Waves* as we see Woolf both yearning for an imagined and attempting to locate an actual reality of the feminine outside of patriarchal and imperial history.

[29] The narrative device of stage setting is witnessed even more clearly in the conclusion of *Between the Acts* which poses the main characters Isa and Giles as if on a dark stage and about to perform: "Isa let her sewing drop. The great hooded chairs had become enormous. And Giles too. And Isa too against the window. The window was all sky without colour. The house had lost its shelter. It was night before roads were made, or houses. It was the night that dwellers in caves had watched from some high place among rocks. Then the curtain rose. They spoke" (219) (New York: Harvest, 1969).

[30] See also characters' comments throughout the episodes in which Woolf claims spaces of darkness and shadow as places of possibility for new identity formation. At Percival's dinner, Bernard comments: "I have been traversing the sunless territory of non-identity. A strange land. I have heard in my moment of appeasement, in my moment of obliterating satisfaction, the sigh, as it goes in, comes out, of the tide that draws beyond this circle of bright light, this drumming of insensate fury" (116). Rhoda, at the same dinner, states: "and look—the outermost parts of the earth—pale shadows on the utmost horizon, India for instance, rise into our purview. The world that had been shriveled, rounds itself; remote provinces are fetched up out of darkness; we see muddy roads, twisted jungle, swarms of men, and the vulture that feeds on some bloated carcass as within our scope, part of our proud and splendid province, since Percival, riding alone on a flea-bitten mare, advances down a solitary path, has his camp pitched among desolate trees, and sits alone, looking at the enormous mountains" (137). In both musings, these territories of opportunity are described in terms of imperialism and sites of the other which are both inherently feminine and colonial. In this way, identity formation is linked again to the feminine, nationalism and imperial activity. Bernard's comment on the "sunless territory of non-identity" confirms the places of darkness and shadow as outside of pre-conceived identity demarcations, again making it a place filled with possibility for the feminine.

Works Cited

Burford, Arianne. "Communities of Silence and Music in Virginia Woolf's *The Waves* and Dorothy Richardson's *Pilgrimage*." *Virginia Woolf and Communities: Selected Papers from the Eighth Annual Conference on Virginia Woolf*. Jeanette McVicker and Laura Davis, eds. New York: Pace UP, 1999. 269-75.

Cain, P.J. and A.G. Hopkins. *British Imperialism, 1688 – 2000*. 2nd Edition. Harlow: Longman, 2002.

Garrity, Jane. *Step-daughters of England: British Women Modernists and the National Imaginary*. Manchester: Manchester UP, 2003.

Goldman, Jane. *The Feminist Aesthetics of Virginia Woolf: Modernism, Post-Impressionism and the Politics of the Visual*. Cambridge: Cambridge UP, 1998. 189.

Hussey, Mark. *Virginia Woolf A to Z: A Comprehensive Reference for Students, Teachers and Common Readers to Her Life, Work and Critical Reception*. New York: Oxford UP, 1995.

Katz, Tamar. "Modernism, Subjectivity, and Narrative Form: Abstraction in *The Waves*." *Narrative* 3.3 (October 1995). 232-51.

Kent, Susan. *Making Peace: The Reconstruction of Gender in Interwar Britain*. Princeton: Princeton UP, 1993.

Laurence, Patricia Ondek. *The Reading of Silence: Virginia Woolf in the English Tradition*. Stanford: Stanford UP, 1991.

Marcus, Jane. "Britannia Rules the Waves." *Decolonizing Tradition: New Views of Twentieth-Century 'British' Canons*. Ed. Karen R. Lawrence. Urbana: U of Illinois P, 1992.

Moran, Patricia. *Word of Mouth: Body Language in Katherine Mansfield and Virginia Woolf*. Charlottesville: U P of Virginia, 1996.

Moore, Madeline. "Nature and Community: A Study of Cyclical Reality in *The Waves*." *Virginia Woolf: Revaluation and Continuity*. Ralph Freedman, ed. Berkeley: U of California P, 1980.

Paccaud-Huguet, Josiane. "The Crowded Dance of Words: Language and Jouissance in *The Waves*." *Q/W/E/R/T/Y* 5.1 (1995): 227-40.

Phillips, Kathy J. *Virginia Woolf Against Empire*. Knoxville: U of Tennessee P, 1994.

Scott, Bonnie Kime. *Refiguring Modernism, Volume Two: Postmodern Feminist Readings of Woolf, West and Barnes*. Bloomington: Indiana UP, 1995.

Sharpe, Jenny. "Figures of Colonial Resistance." *The Post-Colonial Studies Reader*. Bill Ashcroft, Gareth Griffiths and Helen Tiffin, eds. London: Routledge, 1995.

Spivak, Gayatri Chakravorty. "Three Women's Texts and a Critique of Imperialism." *The Post-Colonial Studies Reader*. Bill Ashcroft, Gareth Griffiths and Helen Tiffin, eds. London: Routledge, 1995.

Thane, Pat. "The British Imperial State and the Construction of National Identities." *Borderlines: Gender and Identities in War and Peace 1870-1930*. Ed. Billie Melman. New York: Routledge, 1998.

Torgovnick, Mariana. *Primitive Passions: Men, Women and the Quest for Ecstasy*. New York: Knopf, 1997.

Wilson, John. "Noctes Ambrosianae." *Blackwood's Magazine*. See Roth, Nicole. "The Sun Never Sets on the British Empire." Mooney, Jennifer. The 19th Century British Literature: The Empire Abroad. Course home page. Spring 2003. Dept. of English, U of Vermont. 28 Sept. 2005. http://athena.english.vt.edu/~jmooney/3044annotationsp-z/sunneversets.html .

Woolf, Virginia.*The Waves*. San Diego: Harvest, 1959

"Ce chien est à moi": Virginia Woolf and the Signifying Dog

Jane Goldman

Woolf's signifying dog belongs to the "companion species" that marks the boundaries between the human and non-human. My concern, however, is not primarily with the modality, or dogginess, of the dog but with its status as signifier. It marks the boundary between literal and figurative. In exploring the dog's metaphorical or figurative status, I risk its "erasure," confirming it as "absent referent,"[1] according to animal ethicist-feminist, Carol Adams. "Could metaphor itself be the undergarment . . . of oppression?" she asks, since through the reifying action of metaphor "the object is severed from its ontological meaning," something that also occurs in the discourse of racism and misogyny (Adams 209, 213). But what interests me, in risking the bracketing of Adams's referent, is the behavior of such metaphors in Woolf's modernist free indirect discourse, in texts that also are themselves highly allusive to and citational of other texts. Adams is concerned with the restoration of the "absent referent" of oppressive metaphor, so that the witnessing of its presence would prevent its becoming the object of oppression, whether of racial violence or sexual violence or violence against animals, and, drawing on Marjorie Spiegel's *The Dreaded Comparison: Human and Animal Slavery* (1988), she demonstrates how closely these three oppressive discourses are interrelated in their choice and deployment of metaphor (Adams 211-212). But such a restoration, as the literary history of black and feminist experimental writing makes evident, is no easy matter; nor can we understand the relationship between figurative and literal (language and referent) quite so straightforwardly as Adams has it. Furthermore, we cannot simply abolish or censor metaphor; but it may perhaps be turned to advantage. The sense of turn-

---

[1] "Referent" is Adams's term for the tenor of the metaphor. In this paper I will be discussing the tenor and vehicle of metaphor in ways that emphasize the self-consciously figurative qualities of Woolf's writing, which sometimes seems to posit the status of the tenor of the metaphor, not as a "referent," but as itself another vehicle. Saussurean notions of the sign become relevant here. The sign, in comprising both signifier and signified, disrupts the commonsense notion that language refers to the world, and that words name things in the world. My argument therefore puts at risk the acknowledgement of a canine presence which is central to Adams's concern for the "absent referent." Canine ontology is not the priority of the paper except in so far as it points up the complex politics of historical canine metaphors and tropes which have been deployed to signify human (non-)subjectivity in terms of race, animality and gender.

ing metaphor to advantage informs the canine-feminist ethics of writing and reading that Woolf's signifying dog enables, as this essay will explore.

Woolf's dog is a sliding signifier representing not least the historic, unequal struggles between men and women over artistic subjectivity and voice.[2] Marking and marked by race, gender and class, Woolf's signifying dog is a constructed, monstrous, multivalent figure whose "referent" is certainly not just a dog, but nor, *contra* Adams, does this metaphor cleanly evacuate the dog from its vehicle merely to accommodate "woman" or "slave" (Woolf gestures to both). A few critics have previously noted the metaphoricity of Woolf's dogs, but only as simple allegories of sexuality, particularly of lesbianism, and, in one argument, of incest (Dunn, Eberly, Vanita). But Woolf's dogs are already more complicated than this; already metaphors of metaphor, they have complicated textual pasts, burdened by canine cultural baggage.

Woolf's most obvious signifying dog is the protagonist of her best-selling novel *Flush: A Biography* (1933), but Flush is preceded (and followed) in Woolf's *oeuvre* by numerous important instances, and "turns," in a fascinating chain of canine troping. My focus in this essay will be on Woolf's signifying dogs prior to Flush, particularly their appearance in *A Room of One's Own*. I am interested, most specifically, in the notorious "fine negress" passage (*AROO* 76), and the performance there of Woolf's slippery canine metaphors in her free indirect discourse.[3] These elude Jane Marcus's attention in her illuminating and fine scrutiny of the passage in her book *Hearts of Darkness: White Women Write Race* (2004). But, hunting with canine and animal ethicists, I will chase Woolf's dog in one crucial sentence back through some of the sentences it has previously frequented in Woolf's and others' writing. My aim is to explore and uncover the rich semantic layering at play in this densely allusive and highly citational, multivoiced passage; to build on Marcus's detailed, and nuanced reading, supplying further detail and nuance; but also to depart from it. I am not interested in indicting Woolf or *A Room of One's Own* as racist, or indeed in rescuing either from such indictments; but I am interested in the ways Woolf's writing, which she her-

---

[2] Rachel's virtuoso pianism in *The Voyage Out*, for example, is likened by her fiancé Terence to "an unfortunate old dog going round on its hind legs in the rain," and he imagines Rachel herself as a "drilled dog" (VO 283); and Mrs Ramsay, whose husband is "the very figure of a famished wolfhound," calling for his wife "for all the world like a wolf barking in the snow" (TL 307), thinks of Lily Briscoe as "her little Brisk," while Lily, in turn, at her easel, "wince[s] like a dog who sees a hand raised to strike it" (*TTL* 84).

[3] The Free Indirect Discourse (or Speech) in *A Room of One's Own* is performed by a dispersed first person narrator. See Prince: "Though free indirect discourse may have a special affinity with the third person, it can and does occur in the first and second persons" (35)

self characterized as a "tunnelling process" (*D2* 272), encourages her readers to engage actively in the quite canine business of chasing, unearthing, and *turning* its densely wrought metaphors and tropes. "Tunnelling," as a mode of conduct, applies to the process of reading, then, as much as to that of writing. Indeed, Woolf observes how Marcel Proust's imagery sets his reader "tunnelling logically and intellectually . . . after a shred of meaning" (*E4* 244), and how her sister's paintings "yield their full meaning to those who can tunnel" ("Foreword" 172).

After the introduction, which briefly sets out and explores theoretical and critical frames for examining Woolf's canine tropes in free indirect discourse, this essay is in three parts. The first part offers a view of the broad terrain, the significant canine tropes, and complex models of subjectivity, that *A Room of One's Own* lays out before the reader in its opening pages; the next two parts focus on the "fine negress" passage, chasing down, unearthing, and turning on its key canine tropes. The canine details unearthed in the "fine negress" passage take on further significance when understood in relation to the canine grounds established in the opening pages of Woolf's tract.

Part 1, "Dogs in College and Talking Books" proposes the narrator of *A Room of One's Own* as dog-woman, explores Woolf's feminist engagement with tropes of slavery, and argues for an intertext in *A Room of One's Own* with an early English treatise on dogs by a founding Cambridge scholar, which was in Woolf's library. Part 2, "The 'Fine Negress' and the Chien," discusses the canine qualities of the "fine negress" passage and departs from Marcus's reading of it; it also discloses intertexts with works by Pascal, Leonard Woolf, G.K. Chesterton, and Lord Dunsaney. Part 3, "The 'Fine Negress' and the Shock-Dog," takes up Marcus's disappointing discussion of Woolf's allusions to Aphra Behn, and argues that Woolf's source for these allusions is not exclusively Vita Sackville-West's book on Behn, as Marcus suggests. Whereas Marcus cites Behn's novella *Oroonoko*, only as mediated by Sackville-West, for the source of Woolf's gender and race politics in the "fine negress" passage, I argue that it is worth reading Behn's novella itself as a rich source for its key terms, and then I trace these terms in Behn's text. I also argue that the advantage for Woolf's narrator in not wanting to make an Englishwoman of the fine negress might be understood productively via readings of later stage versions of *Oroonoko*, which are neglected by Sackville-West and not considered at all by Marcus, but were known to Woolf. I draw on recent scholarship on Behn to discuss the gender, race, and canine politics of Woolf's work. The "Conclusion" briefly proposes a canine ethics, a mode of conduct and evaluation, for reading Woolf's sentences, a methodology that seems encouraged by Woolf's canine troping itself.

Introduction

First, a word on the larger project: this work in progress titled *Virginia Woolf and the Signifying Dog* learns a trick or too from Henry Louis Gates's *Signifying Monkey* (except there's no originary feminist trickster-dog.) This reading strategy is not as anachronistic as it might at first seem. W.E.B. DuBois's much cited model of black "double-consciousness" informs Gates's theoretical armature for *The Signifying Monkey*, and it was also available to Woolf, who, we know, owned a copy of Dubois's *The Souls of Black Folk*, in which his theory of black double-consciousness is set out: "It is a peculiar sensation, this double-consciousness, this sense of always looking at one's self through the eyes of others, of measuring one's soul by the tape of a world that looks on in amused contempt and pity. One ever feels his twoness,—an American, a Negro; two souls, two thoughts, two unreconciled strivings; two warring ideals in one dark body, whose dogged strength alone keeps it from being torn asunder" (DuBois; see *Gates* 207-209). Modernist, free-indirect discourse, Gates shows, may express this sense of "twoness" in its simultaneous accommodation of both subjective and objective modes (209). Interestingly, he identifies the second mode of Signifyin(g) in the free indirect discourse or "double-voiced narrative mode" of Woolf's modernist contemporary Zora Neale Hurston (xxv, 170ff.). Signifying on "two signal trickster figures from African and African-American mythology" (Esu-Elegdora and the Signifying Monkey), Gates's "Signifyin(g) Monkey" is a figurative discourse that in its earlier phase, of slave narratives, is the "figure of the double voiced," a "Tropological Revision . . . in which a specific trope is repeated, with differences, between two or more texts," and concerns the "form that repetition and difference take among these texts" (xxv). Clearly, Gates's "Signifyin(g) Monkey" is specifically concerned with identifying a tradition of "black" literary discourse: "Black texts signify upon other black texts." But "perhaps critics of other literatures," he suggests, "will find this theory useful as they attempt to account for the configuration of the texts in their traditions" (xxiv-xxv). The Signifying Dog that I am positing in Woolf's aesthetic, then, has its origins in eighteenth-century white English ethnic culture, in patriarchy's persistent misogynist figure of a dog-trick, and in white racist discourse too. Whereas the Signifyin(g) Monkey signifies *on* an established and endorsed African and African-American mythology of the trickster tradition, Woolf's Signifying Dog trope does not signify *on* an originary feminist trickster-dog, but performs tropological revision on the reviled and alien patriarchal figures of the performing dog and canine slave. She is not signifying *on*, so much as *re*-signifying the misogynist and racist texts of Johnson and Carlyle. But she does signify *on* her own resignified dog figures.

Woolf's process of re-signifying suggests that her signifying dog may also be understood as a relative of the "tropicopolitan." Tropicopolitans, according to Srinivas Aravamudan, are "troublesome tropes that—and colonial subjects who—interrupt the monologue of nationalist literary history" (Aravamudan 12). Aravamadum draws on the definition of the rhetorical term, trope, in Chambers's *Cyclopaedia* (1741) as "a word changed from its proper and natural signification to another, with some advantage" (Aravamudan 1), and turns to advantage the "proper and natural signification" of the adjective used in natural history to describe "species dominant in the tropics." He proposes "the term tropicopolitan as a name for the colonized subject who exists both as a fictive construct of colonial tropology *and* actual resident of tropical space, object of representation *and* agent of resistance" (Aravamudan 4). Woolf's signifying dog *re*signifies (following Aravamudan) patriarchal, racialist canine tropes, and signifies *on* (following Gates) these resignifications.

Virginia Woolf and the Signifying Dog also explores the intersection of feminist theory with philosophical interests in animal ethics, and this essay will briefly refer to Donna Haraway's companion species manifesto,[4] Emmanuel Levinas's essay, "The Name of a Dog," and to Giorgio Agamben's *The Open: Man and Animal*, which considers the aporia in Western thought's shifting caesurae between man and animal. Woolf's signifying dog may occupy the very "zone" Agamben identifies: the empty interval between man and animal that is neither animal life nor human life (Agamben 38).

In "1730: Becoming-Intense, Becoming-Animal, Becoming-Imperceptible," a chapter from their influential work *A Thousand Plateaus: Capitalism and Schizophrenia*, Gilles Deleuze and Félix Guattari invoke Woolf's "thin dog" figure, who both "runs down the street" and "*is* the street," for their key concept of "haecceity," the "rhizome":[5] "This is how we need to feel," they declare (263). The "thin dog" is not strictly Woolf's, however, since it appears in Woolf's "A Terribly Sensitive Mind" (1927), her review of Katharine Mansfield's published journal. Woolf remarks on "The thin dog" in Mansfield's journal who is "so thin

---

[4] See also Marjorie Garber's *Dog Love* (1997).
[5] The rhizome is the tuber-like semiotic chain, with no single originary root or destination, capable of "agglomerating very diverse acts, not only linguistic, but also perceptive, mimetic, gestural, and cognitive" (Deleuze and Guattari 7). Rhizomatic processes, according to Verena Andermatt Conley, are "lines, or trajectories open to becomings. [Being] consists of a temporary assemblage of partial components and effects of subjectivization. Being, the moment of arrest in the roll of the dice, is always open to, and traversed by, becomings that are more than simple transformations of an existing real. [. . .] As a philosopher, Deleuze deals with these concepts and their genesis through arduously creative readings of other philosophers' texts" (Conley 21-22).

that his body is like 'a cage on four wooden pegs'" as it "runs down the street. In some sense, she feels, the thin dog is the street" (*E*4 447). She is quoting from the 1918 section of Mansfield's journal, "The Redcliffe Road."[6] Deleuze's and Guattari's citation of Woolf's citation of Mansfield's "thin dog" precisely alerts us to the "agglomerat[ed]" (Deleuze and Guattari 7) condition and the burden of Woolf's own signifying dog. A marked and marking being, it is Woolf's particular canine creation but it is marked by and marks the other streets it has run in. Woolf may lift a canine trope from someone else's sentence, but while the dog may be out of the street, the street is not altogether taken out of the dog. This is a useful model for understanding the behavior of Woolf's canine tropes. The politics of her dog metaphors are to be read through the mapping of her elastic modernist syntax and of her wide-ranging intertextual referencing and citations. Woolf's signifying dog must be understood both in terms of the syntax and voicing of each sentence in which it is encountered and also in relation to the sentences it has previously run through.

In his book *Before Modernism Was* (2004), the critic Geoff Gilbert includes a chapter, "Dogs: Small Domestic Forms," which demonstrates the significance of the figures of the dog-owner and of the rabid dog in some key modernist texts, but he has only just touched upon the import and complexity of canine tropes in modernist writing and in Woolf's work in particular. As a continuing and dominant influence on modern feminist theory, furthermore, Woolf's work needs to be thoroughly scrutinized for its insights into the discursive function of animality in ideologies and representations of gender, sexuality and race.

Woolf's canine tropes are not only significant in all of her ten novels and many of her short stories, they are also central to the exposition of her influential theories of modernism and feminism, most importantly in *A Room of One's Own*, her founding feminist manifesto. Her dogs are "overdetermined" signifiers, emerging from Woolf's broad, eclectic readings in classical and canonical literatures. Samuel Johnson and Thomas Carlyle, for example, are key patriarchal authorities on caninicity whose work Woolf interrogates; in particular, Johnson's

---

[6] "This is the hour when the poor underfed dog appears, at a run, nosing the dry gutter. He is so thin that his body is like a cage on four wooden pegs. . . . His lean triangle of a head is down, his long straight tail is out, and up and down, up and down he goes, silent and fearfully eager. The street watches him from its creeper-covered balconies, from its open windows—but the fat lady on the ground floor who is no better than she should be comes out, down the steps to the gate, with a bone. His tail, as he waits for her to give it him, bangs against the gate post, like a broomhandle—and the street says she's a fool to go feeding strange dogs. Now she'll never be rid of him./ (What I'd like to convey is that, at this hour, with this half light and the pianos and the open, empty sounding houses, he is the spirit of the street—running up and down, poor dog, when he ought to have been done away with years ago.)" (Mansfield 94)

notorious canine analogy for women preachers is a key trope in her work (*AROO* 72, 82-83). It is this persistent misogynist trope, which denies women subjectivity, authorial and artistic, that Woolf's canine writing is attempting to turn to feminist advantage.[7] Woolf also draws on anthropology, and contemporary culture and politics, including Darwinism, eugenics, anti-vivisectionism, anti-imperialism and militant feminism. I will examine signifying dogs in historical, material culture as well as in aesthetic, literary, philosophical and political discourses. (An alternative title might be *Virginia Woolf and the Overdetermined Dog*).

The "anthropological machine," Agamben shows, in seeking to identify the evolutionary bridge between animal and man in fact "functions by excluding as not (yet) human an already human being from itself, that is by animalizing the human, by isolating the nonhuman within the human: *Homo alalus* [significantly, man without speech], or the ape-man," and conversely by the "humanization of an animal: the man-ape [or non-man], the *enfant sauvage* or *Homo ferus*, but also and above all the slave, the barbarian, and the foreigner, as figures of an animal in human form." This model made possible the Nazi identification of the Jew as "the non-man produced within the man, or the *néomort* . . ., the animal separated within the human body itself" (Agamben 37). Again, a sense of "twoness" becomes apparent in this model of the subject that includes the object within, something that modernist free-indirect style has the capacity to access, as Gates indicates. Interestingly, a dog-ape is identified as a phase in the evolution of the pre-human. Agamben touches on human sexuality, but is silent on the status of women in the anthropological machine. Presumably a non-speaking pre-human ape *woman* is to be posited as giving birth to the non-animal *Homo sapiens*, man, "the animal," according to Linnaeus, "that must recognize [or read] itself as human to be human" (cited Agamben 26). I correlate Agamben's "open" with the shifting caesurae between subject and object in Woolf's metaphors and free indirect discourse, and read Woolf's mobile signifying dogs through Levinas's stray

---

[7] Following on from my conference paper, "Who Let the Dogs Out?" (2001), my forthcoming book traces Woolf's turning of this trope in *A Room of One's Own* and elsewhere. Woolf is in dialogue with Cecil Gray who turns the Johnsonian canine analogy on women composers, which she cites in *A Room of One's Own* (83), and other misogynists such as Peter Quennell, whose comments in *Life and Letters* (June, 1928) on the "limitations" of women writers she also cites (*AROO* 113), and who in turn acknowledges this citation, in his review of *A Room of One's Own* for the same journal, before going on to further expand on the "limitations" of women novelists by comparing them unfavourably to panthers and domestic cats whose "characteristic [. . .] instinctive wisdom and unfathomable dignity" means "that never, never do they attempt to walk upon their hind-legs" ("New Novels," *Life and Letters* 3 (Jul-Dec 1929), 551). Quennell is clearly picking up on Woolf's turning of Johnson's canine trope and then turning it (feline) in turn.

dog. I would correlate this zone too with the "empty deictic centre" that Ann Banfield identifies in free indirect discourse which is produced in a text where no observable, fixed, self is available to which deictic elements are to be aligned (Banfield 273; Fludernik 388). Deictic dysfunctionality and shifting unstable subjectivities in Woolf's densely allusive, citational prose are bound up with, and contribute to the production of, her radically unstable canine metaphors.

Paula Rego, *Dog Woman* (1994)

Part 1: Dogs in College and Talking Books

I invite you to think of Paula Rego's *Dog Woman* (1994), a woman of colour adopting canine morphology, as the opening narrator of *A Room of One's Own*. As will become evident, there is in my reading no one single, consistent, narrator, of fixed identity, narrating *A Room of One's Own*. Rego's *Dog Woman* is a useful figure to keep in mind, precisely because she presents a morphology which is clearly mutable, but nevertheless she is already marked in terms of culturally received notions of animality, gender, and race that very soon become significant in *A Room of One's Own* and that this essay will attempt to explore. The narrator has no fixed, coherent, identity prior to the sentences she finds herself in, and it is quite clear from the text that the main signifier of subjectivity, "I," is critically unstable throughout, as numerous critics have acknowledged,[8] and that it is subjected to numerous turns and to further moments of radical undermining as the text unfolds. Is it possible to identify the later narrator(s) of *A Room of One's Own*, and, indeed, the narrator(s) of the "fine negress" passage itself as form(s) of Rego's *Dog Woman*?[9] As readers, we find ourselves returning to key points in the grounds, or plot, of *A Room of One's Own*, reading and re-reading the "I" of the opening pages with a scent of the later subjectivities on the wind, and vice-versa.

The opening narrator, it is not difficult to infer, has been chased *like a dog* from the hallowed ground of patriarchal learning on to which she has strayed: "It was thus that I found myself walking with extreme rapidity across a grass plot. Instantly a man's figure rose to intercept me. . . . His face expressed horror and indignation. Instinct rather than reason came to my help; he was a Beadle; I was a woman. This was the turf; there was the path. Only the Fellows and Scholars are allowed here; the gravel is the place for me" (*AROO* 9). Haraway makes only a little more explicit this famous Woolfian analogy in recognizing: "Woolf understood what happens when the impure stroll over the lawns of the properly registered . . . when these marked (and marking) beings get credentials and an income" (Haraway 88). That animals and women are excluded from traditional notions of enlightenment is inferred from the "instinct" rather than "reason" that assists the speaker to realize her ironic identification by the Beadle, himself only one consonant away from the canine, as alien to the institution of education. As

---

[8] For discussion of the text's open construction and resistance to intellectual closure, see Stimpson, p.164; and Laura Marcus, p. 241.
[9] Alice A. Kuzniar examines Rego's *Dog Woman* paintings in *Melancholia's Dog: Reflections on Our Animal Kinship* (2006), which has come to my attention too late to address in the present essay.

patriarchy's dutiful watchdog, he has hardly been secured on the side of "reason" in this sentence. His double designation of the trespasser as both a woman and, implicitly, a dog shocks the wandering "I" who finds herself merely "walking," a self-definition by action, process, behavior or conduct, before she is so rudely hailed. *A Room of One's Own* becomes a lesson in how to resist this interpellation.

Interestingly, this scene of the barking Beadle, interpellating the stray walker as a dog-woman, is the very inverse of the famous scene in Levinas's essay where the bark of the stray dog, "Bobby," in his daily greeting, restores to Levinas, and his fellow prisoners of war, the subjectivity that the Nazi guards, and "the other men, called free, who had dealings with us," have robbed them of. "We were" to the oppressors, Levinas observes, "subhuman, a gang of apes" (Levinas 152, 153). But a "wandering dog," whom they come to call "Bobby," "would appear at morning assembly and was waiting for us as we returned, jumping up and down and barking in delight. For him, there was no doubt that we were men" (Levinas 153). The appearance and conduct of this passing, stray dog, with no fixed origin or identity, are the means by which the prisoners have their subjectivity affirmed. For Levinas, this dog "was the last Kantian in Nazi Germany" (Levinas 153).

But, returning to the Beadle and the dog-woman in *A Room of One's Own*, what may have slipped our notice is that Woolf's canine trope has *already* been initiated in the previous paragraph, where the narrator refers to the burden of her agreed talk: "That collar I have spoken of, women and fiction, . . . a subject that raises all sorts of prejudices and passions, bowed my head to the ground" (*AROO* 8). The very invitation to speak has already interpellated her as a dog. Given the later, overt, citations of Johnson's canine analogy (*AROO* 72, 82-83), we might wonder whether the tug of the collar is here in danger of taking the canine narrator off her hind legs and forcing her back on to four, nose to the gravel. To speak of women and fiction is to acknowledge "prejudices and passions," including misogynist, canine epithets.

Yet the collar metaphor speaks also of the shackles of human *slavery*.[10] "Like a good deal of feminist protest literature," Marcus reminds us, *A Room of One's Own* "uses the tropes of slavery to make the case for women's oppression,"

---

[10] As if to confirm that "the train of thought" is canine, a dog's view of the terrain is offered: "To the right and left bushes of some sort, golden and crimson, glowed with the colour, even it seemed burnt with the heat, of fire. On the further bank the willows wept in perpetual lamentation, their hair about their shoulders," (*AROO* 8). And again, the Biblical allusions to lamentation and to the burning bush (from where God spoke to Moses of delivery to the promised land) speaks of slavery and the prospect of emancipation.

"brilliantly link[ing]" scenes of violence against Englishwomen to violence against slaves (Marcus 48). It would, however, limit the resonance of Woolf's rhetoric here, I would suggest, to confine this convergence of racially marked and gendered tropes of oppression to the prior historical record of the centuries of Atlantic slavery, or indeed to the continuing British imperial context she was writing in. The slave economies of classical Greece, and of Biblical times, are cited too; Woolf also addresses, directly in places, the emergence of fascist and Nazi powers in Europe and their attendant racism and misogyny. Woolf's elusive narrator, who refuses a stable nomenclature or identity is doubly yoked by the metaphors of "dog" and "slave," but the third yoke is surely "woman." The three terms coalesce at several points in the book, most strikingly in the clinching argument on the prospects for women's writing, which rearranges and amplifies a statement by Sir Arthur Quiller Couch: "Intellectual freedom depends upon material things. Poetry depends upon intellectual freedom. And women have always been poor . . . . Women have had less intellectual freedom than the sons of Athenian slaves. Women, then, have not had a dog's chance of writing poetry" (*AROO* 162-163).

The troika slave-woman-dog is rooted in the legacy of counter-enlightenment discourse that links slaves and dogs, as well as an equally entrenched patriarchal discourse that links women and dogs. The significance of dogs in the history of slavery is powerful and complicated, not least because of the way certain dogs were bred to discipline and hunt down fugitive slaves. "I am the hounded slave, I wince at the bite of the dogs," declares Walt Whitman in *Song of Myself*. But there is also a connected discourse that figures slaves themselves *as* dogs. Canine slave metaphors are simultaneously engaged and refigured when Woolf interferes with the patriarchal legacy of misogynist canine troping, which, I have shown elsewhere, she sources in Johnson and Carlyle.[11] The collar imagery is key here. In British aristocratic households of the eighteenth century, black servants and dogs "shared the same status," as David Dabydeen's study of English painting has pointed out (Dabydeen 22). Dabydeen examines the frequent portrayal of white men and women posing with pet dogs and/or pet black people: "Sometimes both dog and black are present in the same picture, both gazing respectfully at their owner, as in Dandridge's *Young Girl with Dog and Negro*

---

[11] Woolf makes explicit her engagement with misogynist canine troping, in *A Room of One's Own*, when she invokes Dr. Johnson's infamous analogy for women preachers: "Sir, a woman's preaching is like a dog's walking on his hinder legs. It is not done well; but you are suprized to find it done at all" (Boswell; *AROO* 72, 82-83). I've shown (Goldman 2006) how Woolf also derives, in her *London Scene* essays, a racially marked canine trope from Thomas Carlyle's pamphlet, "The Nigger Question." Another source is Conrad's canine figuring of Africans in *Heart of Darkness*.

Attendant" (Dabydeen 23). Indeed, the parallel reification of both dogs and black servants extended to the issuing of collars. "It was not uncommon," according to historian J. Jean Hecht, "for a black servant to be obliged to wear a collar of silver or brass on which either his owner's arms or initials were inscribed—a device obviously suggestive of the modern dog collar" (Hecht 40). This is evident, Dabydeen shows, in Matthew Dyer's advertisement in the *London Advertiser* of 1756 of his "silver padlocks for Blacks or Dogs; collars etc.," and in a spoof letter from a black boy to *The Tatler* of 1710 "complaining that his lady's 'parrot who came over with me from our country is as much esteemed by her as I am. Besides this, the shock dog has a collar that cost as much as mine" (Dabydeen 22-23). Domestic African slaves, Aravamudan points out, "wore ornamental collars made of precious metals such as gold and silver, on which were stamped the owner's name, initials, and coat of arms" (Aravamudan 38). These "ornamental collars became markers that exhibited the subject's special status as aristocratic property. These external markers recalled the status of these Africans not only as pets but as commodities that could, at any time, be converted to cash" (Aravamudan 38-39).

English women too, historical records show, might also literally be collared. Keith Thomas cites "bridles for scolding women" and "halters for wives sold by auction in the market" (Thomas 45). He also demonstrates that "above all, common people were repeatedly portrayed as animals who needed to be forcibly restrained"; and he cites Timothy Nourse's recommendation in 1700 "to bridle them, and to make them feel the spur too." Nourse repeats the "saying of an English gentleman . . . that three things ought always to be kept under: a mastiff dog, a stone horse [i.e. a stallion] and a clown; and really I think a snarling, cross-grained clown to be the most unlucky beast of [the] three" (Nourse 15-16; Thomas 45). In such a culture, women of any class or colour might also sport "decorative" collars designating their status as the property of a man, such as the one worn by the "hind" in Thomas Wyatt's famous poem on Anne Boleyn: "And graven with diamonds in letters plain,/ There is written her fair neck round about;/ 'Noli me tangere; for Caesar's I am, /And wild for to hold, though I seem tame.'" Caesar, of course, is in turn an example of the "pompous classical name[s]" that black servants and slaves were given, "the exalted associations of which contrasted sharply with [their] lowly estate. Scipio, Zeno, and Socrates were among the more common appellations; Pompey was the favourite, indeed almost becoming a generic soubriquet for black servants" (Hecht 40). "Names such as Zeno, Socrates, Scipio, and Scipio Africanus were common for slaves, but," Aravamudan points out, "such names were also later adopted for dogs" (65). He points to Francis Coventry's popular novella of 1751, *The History of Pompey the Little or the Life and Adventures of a Lapdog* (Aravamudan 66-67).

Woolf's narrator, then, embodies her own predicament: attempting to speak of Women and Fiction, she represents herself as already collared by the fiction "woman" and its implicit synonyms "dog" and "slave." This collar, as in George Herbert's poem (1633), may also be understood to be a pun on and the source of the narrator's much discussed anger.[12]

We know that Woolf's narrating dog-woman is (already) well read. After all, she is heading to a university college library, in the grounds of the fictional and composite university site of "Oxbridge," to settle a matter of textual scholarship concerning an essay by Charles Lamb on the composition of John Milton's great elegy, *Lycidas*.[13] The manuscript of *Lycidas* is owned by Trinity College, Cambridge, and is held in the college library. It is therefore this "famous library" that Woolf's narrator curses, having been waved back at its entrance by "a deprecating, silvery, kindly gentleman, who regretted in a low voice . . . that ladies are only admitted to the library if accompanied by a Fellow of the College or furnished with a letter of introduction" (*AROO* 12). Woolf is here inscribing a scene of thwarted education which stands as a figure of the historical exclusion of women from literacy and education; but given that the narrator is clearly literate

---

[12] I am most grateful to the Woolf critic and editor Linden Peach, who has confirmed to me in recent correspondence "the way in which the dog metaphor points through references to collars and chains to slavery is very pronounced in *Flush*. Chapter 2 is very interesting in this respect. Flush being taken for a walk along Wimpole Street by Miss Barrett recalls a slave's confusion and fear on arriving in the New Country: 'he stopped, amazed; defining and savouring, until a jerk at his collar dragged him on' (37). Interestingly, Woolf suggests that the chain actually protects the dog from the danger in this new world: 'Mercifully the chain tugged at his collar: Miss Barrett held him tight, or he would have rushed to destruction.' (37) Also: 'He gladly accepted the protection of the chain'. Allusions to the country from which slaves came are overt: 'the old hunting cry of the fields hallooed in his ears and he dashed forward to run as he had run in the fields at home. . . But now a heavy weight jerked at his throat; he was thrown back on his haunches' (38) The text goes on to ask 'Why was he a prisoner here?' Also: 'Miss Barrett could not divine what Wilson's wet umbrella meant to Flush; what memories it recalled, of forests and parrots and wild trumpeting elephants. . . . [and] Flush heard dark men cursing in the mountains' (44)."

[13] "I had thought of the 'Lycidas' as a full-grown beauty—as springing up with all its parts absolute—till, in an evil hour, I was shown the original copy of it, together with the other minor poems of the author, in the library of Trinity, kept like some treasure to be proud of. I wish they had thrown them in the Cam, or sent them after the latter Cantos of Spenser, into the Irish Channel. How it staggered me to see the fine things in their ore! interlined, corrected as if their words were mortal, alterable, displaceable at pleasure! as if they might have been otherwise, and just as good! as if inspiration were made up of parts, and these fluctuating, successive, indifferent! I will never go into the workshop of any great artist again." Charles Lamb, note to "Oxford in the Vacation," *Essays of Elia* (1823).

and already educated enough to be interested in the manuscript of *Lycidas*, this self-conscious act of re-representing, or revisiting, a primal scene of thwarted education suggests that the threshold to the library has already been breached. There are clear parallels with the trope of what Gates has termed "the scene of instruction of the black author's literacy" (47), a trope that continues to be signified on by black authors in a tradition he traces from early slave narratives to present-day literature, from Olaudah Equiano, and antecedents, to Jean Toomer and Zora Neale Hurston, to Ishmael Reed and Alice Walker (Gates 127-169).

This trope Gates identifies more precisely as "the trope of the Talking Book . . . the first repeated and revised trope of the tradition, the first trope to be Signified upon" (131). Gates considers the first text in which it appears, the slave narrative (widely published and republished between 1774 and 1840) of James Albert Ukaawsaw Gronniosaw, where the narrator recounts the formative moment of his opening a book discarded by his master: "I . . . put my ear down close upon it, in the great hopes that it would say something to me; but I was very sorry, and greatly disappointed, when I found that it would not speak. This thought immediately presented itself to me, that every body and every thing despised me because I was black" (Gronniosaw 8; Gates 132, 136). Gates understands Gronniosaw to be a self-styled "Noble Savage," an "Oroonoko, in other words," who along with "his fellow black princes-in-bondage are made noble by a dissimilarity with their native countrymen" (133). Under the pens of other black writers, the trope was resignified, and indeed "turn[ed] back upon itself" (Gates 150) by writers such as Quobna Ottobah Cugoano and Equianio. In a highly wrought, self-conscious refiguration of the trope, Cugoano has a beleaguered Inca throw the ("Spanish banditti") masters' "silent" book "with disdain to the ground," an heroic act of defiance that prompts the Christian "assassinators" to "avenge this profanation on these impious dogs" (Cugoano 78-81; Gates 149-150). The canine metaphor here, needless to say, is the mark of the Other's exclusion from a subjectivity and from a model of literacy that already demonstrably fails to speak to the Other.

Before returning to Woolf's dog-woman, it is worth attending to Equiano's treatment of the trope of the Talking Book, and to Gates's reading of it. In his sophisticated re-writing of the trope, shifting between past and present, earlier and later selves, Equiano explains:

> I had often seen my master and Dick employed in reading; and I had a great curiosity to talk to the books, as I thought they did; and so learn how all things had a beginning: for that purpose I have often taken up a book, and have talked to it, and then put my ears to it, when alone, in hopes that it would answer me; and I have been very much concerned when I found it remained silent. (Equiano 106-107; Gates 155)

"Under the guise of the representation of his naïve self," Equiano's achievement here, according to Gates, is that "he is naming or reading Western culture closely, underlining relationships between subjects and objects that are implicit in commodity cultures" (156). Gates recognizes that books "do speak to Europeans, and not to the Africans of the eighteenth century." In recognizing the master and Dick, the book acknowledges "both their voices and their faces by engaging in dialogue with them; neither the young African's voice nor his face can be recognizable to the text, because his countenance and discourse stand in Western texts as signs of absence, of the null and void" (Gates 156). Gates identifies the crux of Equiano's sophisticated politics of grammar in his "narrator's account of his own movement from slave-object to author-subject," a process, I would suggest, that is also implicit in the grammar of Woolf's *A Room of One's Own* in its return to the scene of literacy. Gates's further observations are helpful too for reading Woolf's narrator(s) where he talks of "Equiano's grammatical analogue of this process of becoming—of becoming a human being who reads differently from the child, of becoming a subject by passing a test (the mastery of writing) that no object can pass, and of becoming an author who represents, under the guise of a series of naïve readings, an object's 'true' nature by demonstrating that he can now read these objects in both ways, as he once did in the Middle Passage but also as he does today" (Gates 157). Equiano's virtuoso, erudite, "mastery of the text" is an indictment of the racist stereotypes of "trained" Africans that Joseph Conrad deals in, in *Heart of Darkness*, when he has Marlow describe "the savage who was fireman" as "an improved specimen," given enough instruction to be able to "fire up a vertical boiler." He is "full of improving knowledge" and "useful because he had been instructed" (1916). Like Rachel in *The Voyage Out*, he is imagined as a Johnsonian drilled dog: "to look at him was as edifying as seeing a dog in a parody of breeches and a feather hat, walking on his hind-legs. A few months of training had done for that really fine chap" (1916). Education apparently ruins the innate fineness of the "savage": "Fine fellows—cannibals—in their place" (1915).

I would further invite you to think of Woolf's well-read narrating dog-woman as being already acquainted, like Woolf herself, with the first treatise on English dogs, published in 1576: *De Canibus Britannicis*. Woolf had several books on dogs in her library, many of them publications of the anti-vivisectionist National Canine Defence League, with titles such as *How to Keep a House Dog, Dog Welfare*, and *Canine Distemper*, all of which were published in the 1920s. But she also owned an 1880 edition of *De Canibus Britannicis,* a treatise by the Cambridge scholar John Caius, translated from the Latin by one his students, Abraham Fleming. The eminent John Caius (1510-1573) was a founder of Gonville and Caius College, Cambridge, and President of the Royal College of

Physicians. "His most visible legacy to the College," the College website informs us, "remains the very beautiful Caius Court and the College's three famous gates—of 'Humility', 'Virtue' and 'Honour'." Caius's body lies in a crypt in the college chapel, and his statue overlooks King's Parade. More interestingly, a cast of his skull is prominently exhibited in a glass case at the entrance to the library (I have it on good authority). A renowned scholar and physician, he published on many subjects and spent his latter years writing a history of Cambridge. While his treatise on dogs is not perhaps his most famous work, it was sufficiently known to prompt a pointedly canine aside in Act 1 Scene IV of Shakespeare's *Merry Wives of Windsor* where Dr. Caius is parodied. "When presented with Dr Cauis's monograph on the antiquity of Cambridge University," King James I, Thomas reminds us, "is said to have remarked rather ungraciously, 'What shall I do with this book? Give me rather Dr Caius's *De Canibus*'" (Thomas 103).

As his fawning translator tells us in his fulsome dedication, Cauis was "a man most advised in every branch of life; one who has deserved well of the company of the learned . . . a most shining light of the University of Cambridge; its jewel and glory." John Cauis, he continues, "wrote an epitome concerning British dogs, not so concise as elegant and useful; an epitome compact of various arguments and experiences of many minds; a book which when by chance I had met with it, and was covered with delight with the novelty of its appearance, I attempted to translate into English." The treatise describes and categorizes hunting dogs, fowling dogs, gentle dogs, shepherd dogs, mongrels and rascal dogs, including tumblers and dancing dogs. It bears an uncanny resemblance to the many books the narrator of *A Room of One's Own* discovers in the British Library catalogue on the subject of women. Knowledge of Caius's book certainly lends an ironic resonance to the narrator's expulsion from the lawn on the way to the "famous" composite Oxbridge library, to which she is then denied access, in the opening pages. Women and dogs appear equal in their status as the lowly objects of patriarchal scientific inquiry, and in being denied the status of enquiring rational subjects. But further layers of irony are made possible if we attend to the fetching poem composed by Caius's translator, Fleming, to serve as the book's epigraph. As its title indicates ("A Prosopopoicall Speache of the Booke"), Fleming's poem is in the voice of the book itself. I would suggest that this convention of personifying the text is one that Woolf is experimenting with in *A Room of One's Own*, and that this tradition may be linked in her text to the black trope of the Talking Book. Interestingly, this speaking book introduces itself as possessing human form in drawing attention to "My forhed . . . baulde and bare" and "bod'y beutifull," but then immediately seems to transform itself into a speaking "plot" of land. The flower imagery and declaration of bodily beauty may also suggest the self-celebration of the Queen of Sheba in the Song of Solomon (who is "black but comely," as well as fragrant and flower-like.) No sooner has it become a talking garden than it boasts of its hospitality to the dogs trampling through it, and of its own magical properties in remaining unsoiled and sweet smelling despite such canine traffic.

> And though my garden plot so greene,
>   Of dogges receaue the trampling feete,
> Yet it is swept and kept full cleene,
>   So that it yields a sauour sweete.

Woolf's "grass plot" surely alludes to Cauis's "garden plot so greene." The dog-woman is excluded from the library yet seems already to know of the books in there that happily would receive her trampling feet, books that would talk to her as a presence. Woolf seems, then, to be revising the scene of literacy, and revising an embedded trope of the Talking Book; and she achieves this, like Equiano, "by shifting from present to past and back to present" and demonstrating her narrator(s)' "true mastery of the text of Western letters and the text of [their] verbal representation of his [their] past and present selves" (Gates 157). Shifting between past and present, earlier and later selves, the opening narrator ironically departs from reason and turns to "instinct" in finding "he was a Beadle; I was a woman. This was the turf; there was the path. Only the Fellows and Scholars are allowed here; the gravel is the place for me" (*AROO* 9). This narratorial shifting between past and present, between earlier and later selves, and the sense of the slave, woman, and dog as coalescing excluded subjectivities, inform the narrative complexities of the entire tract, and, not least, of the "fine negress" passage itself. Equiano, "the author and subject of his narrative, is now able," Gates insists, "to make the text speak in his own tongue" (Gates 159); whereas Woolf, we should note, is the author, but pointedly *not* the narrator, of *A Room of One's Own*, which, quite self-consciously, speaks in numerous voices and personae. In doing so, it encourages its readers to reflect on narrative authority itself, writerly and readerly, and, if not to make the text speak entirely in their own tongue, at least to actively enter into dialogue with it.

Part 2: The "Fine Negress" and the Chien

Marcus's thoroughgoing examination of the "fine negress" passage notes parenthetically the association "of the Negress with the dog [as wild creatures to be tamed and domesticated]," linked to Woolf's earlier citation of Johnson's canine analogy for a woman preaching (Marcus 49), but she does not address the more complicated canine troping at play in this passage (indeed, in the same sentence), nor the complexities of its racial marking. She does, however, judge Woolf's conjunction of "Negress" with "woman" and "Englishwoman" that the embedded citation of Johnson's dog makes available as "unfortunate" (Marcus 50). Can Woolf's text, and Woolf herself, slip the collar of "racist" that Marcus's persuasive argument seems inevitably to secure? She finds Woolf "has robbed her 'very fine negress' of subjectivity in much the same way as men appropriated hers" (Marcus 52). Marcus is persuasive on the alarming sense of appropriation in Woolf's text. After all, ownership is overtly in the tract's title. "Is she not saying," Marcus asks, "we have rooms of our own because they don't—our sisters in the former colonies on whose labor the 'first' world largely functions?" (Marcus 42). A "room" of one's own discloses in mirror form the "moor" of one's own, then, standing for the black dispossessed who make white freedom possible.

Marcus's concern for the subjectivity of the "fine Negress" is reasonable especially considering the slippery metaphoric, and free indirect discourse of the sentence and the larger tract that the "fine Negress" inhabits. In such a multivocal text, one that is at pains to explore the connected politics of voice and subjectivity, *why*, we must ask, is there no clear and direct citation of a black woman's words? A more difficult, and radical, concern to raise would be the subjectivity of the dog. Is it possible that the mutable speaker of this book, who famously acknowledges a destabilised subjectivity by declaring "'I' is only a convenient term for somebody who has no real being . . . (call me Mary Beton, Mary Seton, Mary Carmichael or by any name you please)" (*AROO* 7), does herself inhabit a canine morphology? In one version of the cited "Four Maries" Ballad, Mary Hamilton, whom Woolf pointedly elides and leaves unnamed, sings from the gallows of "This dog's death I'm to die."[14]

In the controversial "fine negress" passage, women are distinguished from men by their historical, inured, "anonymity": "They are not even now as concerned about the health of their fame as men are, and, speaking generally, will pass a tombstone or a signpost without feeling an irresistible desire to cut their names on it, as Alf, Bert or Chas. must do in obedience to their instinct, which murmurs if it sees a fine woman go by, or even a dog, Ce chien est à moi" (*AROO* 76). Here Woolf prefigures patriarchal colonialism and inscription as a dog marking its territory: women, unlike men, then, do not mark out territory as a matter of "irresistible desire" and "obedience" to "instinct." The act of writing is expressed as "a reflex reaction ingrained in any European male" to appropriate and colonise (Phillips 73). But even as she reproachfully figures men writing as

---

[14] "I charge ye all, ye mariners, /That sail upon the sea, /Let neither my father nor mother get wit, /This dog's death I'm to die." Made up version from Scott's edition of 1833.

colonial patriarchs, which are in turn figured as dogs pissing on signposts and monuments to the dead (themselves figures of signification), she is also aligning —in the same sentence—the object of this very process, the "fine woman" with dogs: "Ce chien est à moi." Marcus recognizes that this crucially presents women's signature as erasure, but while she connects "ce chien" to Woolf's earlier citation of Johnson's canine trope, she ignores the dogginess of Alf, Bert and Chas. The double-gendered dog is both subject and object of colonialism. The repeated "even" ("*even* a dog"; "*even* a very fine negress," herself reprising the "fine" of "fine woman") strengthens the analogy between dog and negress, amplified in the next sentence, where the dog is shown to be interchangeable with "a piece of land or a man with curly black hair." The dog as usual performs a number of vehicular tasks: its tenors are both men and women, English and African, coloniser and colonised.

But who is speaking in this sentence? It is not a simple matter of plumping for either Woolf or her narrator: there are too many voices, citations and ventriloquised citations compressed here. We must also attend to the question of who is listening to or reading this sentence, which first addresses the intradiegetic audience of "women who attended Woolf's original talks," Melba Cuddy-Keane reminds us, whereas the extradiegetic readers "make up an unlimited number of possibilities, but whoever we are, we read *through* the audience of young university women in the late 1920s" (Cuddy-Keane 153). The sentence begins by "speaking generally" of canine, perhaps working class, men provisionally called "Alf, Bert or Chas." who are then the murmurers of "Ce chien est à moi" ("this dog is mine"), itself a citation of Blaise Pascal, but which comes to Woolf, as Phillips points out, via her husband Leonard Woolf's book, *Empire and Commerce in Africa* (1920)—a book, we know, Virginia Woolf helped to research, closely read twice, and thought "superb" (*L2* 413).[15] Already, deictic functioning is in crisis: the "ce" of "ce chien," the this-ness of "this dog," is receding just as "Alf, Bert or Chas." recede. The proposition "Ce chien est à moi," in keeping with Woolf's free indirect mode, has no speech marks to collar it as the direct speech of "Alf, Bert or Chas.," nor as the verbatim citation of Pascal, albeit a citation of Leonard Woolf's citation of Pascal in the epigraph to his book on Africa: "'This dog is mine,' said those poor children; 'that is my place in the sun.' Here is the beginning and the image of the usurpation of all the earth" (*Pensées* 295).

---

[15] See also Marcus (45, 189) who cites Wayne Chapman's paper at the 1992 Virginia Woolf Conference in New Haven, which "indicated that Virginia Woolf's participation in the research and writing of this book was extensive."

Virginia Woolf has omitted from the epigraph Pascal's amplification of the claim "*Ce chien est à moi*" as the originating cause but also the *image* of all colonial appropriation. "Ce chien est à moi" has, then, a self-consciously figurative pedigree. But Woolf also elides the information that these words constitute the directly quoted speech of "ces pauvres enfants." Pascal has "poor children" as the origin of the primary utterance of appropriation, the universal image. Pascal universalises an instinct to appropriate by making the most innocent and the least wealthy his image of possessiveness—a reactionary gesture, I would suggest. But Woolf sheds Pascal's "pauvres enfants," and the didactic "voilà" that Leonard Woolf retains. In her analysis, the poor are themselves the objects of appropriation, and the prospects of the poor to become poets is the basis of her argument, something she presses at the close of her book in her adapted citation from Quiller-Couch that embraces the images of the poor, women, slaves and a dog. Her characterization of this utterance as a murmuring instinct collocates the instinct to appropriate with the bodily drives to urinate or to foul as well as to sexually possess, to rape.

The sentence that comes between those of "ce chien" and the "fine negress" is also slippery: "And, of course, it may not be a dog, I thought, remembering Parliament Square, the Sieges Allee and other avenues; it may be a piece of land or a man with curly black hair" (*AROO* 76). Without quotation marks, a full stop is all that comes between "Ce chien est à moi" and the sentence presented, also unadorned by quotation marks, as the thought of the narrator. Is "Ce chien est à moi" therefore also the thought of the narrator? Does "of course" indicate a moment of recognition, the dawning of a new thought, or is it merely the confirmation of a commonplace? As if in Socratic dialogue with the citation clipped from Pascal's dictum, it implicitly seizes on an absent "voilà," and offers an interpretation of the "chien": "And, of course, it may not be a dog." This suggests first that any other object may come into the sights of the colonisers, but it also confirms Pascal's sense of the figurative work that the dog performs here: the dog is the very *image* of the appropriated object, yet it is at the same time a sliding signifier whose signified is something *not* a dog. The switch from French to English is interesting: the act of translation may suggest the signified (or the tenor of the metaphor, or Adams's "referent") remains untouched by the change of signifier from "chien" to "dog," but it occurs in a proposition that states that the signifier and signified "may not be a dog" after all! Aside from raising linguistic questions concerning translations and questions of the national identity of the dog (is it French or English?), it also confirms the status of the dog (or chien) as metaphoric vehicle for other tenors. This thought is prompted (or accompanied) by the speaker's "remembering Parliament Square, the Sieges Allee and other avenues," places which are "favoured sites of memorial statues" (Shiach 417-418).

Parliament Square became in 1926 Britain's first roundabout, and the traffic circulated around the statues of Britain's eminent statesmen: Sir Robert Peel (1788-1850), Lord Palmerston (1784-1865), Lord Derby (1799-1869), Lord Beaconsfield (1804-1881), George Canning (1770-1827), and a replica of an American statue of Abraham Lincoln (1809-65), which was placed there in 1920. In 1928, the year prior to the publication of *A Room of One's Own*, the death of Emmeline Pankhurst (1858-1928), the militant feminist who in the 1920s became an establishment figure and Conservative candidate, prompted a lobby to raise a statue in Parliament Square to her memory. It was dedicated in March 1930 (see Mayhall). *A Room of One's Own* was drafted, then, during the period when the first statue of a woman was being proposed to join the symbolic order of statuary of historical patriarchal statesmen, credited in Woolf's paragraph with the canine instinct for imperial colonisation.

"Sieges Allee" may look French to the untutored eye, and seems to continue the French slant of Pascal, but it is in fact German in location and culture: it is "The Avenue of Victory" in Berlin. What "other avenues," what other sentences has Woolf's Signifying Dog run in before finding itself in this one? The Sieges Allee is a place that G.K. Chesterton, for one, remarks on, in *The Crimes of England* (1915). Commenting on German "Superman" culture, Chesterton (an acquaintance of Leonard's, and whose work Woolf herself knew), remarks "I am all for 'going out into the world to seek my fortune,' but I do not want to find it—and find it is only being chained for ever among the frozen figures of the Sieges Allee" (Chesterton 79). Lord Dunsany's *Tales of War* (1918), furthermore, includes an eerie vision of this avenue, haunted by the ghosts of fallen comrades:

> And before the flags, and before the generals, I saw marching along on foot the ghosts of the working party that were killed at X, gazing about them in admiration as they went, at the great city and at the palaces. And one man, wondering at the Sieges Allee, turned round to the Lance Corporal in charge of the party: "That is a fine road that we made, Frank!" he said. (24)

Dunsany contrasts this "fine road" with the sites of the primal scenes of war in the battlefields of France: "We have come to the abomination of desolation. And over it broods, and will probably brood for ever, accursed by men and accursed by the very fields, the hyena-like memory of the Kaiser, who has whitened so many bones" (27). This clearly marks the avenue canine imperialist.

Woolf's allusion to the site of Berlin's imperial monuments, furthermore, also returns us again to Leonard Woolf's book *Empire and Commerce in Africa*, which, marked by Pascal's "chien," addresses the Final Act of the historic Congo

Conference in Berlin, and turns a canine simile to describe the rapacious actions of imperial colonial powers unleashed after the Conference: "the nations of Europe . . . [fell] upon Africa like a pack of snarling, tearing, quarrelling jackals." The simile allows agency and choice, rather than instinct. "And when Africa in a few years had been completely divided up amid a yapping and yelping of mutual recrimination, it saw the same pack take itself off to Asia" (Leonard Woolf 44). The turn to metaphor, itself an act of violence, returns the violence of the oppressors' own impositions of metaphorical discourse. The status and subjectivity of African people occupies Leonard Woolf, as he turns on European marauders their own dogs (their racist, canine figurations).

The thought of the appropriated, marked dog, in Virginia Woolf's sentence, where previously a canine trope has the dog appropriating and marking tombstones and signposts, prompts thoughts on two locations of imperial monuments, which themselves represent the acts of colonial appropriation figured as dogs pissing on tombstones and signposts, but which simultaneously present themselves (as monuments) as the very targets for this canine practice. This heady metanarrative arabesque, which has tombstones, monuments and signposts figured as both the subject and object of canine marking, mediates the thought "it may not be a dog" with the corresponding thought on the figurative burden of the dog: "it may be a piece of land or a man with curly black hair." If the dog is both a marked and marking being, this contradictory double status is also conferred to its tenors, "land or a man with curly black hair." It is difficult to read "Ce chien est à moi," then, as merely parroting Pascal on colonial appropriation (Shiach 417), or parroting Woolf's husband's citation of Pascal (Phillips 73), although this latter intertext with Leonard Woolf's book also marks her citation with further anti-imperialist discourse that brings canine resonance to the allusion to Berlin's Sieges Allee. Woolf clearly leaves her own passing canine mark on Pascal's pensée, a rhetorical feat she performs in tandem with her resignification of Dr. Johnson's dog.

The canine signifying on canine signifiers, in the two sentences that precede the sentence in which the "very fine negress" finds herself, strain the collar on the gender and racial and national markers of both the subjects and objects of the act of colonial inscription and appropriation explored here. Is the "fine negress" the equivalent of the "really fine chap" in *Heart of Darkness*? The proximity of both to a version of Johnson's canine metaphor suggests a conscious echo by Woolf; but in engaging the trope, Woolf's sentence turns it in an arabesque of canine signification. As well as attending to her sources in the writings of others, it is instructive to observe how Woolf herself has already marked similar territory in her own writing prior to *A Room of One's Own*. In *Jacob's Room*, for example, Clara's dog "Troy" fouls the statue of "Achilles," monument to colonial imperialism (*JR* 273; Phillips 73); and Jacob himself employs the familiar Johnsonian analogy for his account of the reviled presence of women in King's College Chapel: "No one would think of bringing a dog into church. For though a dog is all very well on a gravel path . . ., the way he wanders down an aisle, . . . approaching a pillar with a purpose . . ., a dog destroys the service completely. So do these women—" (*JR* 50). Likewise the gravel path here returns in *A Room of One's Own*, as does the sacred architecture of Cambridge University. But in the "fine negress" passage, the canine trope is also doubly *racially* marked, while similarly mobile between subject and object status. Furthermore, following the scent of the Johnsonian dog trope in *The Voyage Out*, I have shown Woolf to smuggle in a semitically marked and marking dog to the already unsettling "fine negress" passage (Goldman 2001).[16] "Fine woman" and "fine negress" recall Mary Datchet's epithet for "Sailor," the pet dog of the Suffragist leader Miss Markham, in *Night and Day*: "A very fine dog, too" (*ND* 170). The suffragist dog, Sailor is also an allegory of lesbianism, according to Dunn (177).[17]

Marcus exposes the colliding historical, aesthetic and colonial discourses that inform the term "fine negress." She also scrutinises the term "pass": "The narrator's gaze is raced as well as gendered and powerfully erotic. . . . Was Woolf aware of the racial meaning of the word *pass*?" (Marcus 44). Indeed, yes: Woolf, I suggest, would be able to find in her copy of DuBois's *The Souls of Black Folk*

---

[16] There is a Johnsonian canine pedigree to the term "rake," used by Terence when he taunts Rachel about feminine qualities: "'"Every woman not so much a rake at heart, as an optimist, because they don't think." What do you say, Rachel?'" (*TVO* 275) Rachel's own name is close to the etymological sources supplied by Johnson where "rake" is also derived from "rekel, Dutch, a worthless cur dog." The warmer end of the spectrum of Johnson's canine epithets reserved for men, indeed, may derive from this canine reading of "rake," which he defines as "A loose, disorderly, vicious, wild, gay, thoughtless fellow; a man addicted to pleasure." Among Johnson's literary citations, however, under his definition of the adjective "CU'RRISH" (as "Having the qualities of a degenerate dog; brutal; sour; quarrelsome; malignant; churlish; uncivil; untractable; impracticable"), are lines from Shakespeare that racially and culturally mark the epithet as semitic: "I would she were in heaven, so she could/ Entreat some pow'r to change this currish Jew." And the third definition of "DOG" likewise cites Shakespeare's reproachful "dog jew" in the *Merchant of Venice*. On the other hand, elsewhere he cites "the reproachful name of dog, commonly used by the Jews of the heathen." Again, Johnson shows how dog is a floating signifier in its racial and cultural aspects too. Terence's pointed etymological definition of Rachel as rake, in proximity to his Johnsonian canine analogy of her musical ability, does encourage us to retrieve "rekel" and "cur dog," from where the Johnsonian scent takes us to Shakespeare's "currish Jew" and "dog jew." Terence interpellates Rachel in these terms. Rachel is in any case a recognized Jewish name.

[17] "Fine" is also a key term in *To the Lighthouse*, associated, from the opening sentence, with the affirmative Mrs. Ramsay.

reference to "that frightful chasm at the color-line across which men pass at their peril" (DuBois). She certainly seems aware of the *canine* qualities of passing (Levinas's passing, stray dog becomes relevant here, as we have seen). For Marcus, the narrator's gaze is the racist, "specimen-making gaze" that also reifies the "very fine negress" as "art object" and "sexual object." She posits "a polished figurine [that] the viewer conflates with the African woman it resembles" (Marcus 45, 55, 57). And why not a statue, too? The slippery canine turns of Woolf's preceding sentences certainly encourage this reading of the negress as a co-sign of the tombstone, signpost and monument that the canine Alf, Bert or Chas. mark when they pass, but that women do *not* mark when they pass, *and* as a cosign of the "fine woman" who when passed by Alf, Bert or Chas. causes them to murmur, "Ce chien est à moi." Again, the subject and object of passing perform an intricate dance.

Just how firmly is the "narrator" collared by the term "woman"? Not a unified subject, famously, she speaks in many personae, but, I suggest, she is always and already speaking through a canine morphology. Her citation of the primary utterance of appropriation "Ce chien est à moi" is thus complicated by her own demonstrable canine morphology, hailed (interpellated) as she has been all through *A Room of One's Own* as woman, slave and dog. Momentarily accepting the collar of "woman," she reflects on "one of the great advantages of being a woman." But how far is she speaking as a woman at all (she is pointedly not a self-designated "*English*woman"), and how far as a woman in the first person, when she admits "one can pass even a very fine negress without wishing to make an Englishwoman of her"? "One" is nominative here but it may be read as accusative, and it has a certain distance from both. Is "one" a dog? The canine instinct of "Alf, Bert or Chas." is aligned through Woolf's citation of Pascal, to the "pack of snarling, tearing, quarrelling jackals" in her husband's simile for Europe's rabid colonisation of Africa, the jackals whose choice is to subordinate African peoples to national, imperial order. The speaker of Woolf's sentence is aligned with the canine objects, not subjects, of canine "instinct": the "woman," the "fine woman," the "very fine negress" and the "dog," all of whom are aligned with "ce chien." And the very notion of "instinct" itself has already been undermined by the "dog woman" narrator's encounter with the Beadle.

It would be a grotesque misreading to conclude that Woolf herself runs with the jackals and not the dogs in this sentence, or even that she has clumsily but unintentionally aligned herself with the jackals in using the terms "Englishwoman," "fine woman" and "very fine negress."

Part 3: The "Fine Negress" and the Shock-Dog

Jane Marcus's chapter on the "fine negress" makes a powerful case for indicting Woolf as an imperialist, colonialist jackal. Her prosecution of Woolf partially rests on her interpretation of Woolf's allusions in *A Room of One's Own* to the notorious Restoration writer Aphra Behn (1640-1689), acknowledged as the first professional woman writer in English. "All women together," it is argued in *A Room of One's Own*, "ought to let flowers fall upon the tomb of Aphra Behn, which is, most scandalously but rather appropriately, in Westminster Abbey, for it was she who earned them the right to speak their minds. It is she—shady and amorous as she was—who makes it not quite fantastic for me to say to you tonight: Earn five hundred a year by your wits" (*AROO* 98-99). Woolf's tandem deployment of the adverbs "scandalously" and "appropriately" is unsettling— unsettling enough perhaps to let loose among the garlands falling on Behn's tomb a less than reverential dog. (After all, dogs are never far from Woolf's statues, monuments, or tombstones.)

Marcus is not so unsettled. She approaches Woolf's citation of Behn's memorial with a singular purpose. First she points to the "pioneering but embarrassing" book on Behn written by Woolf's lover, Vita Sackville-West: *Aphra Behn: The Incomparable Astrea* (1927). "That Woolf should have adopted her friend's heroine as her own is strange," according to Marcus, "for Aphra Behn seems as unlike Virginia Woolf as a professional writer as she was like Vita Sackville-West: Tory, conservative, amorous, and adventurous, not to mention male identified" (Marcus 33). Marcus rightly points to Behn's novel, *Oroonoko, Or The Royal Slave. A True History* (1688), as a significant intertext for *A Room of One's Own*, and particularly for the "fine negress" passage. *Oroonoko*, narrated by a white colonial woman, in the turbulent West Indian colony of Surinam, tells the story of Oroonoko, an enslaved African Prince, and of his tragic martyr's death after his ill-fated reunion with his beautiful African lover, Imoinda, who, as the exquisite object of every man's desire in the novel (African or European), has likewise been sold into slavery by Oroonoko's vindictive and sexually jealous grandfather. Their love did not flourish in Africa; nor can it in Surinam. "Imoinda, the totally tattooed princess of Oroonoko," Marcus contends, "may seriously serve as the origin of the figure of the 'fine negress' who compels the gaze of the narrator of *A Room of One's Own*, as she is an erotic object to Aphra Behn. Virginia's 'very fine negress' may be simply another appropriation of Vita's heroine Aphra's 'very fine negress', the visually spectacular Imoinda" (Marcus 33). I agree with Marcus that Woolf's "very fine negress" appears to be in part an allusion to Behn's Imoinda, but I read Woolf's citation of her in that vexatious sentence somewhat differently. I would also dispute that Woolf's citation of Imoinda in that sentence has its source wholly in Sackville-West's book on Behn. Imoinda, like Pascal's chien, is a piece of property that is fought over, not only by various characters in the novel, but by numerous authors who have adapted Behn's work, and by generations of critics seeking to interpret Behn's novel, its antecedents, and its various adaptations. Along with Oroonoko, Imoinda embodies or personifies here (or indeed is a metaphor for) the violence of appropriative metaphor; she is an object severed from its ontological meaning.

Marcus, meanwhile, has Woolf running with the jackals when she follows recent critical consensus on *Oroonoko* in suggesting that this novel "participates in a special brand of racial pornography concerned with representing the castration of the black male and disfiguring the black female," and that its "(supposedly) . . . antislavery appeal" in fact stages "a European fantasy of black slaves in total submission to the knives of white people, cut down in their prime without struggle. *Oroonoko* is about cutting and writing, deforming and defacing the Other to create the self. If it is only a female pen Behn is brandishing, she uses its blade to cut her black characters to shreds. That is clearly why Vita Sackville-West admired it. Why does Virginia Woolf, otherwise holding her own in a battle with Vita about feminism, seem to condone her lover's sadistic racism?" (Marcus 34). I would suggest that before we leap to such conclusions we might attend more closely to the "fine negress" both in the context of Behn's novel, and in the context of its later adaptations (something Marcus neglects to do), and then in the context of Woolf's sentence, and the paragraph in which it is placed (which Marcus also neglects).

First, we can agree with Marcus that Woolf is clearly in dialogue with Sackville-West's book on Behn, when she cites, in *A Room of One's Own*, the same two poems by Behn that Sackville-West herself cites. Behn, Woolf writes, "had to work on equal terms with men. She made, by working very hard, enough to live on. The importance of that fact outweighs anything she actually wrote, even the splendid 'A Thousand Martyrs I have made', or 'Love in Fantastic Triumph Sat', for here begins the freedom of the mind, or rather the possibility that in the course of time the mind will be free to write what it likes" (*AROO* 95). Susan Wiseman, not alert to Sackville-West's citation of these very poems in her book on Behn, nevertheless notes that "Woolf does not say *why* she chose ['Love Arm'd'] to represent the height of Behn's achievement, but it is a choice which, in reminding the reader of Behn's use of formal antecedents and particularly Behn's use of Petrarchan convention, steers them to think formally" (Wiseman, "Aphra" 19). In emphasizing the economic independence achieved by Behn along with her formal technique, then, Woolf seems to be creating a critical distance from the perceived political content of her work. Indeed, such a stance is somewhat distant from Sackville-West's own salacious account of the spectacle of sexualized violence committed on African bodies, when she speculates on the truthfulness of Behn's "True History": "As it is, we must be content with the hope that Oroonoko and Imoinda, glistening ebony, tortured figures that they are, running with little rivulets of blood, crowned with their martyrdom, bear little resemblance to life on the plantations, even in the seventeenth century, but rise as splendid evocations complete in themselves, from the odds and ends of legend that drifted about the verandahs of Surinam" (Sackville-West 25).

Sackville-West also dwells on Behn's "accounts of Oroonoko's feats of heroism and endurance; of his continuing to smoke while his ears, his nose, his private members, and one of his arms were hacked off; all seen through the magnifying glass of romance" (Sackville-West 26). So, does the term "very fine negress" import Sackville-West's sadistic racist account of Behn's racial pornography, in the way Marcus is suggesting? I think not. Before coming to why I think not, it is worth establishing just how precisely Woolf's "fine negress" alludes to Aphra Behn's Imoinda, rather than to Sackville-West's mediated and very brief account of Imoinda.

In Behn's *Oroonoko*, which Woolf probably read in Montague Summers' 1915 edition (Wiseman, "Aphra" 19), Imoinda is notably described as "the beautiful black Venus" (Behn 81), "this fair Queen of Night," whose soul "would be always fine" (Behn 82, 83); as "the most charming black" on the plantation; as "a fine she slave" (Behn 109); as "this fine creature" (Behn 110), and "carved in fine flowers and birds all over her body" (Behn 112). In Africa, Imoinda is envied by Onahal, an aging mistress of the old king, a "decayed beauty" of "declining charms" who "find[s] those caresses paid to new beauties to which she once laid claim" and "hears them whisper as she passes by, 'That once was a delicate woman'" (Behn 90). There is a whisper of such whispers, I suggest, in the instinct of Woolf's "Alf, Bert or Chas." that "murmurs if it sees a fine woman go by, or even a dog." Behn's Imoinda, furthermore, causes Oroonoko to "sigh" when he hears of her anonymously as the "fine she slave" (Behn 109). We are told she also had "an hundred white men sighing after her" (Behn 81), including Trefry, who "had nothing but sigh for her ever since she came" (Behn 110)

It is not only Imoinda who is given the epithet "fine" in Behn's novel. Oroonoko too, who, in a reifying account of his "perfect ebony... polished jet," statue-like form, is credited with the "finest shaped" mouth, and also with a perfect mind of "fine wit" (Behn 81). Oroonoko's own captive enemy in Africa, Jamoan, is described as a man of "fine parts" (Behn 100). The white English woman narrator, furthermore, and her companions of both genders are themselves termed—*by themselves* on behalf of the native Indian population—"extremely fine" (Behn 121) in the moment in the novel where they travel to an Indian town, and enact what Suvir Kaul has identified as an instance of Mary Lou Pratt's notion of "an idealized drama of reciprocation" (Kaul 82). "They were all naked," declares Behn's narrator, who adds a frisson of gender slippage in her self-reflexive account of the reversed ethnographic-drama, "and we were dressed, so as is most commode for the hot countries, very glittering and rich, so that we appeared extremely fine. My own hair was cut short, and I had a taffeta cap, with black feathers on my head. My brother was in a stuff suit, with silver loops and buttons, and abundance of green ribbon. This was all infinitely surprising to them" (Behn 121). This encounter is "less culturally reciprocal than it might seem," as Kaul shows, for "[a]lmost immediately, the visiting party of whites establish their technological and rational superiority" (Kaul 83). The representational politics here, according to Kaul, work "toward establishing both the sentimental innocence and the cultural and material dominance of the imperial subject" (Kaul 83).

It is not only Behn's mobile epithet "fine" that makes its way into Woolf's highly wrought "fine negress passage"; there is also a notable canine trope in Behn's novel that Woolf's text may be (re)signifying on further. Most crucially, a dog appears at the key moment when Oroonoko, enslaved under the ironically imperial name Caesar, is reunited with his Imoinda, herself enslaved as Clemene, and now owned by the equally smitten white "gentleman," Trefry:

> Caesar assured him, he was proof against all the charms of that sex, and that if he imagined his heart could be so perfidious to love again, after Imoinda, he believed he should tear it from his bosom. They had no sooner spoke, but a little shock-dog, that Clemene [later editions: Trefry] had presented her, which she took great delight in, ran out, and she, not knowing anybody was there, ran to get it in again, and bolted out on those who were just speaking of her. (Behn 111)

Behn has the black slave woman Clemene/Imoinda bolting just like the poodle bolts, itself the gift of her white owner, Trefry. Later Oroonoko rouses an ill-fated rebellion, declaring the slaves "suffered not like men who might find a glory, and fortitude in oppression, but like dogs that loved the whip and bell, and fawned the more they were beaten. . . . they had lost the divine quality of men" (Behn 126). As slaves, he declares, "we are bought and sold like apes, or monkeys, to be the sport of women, fools and cowards"; he refuses "obedience" to the "degenerate race" of slave owners, themselves with "no one human virtue left, to distinguish them from the vilest creatures" (Behn 126). In submissive defeat these cowardly slaves become to him "dogs, treacherous and cowardly"; he declares "he had rather die than live upon the earth with such dogs" (Behn 130, 131); and his captors finally ensure that "he should die like a dog" (Behn 140). The lap dog and pet ape imagery suggest the sexualized nature of the slave's commodification. Aravamudan's illuminating chapter, "Petting Oroonoko," confirms this reading of both Oroonoko and Imoinda as positioned in the "contemporaneous discourses of pethood and virtual subjectivity" (Aravamudan 33). As "domestic pet" each becomes a "privatized fetish" rather than the "public commodity" of plantation laborer (Aravamudan 38). "The initial status of the pet subject," Aravamudan explains, "is honorary, or virtualized, because it depends on the contingent and fetishized investment of the owner. The owner's disinvestment returns the pet to the identity of an objectified commodity in the market-place" (Aravamudan 44). The racial pornography of *Oroonoko* exploits stereotyped, commodified African sexuality. Imoinda's "shock-dog" initiates the extending canine trope for a hierarchized, commodified humanity never rising above animality. Woolf's "fine negress" passage similarly freights its canine trope with this sexualized property chain. Yet, as Aravamudan indicates, the virtualization of subjectivity in pethood, although reversible, "soon acquires an autonomy of its own" (44); and I would therefore interpret the crucial momentary bid for freedom made by Imoinda's shock-dog as a representative gesture of such potential autonomy. The "beginnings of social contract discourse," Aravamudan explains, "allowed the theorization of subjectivity on the basis of 'natural' rights that rationalized the possession of property; Africans and women, variously extraneous to such ideas, begin challenging those who claim ownership of them by exerting subjective authority over themselves as objects" (Aravamudan 44).

Yet Behn's Imoinda does not go so far as to claim "This shock-dog is mine" (never mind, "*I* am mine"). In the hierarchized, sexualized property chain, Behn's silent subaltern "fine negress" remains "obedient" to her husband, Oroonoko, loyally joining him in death. She never speaks. Whereas she is a gift in Africa, she becomes a commodity in America, as Laura J. Rosenthal observes. Noting that "Behn did not hesitate to tell stories of miscegenation elsewhere and could have easily done so in *Oroonoko*," Rosenthal controversially takes Behn's "choice to create faithful black African lovers . . . as one both embedded in and resistant to stereotypes of African sexuality. Behn uses myths of Africa—the only Africa to which she has access—to represent an alternative to the brutality of British commodification and a place from which to offer a sceptical view of colonialism" (28). She also argues that Behn is not fuelling the problematic "main stream," white feminist tendency that Marcus and others before her have critiqued, because Behn's "narrative further avoids racist and sexist comparisons between 'women' and 'Africans' by keeping an African woman central to its unfolding. If we cannot praise Oroonoko for being an abolitionist text," Rosenthal continues, "we can appreciate its critique of colonialism and resistance to some colonialist stereotypes of African sexuality, as well as its representation

—however ethnocentric—of an Africa with a culture prior to and independent of the British slave trade. This, too, becomes possible through the narrative centrality of an African woman." She reads the "passionate love between Oroonoko and Imoinda" as "an emblem for this cultural independence" (36).

Very few critics, however, including Rosenthal and Aravamudan, arrive at their interpretation of the blackness of Behn's Imoinda by reading *Oroonoko*, the novel, only in relation to Behn's other works or in isolation from its later adaptations, particularly Thomas Southerne's influential dramatization of 1695. Southerne's stage adaptation not only adds a comic subplot to Behn's tragedy, complete with trans-gendered masquerade, it also turns Behn's black African Imoinda white. Set entirely in Surinam, it also elides most of the African back story. Southerne makes much of the term "pass," furthermore, in dialogue concerning the cross-dressing of the "husband-hunting," white woman protagonist of the subplot; and he makes comedic comparison between the marriage market and the slave trade. Southerne's dedicatory epistle makes much of Behn's own reluctance to put her African protagonists on stage, and critics have speculated that whereas Southerne's Oroonoko could be played by an actor in blackface, there would be anxieties over an actress in blackface, and that Southerne was also pointing up Aphra Behn's rumored dalliance with a real-life Prince Oroonoko.[18] This reading of Imoinda's whiteness fuels the critical debate on questions of authorial subjectivity, artistic property, and biographical interpretation raised by Southerne's rewriting of Behn's work. It has, furthermore, been suggested that in whitening Imoinda, Southerne is tempering the political force of Behn's novel. Rosenthal argues that: "By eliminating the history of African characters and by changing Imoinda into a white woman, Southerne inscribes precisely the progressive ideology that helped enable colonialism and that Behn's novel holds up for scrutiny. Further, authorship itself becomes a site of contestation over property as Behn and Southerne take up various strategies to negotiate their differently gendered positions and thus their differing capacities to own discourse" (Rosenthal 27; see also Vermillion). Authorship as a site of contestation over property is likewise central to the argument of Woolf's *A Room of One's Own*.

Furthermore, Kaul argues that Behn's narrative, "in its encounters with the Indians of Surinam, and its obsessive detailing of bodily mutilation, is much less able (than its adaptations) to *manage* the telling of contact tales, or to repress the violence that defines the Caribbean plantation economy with whose culture it engages. The form of the heroic tragedy, of course, is her generic strategy for the retelling of a tale of slavery and culturally-specific cruelty as a story of heroism

---

[18] See: Kaul (90); Wiseman (35); Nussbaum (158-159, 16, 163); Spencer (234).

and transcultural nobility. Her novella at least partially orders its narrative energies and interests in the terms of heroic tragedy; Southerne's play, on the other hand, finds in the cadences of heroic verse a language for the redemption of the brutality and ugliness of slavery and the slave trade" (Kaul 80). Certainly Behn's heroic Oroonoko is reduced by Southerne to concurring with his own enslavement, when he tells his fellow slaves "we are now/ Their property" (Southerne III.ii.111-112), and to concurring with the white male slave-owning class about the "worth" of having Clemene/Imoinda and the status of her "consent" as a slave (Southerne II.iii.50-61). Imoinda's whiteness is crucial here, as Wiseman points out, since it "naturalises the representation of the governor's attack on her as rape," for, in the world of Southerne's play, she asks, "could a black Imoinda have been 'enough' of a subject to be raped" (Wiseman, "Abolishing" 35)? The legal answer is no. And we might compare the historical legal resistance to the notion of rape in marriage. Wiseman's comparative observations on the status of Imoinda's subjectivity in Behn's novel and Southerne's play, may also throw light on the contested subjectivity of Woolf's "fine negress."

> Behn's text situated subjectivity in behavior: Africans—including African women—as much as Europeans, might be noble. Perhaps this emphasis on behavior contributes to the instability of her text in ideological terms. For Southerne, what guarantees Imoinda's status as subject is her white lineage: a white slave is already [enough of] a subject . . . to be raped. Clearer still, the audience are not required to negotiate the question of black female subjecthood and slavery. (Wiseman, "Abolishing" 36)

Wiseman's identification in Behn's text of behavior or conduct as the locus of subjectivity, rather than fixed essence or prior identity, may extend to Woolf's too, as we have seen. The stray speaking subjects in Woolf's sentences have no fixed identity, prior to entering the text. If "whiteness" is the "key to subject status" for Southerne's Imoinda, as Wiseman suggests, then it appears that he has made an Englishwoman of her in order to make more feasible, in the logic of his racist colonial discourse, her potential to be raped. The narrator of Woolf's sentence, in re-establishing Imoinda's blackness, may be undoing such logic. She may also be refuting Southerne's biographical reading of Imoinda as merely a cipher for Behn herself.

The "notable absence of a black woman in Southerne's play, should alert us," Aravamudan warns, "to the limits of the analogical use of slavery in the advancement of a metropolitan agenda of women's rights" (Aravamudan 57). But "bleaching Imoinda white," for Aravamudan, does not prevent her contribution to Southerne's juxtaposition of "the success of the Englishwomen with the failure of the slave rebels," since he finds Imoinda ultimately to be positioned as an exemplar of "failed whiteness" by her designation as *Indian* in Charlot's epilogue to the play, written by Congreve, where she urges the audience to "Forgive this Indians fondness for her Spouse" (Southerne *Epil.* 29; Aravamudan 57). Although Southerne's Imoinda is white, she remains "ethnic" (Aravamudan 57).

Virginia Woolf owned a 1751 edition of Southerne's *Oroonoko*, which came from her father's library. And in Summers' preface to Behn's novel she would have read of the popular German translation of Southerne's *Oroonoko* (1789) whose "somewhat grotesque frontispiece," depicts Oroonoko and Imoinda, "both . . . black 'as pitch or as the cole'" (Summers 5: 127). This merely adds to the ironic destabilizing of Imoinda's colour which has been the case ever since the black Imoinda of Behn's novel came to co-exist with the white Imoinda of the plays (see Spencer; Wiseman, "Abolishing" 37). Sackville-West's book mentions Southerne's play in passing but says nothing of his whitening of Imoinda. Jane Marcus is altogether silent on this.

Woolf's well-read tropicopolitan dog-woman narrator appears to have read and to be (re)signifying on both Behn's novel and Southerne's play. Such allusions mark that vexatious sentence as a clear riposte to Southerne's elision of Behn's ambivalently positioned black African princess Imoinda: "It is one of the great advantages of being a woman that one can pass even a very fine negress without wishing to make an Englishwoman of her" (*AROO* 76). Following Aravamudan, we must continue to question whether such tropes *can* be turned to advantage. We might try to make sense of this sentence, in which lurks Imoinda's shock-dog, by reading it in relation to the preceding sentences, inhabited by Pascal's chien. We can pursue both dogs to their textual origins in critiques of the continuing history of Europe's violent appropriation of Africa. And we can compare Sackville-West's notable dismissal of the abolitionist readings of Behn's novel:

> It was a new departure in fiction, even if we reject the theory that it was 'the first novel of emancipation'. Reject it I think we certainly must, in the absence of all internal evidence to prove that Mrs Behn, despite her proper indignation at any definite ill-treatment of the natives, held views upon the abolition of slavery. She probably took it quite as a matter of course that black people should exist in subjection to white; she was not preaching; she was telling a story. And telling it extremely well. Oroonoko goes with a vigour, an energy, a picturesqueness, which make it readable to-day. (Sackville-West 20)

It is the "vividness" of Behn's writing, she claims, "that is really moving" in this "remote and improbable" story. "What could be further from us than the scene of her tragedy, an obscure little colony in the seventeenth century?" (Sackville-West 20-21). Her question may well be answered by *A Room of One's Own* whose secret project is perhaps that of "Educating Vita." Vita may be re-educated, then, by chasing the chien who keeps the "fine negress" company in Woolf's text. This dog would lead her, via Pascal and the Sieges Allee, to the indictment of the all too recent exploitation of Africa recorded in Leonard Woolf's *Empire and Commerce in Africa* (1920).

Conclusion: A Canine Ethics for Reading Woolf

Woolf as jackal or as dog aside, we must attend to how her "fine negress" sentence and paragraph have been engineered to interpellate the reader as canine. Nor is it simply a matter of the reader running either with the jackals, or with the dogs, or of realizing, as Woolf's slippery syntax and sliding canine signifiers encourage us to realize, that the potential for jackal and dog, for "reason" and "instinct," is there in us all. It is also the way her slippery, rhythmical repetitive syntax and her sliding canine signifiers have the reader reading and re-reading, returning to images and figures, marking and re-marking their significance, digging up her half-buried allusions and chasing them down.

Woolf's writings provide "*an ethics without identification*," according to Pamela Caughie. "What they teach us is not how to read characters as if they were people, but how to read people as if they were texts. Her narratives relocate ethics in the material practices of reading and writing, and thus textual analysis becomes an ethical imperative." These material practices, I would add, extend to the politics of writing and reading metaphor. Woolf's shifting canine metaphors, deployed in the sophisticated syntax of her free-indirect discourse, undermine simplistic notions of readerly identification and eschew models of coherent identity prior to language, but they nevertheless engage us in an ethics of conduct and of *interpellation*. Woolf's canine metaphors do not merely teach us to read in the ways Caughie suggests; they also read us.

Woolf's sentences engage us in an ethical process, as we track and tunnel logically and intellectually after shreds of meaning—a process of turning tropes to advantage. As readers, tracing how Woolf's writing is engaged in such a process, we find that we too have become engaged in it ourselves as we attempt to make sense of the shreds of meaning we unearth, and of the metaphors we encounter. This ethical process asks, then, where we are to position ourselves in relation to, and, more crucially, where we find ourselves (indeed) positioned by, the turning politics of canine metaphors. "The act of metaphor then," according to Thomas Pynchon's novel *The Crying of Lot 49*, "was a thrust at truth and a lie, depending where you were: inside, safe, or outside, lost. Oedipa did not know where she was" (89). It may be that "inside, safe" is the idealized position of the tenor, a secure subjectivity, and "outside, lost" is that desolate place of the figurative vehicle, the reified, object world of the Other. What is at stake in negotiating the politics of metaphor and in the turning of an historical legacy of tropes, then, is our status as subjects or objects, or as something between the two. The shifting caesura between the two, a zone occupied by the virtual subjectivity of caninicity, unsettles that status and is the site, too, of resistance. Marked and marking beings, we (dog) readers, when we enter, or find ourselves in, a sentence by Woolf, leave (by choice, reason or instinct?) our own traces on her tombstones and signposts. And they mark us too. *A Room of One's Own*, in applying its own turns on misogynist and racialist canine troping, in resignifying and signifying on an historical tradition of signifying dogs, demonstrates some of the ethical advantages of the narratorial adoption of a canine morphology (whether on hind legs or all fours). "To be a dog woman," for Paula Rego, "is not necessarily to be downtrodden . . . but powerful" (McEwan 216). Meanwhile Woolf, celebrating the morphological fluidity of the figurative, declares herself quite a different animal: "I'm the hare," she records in her diary of 1931, "a long way ahead of the hounds my critics" (*D4* 45).

Works Cited

Adams, Carol J. "The Rape of Animals, the Butchering of Women" (from *Sexual Politics of Meat: A feminist-vegetarian critical theory* [Continuum, 1990]). *The Animal Ethics Reader*. Ed. Susan J. Armstrong & Richard G. Botzler. London: Routledge, 2003: 209-215.

Agamben, Giorgio. *The Open: Man and Animal*. Trans. Kevin Attell. Stanford: Stanford UP, 2004.

Aravamudan, Srinivas. *Tropicopolitans: Colonialism and Agency, 1688-1804*. Durham and London: Duke University Press, 1999.

Banfield, Ann. "Describing the Unobserved: Events Grouped around an Empty Centre." *The Linguistics of Writing: Arguments between Language and Literature*. Ed. Nigel Fabb, Derek Attridge, Alan Durant, and Colin MacCabe. New York: Methuen, 1987.

Behn, Aphra. *The Works of Aphra Behn*. 5 vols. Ed. Montague Summers. London, 1915.

Behn, Aphra. *Oroonoko, The Rover and Other Works*. Ed. Janet Todd. Harmondsworth: Penguin, 1992.

Boswell, James. *Life of Johnson* (1791). http://www.gutenberg.org/files/1564/15640h/1564-h.htm

Caius, John. *Of Englishe dogges, the diuersities, the names, the natures, and the properties: a short treatise written in latine / by Iohannes Caius of late mem-*

orie, ... and newly drawn into Englishe by Abraham Fleming. [*De Canibus Britannicis*] [1576] (1880) London: A. Bradley, 1880.

Caughie, Pamela. "Ethical Prose: Woolf's Writing Across Identity Boundaries." Unpublished Conference Paper. International Virginia Woolf Society Panel, 20th-Century Literature Conference, University of Louisville, February 24, 2006.

Chesterton. G.K. *The Crimes of England*. London: Cecil Palmer & Hayward, 1915.

Conley, Verena Andermatt. "Becoming Woman Now." *Deleuze and Feminist Theory*. Ed. Ian Buchanan and Claire Colebrook. Edinburgh: Edinburgh University Press, 2000.

Conrad, Joseph. *Heart of Darkness* (1902). *The Norton Anthology of English Literature*. Eighth Edition. Vol. 2. Ed. Stephen Greenblatt. New York and London: Norton, 2006.

Cuddy-Keane, Melba. "The Rhetoric of Feminist Conversation: Virginia Woolf and the Trope of the Twist." *Ambiguous Discourse: Feminist Narratology and British Women Writers*. Ed. Kathy Mezei. Chapel Hill & London: University of North Carolina Press, 1996.

Cugoano, Quobna Ottobah [aka John Stuart]. *Thoughts and Sentiments on the Evil and Wicked Traffic of the Slavery and Commerce of the Human Species, Humbly Submitted to the Inhabitants of Great-Britain, by Ottobah Cugoano, a Native of Africa* (1787). Ed. Paul Edwards. London: Dawsons of Pall Mall, 1969.

Dabydeen, David. *Hogarth's Blacks: Images of Blacks in Eighteenth Century English Art*. Surrey: Dangaroo Press, 1985.

Deleuze, Gilles, and Félix Guattari. *A Thousand Plateaus: Capitalism and Schizophrenia*. Trans. Brian Massumi. London & New York: Continuum, 1992.

DuBois, W.E.B. *The Souls of Black Folk: Essays and Sketches* (1903). http://etext.virginia.edu/toc/modeng/public/DubSoul.html.

Dunn, June. "'Beauty Shines On Two Dogs Doing What Two Women Must Not Do': Puppy Love, Same-Sex Desire and Homosexual Coding in Woolf." *Virginia Woolf: Turning the Centuries*. Ed. Ann L. Ardis and Bonnie Kime Scott. New York: Pace UP, 2000: 176-182.

Dunsany, Lord. *Tales of War*. London & New York: G.P. Putnam's Sons, 1918.

Eberly, David. "Housebroken: The Domesticated Relations of *Flush.*"*Virginia Woolf: Texts and Contexts: Selected Papers from the Fifth Annual Conference on Virginia Woolf.* Ed. Beth Rigel Daugherty and Eileen Barrett. New York: Pace UP, 1996: 21-25.

Equiano, Olaudah. *The Interesting Narrative of the Life of Olaudah Equiano, or Gustavus Vassa, the African. Written by Himself* (1789). Ed. Paul Edwards. London: Dawsons of Pall Mall, 1969.

Fludernik, Monika. *The Fictions of Language and the Languages of Fiction*. London and New York: Routledge, 1993.

Garber, Marjorie. *Dog Love*. New York: Touchstone, 1997.

Gates, Henry Louis. *The Signifying Monkey: A Theory of African American Literary Criticism*. New York: Oxford, 1988.

Gilbert, Geoff. *Before Modernism Was: Modern History and the Constituencies of Writing 1900-30*. Basingstoke: Palgrave, 2004.

Goldman, Jane. "Who Let the Dogs Out?: From Dr Johnson to Horatian Woolf." Unpublished Conference Paper. 11th Annual Conference on Virginia Woolf. University of Bangor. June 2001.

———. "'Who let the dogs out?': Statues, Suffragettes, and Dogs in Woolf's London" *Back to Bloomsbury, the 14th Annual International Virginia Woolf Conference Proceedings,* published online by the Woolf Center: http://www.csub.edu/woolf_center. September, 2006. *Virginia Woolf's Bloomsbury*. Ed. Lisa Shahriari and Gina Vitello Potts. Basingstoke: Palgrave, 2007.

Gronniosaw, James Albert Ukawsaw. *A Narrative of the Most Remarkable Particulars in the Life of James Albert Ukawsaw Gronniosaw, An African Prince, As Related by Himself* (1770; 1840). http://docsouth.unc.edu/neh/gronniosaw/gronnios.html

Haraway, Donna. *The Companion Species Manifesto: Dogs, People and Significant Otherness*. Chicago: Prickly Paradigm Press, 2003.

Hecht, J. Jean. *The Domestic Servant Class in Eighteenth-Century England*. London: Routledge & Kegan Paul, 1956.

Kaul, Suvir. "Reading Literary Symptoms: Colonial Pathologies and the Oroonoko Fictions of Behn, Southerne, and Hawkesworth." *Eighteenth-Century Life* 18.3 (1994): 80-96.

Kuzniar, Alice A. *Melancholia's Dog: Reflections on Our Animal Kinship*. Chicago: University of Chicago Press, 2006.

Lamb, Charles. "Oxford in the Vacation." *Essays of Elia* (1823)

Levinas, Emmanuel. "The Name of a Dog, or Natural Rights." *Difficult Freedom: Essays on Judaism*. Trans. Seán Hand. Baltimore: The Johns Hopkins University Press, 1990.

McEwan, J. *Paula Rego*. London: Phaidon Press, 1997.

Mansfield, Katherine. *Journal of Katherine Mansfield 1914-1927*. Ed. J. Middleton Murry. London: Constable, 1927.

Marcus, Jane. *Hearts of Darkness: White Women Write Race*. New Brunswick, NJ: Rutgers University Press, 2004.

Marcus, Laura. "Woolf's Feminism and Feminism's Woolf." *The Cambridge Companion to Virginia Woolf*. Ed. Sue Roe and Susan Sellers. Cambridge: Cambridge University Press, 2000.

Mayhall, Laura E. Nym. "Domesticating Emmeline: Representing the Suffragette, 1930-1993." *NWSA Journal* 11. 2; http://www.iupress.indiana.edu/journals/nwsa/nws11-2.html

Nourse, Timothy. *Campania Foelix* (1700). New York: Garland, 1982.

Nussbaum, Felicity. *The Limits of the Human: Fictions of Anomaly, Race, and Gender in the Long Eighteenth Century*. Cambridge: Cambridge University Press, 2003.

Pascal, Blaise. *Pensées* (1660). http://www.gutenberg.org/files/18269/18269-8.txt.

Phillips, Kathy. *Virginia Woolf Against Empire*. Knoxville: University of Tennessee Press, 1994.

Prince, Gerald. *A Dictionary of Narratology*. Aldershot: Scolar Press, 1987.

Pynchon, Thomas. *The Crying of Lot 49*. London: Vintage, 1966.

Quennell, Peter. [Review]. *Life and Letters*. Vol. 1 (June 1928): 221.

———. "New Novels." *Life and Letters*. Vol. 3 (July-December 1929): 551-555.

Rosenthal, Laura J. "Owning Oroonoko: Behn, Southerne, and the Contingencies of Property." *Renaissance Drama* 23 (1992): 25-38.

Sackville-West, Vita. *Aphra Behn: The Incomparable Astrea*. London: Howe, 1927.

Shiach, Morag. Ed. *A Room of One's Own* by Virginia Woolf. Oxford: Oxford University Press, 1992.

Scott, Walter. "The Queen's Marie." *Minstrelsy of the Scottish Border* (1802-03). http://electricscotand.com/history/other/scott/queens_marie.htm.

Southerne. Thomas. *Oroonoko: A Tragedy* (1695). Ed. Maximillian E. Novak and David Stuart Rodes. London: Edward Arnold, 1977.

Spencer, Jane. *Aphra Behn's Afterlife*. Oxford: Oxford University Press, 2000.

Spiegel, Marjorie. *The Dreaded Comparison: Human and Animal Slavery*. Philadelphia: New Society Publishers, 1988.

Steeves, H. Peter. "Lost Dog, or, Levinas Faces the Animal." *Figuring Animals: Essays on Animal Images in Art, Literature, Philosophy, and Popular Culture*. Ed. Mary Sanders Pollock and Catherine Rainwater. Basingstoke: Palgrave, 2005.

Stimpson, Catherine. "Woolf's Room, Our Project: The Building of Feminist Criticism." *Virginia Woolf: Longman Critical Readers*, ed. Rachel Bowlby, London: Longman, 1992.

Thomas, Keith. *Man and the Natural World: Changing Attitudes in England 1500-1800*. London: Allen Lane, 1983.

Vanita, Ruth. "'Love Unspeakable': The Uses of Allusion in *Flush*." *Virginia Woolf: Themes and Variations*. Ed. Vara Neverow-Turk and Mark Hussey. New York: Pace University Press, 1993. 248-257.

Vermillion, Mary. "Buried Heroism: Critiques of Female Authorship in Southerne's Adaptation of Behn's Oroonoko." *Restoration: Studies in English Literary Culture, 1660-1700* 16. 1 (1992 Spring): 28-37.

Wiseman, Susan. "Aphra Behn (1640?-89): Virginia Woolf and the 'Little Gods of Love.'" *Women and Poetry, 1660-1750*. Ed. Sarah Prescott and David E. Shuttleton. Basingstoke: Palgrave, 2003.

——. "Abolishing Romance: Representing Rape in *Oroonoko*." *Discourses of Slavery and Abolition: Britain and its Colonies, 1760-1838*. Ed. Brycchan Carey, Markman Ellis and Sara Salih. Basingstoke: Palgrave, 2004.

Woolf, Leonard. *Empire and Commerce in Africa: A Study in Economic Imperialism*. London: Macmillan, 1920.

Woolf, Virginia. *A Room of One's Own*. London: Hogarth, 1929.

——. *Flush: A Biography*. London: Hogarth, 1933.

——. Foreword. *Recent Paintings by Vanessa Bell* (1930). *The Bloomsbury Group: A Collection of Memoirs, Commentary and Criticism*. Ed. S.P. Rosenbaum. London: Croom Helm, 1975.

——. *Jacob's Room*. London: Hogarth, 1922.

——. *Night and Day*. London: Duckworth, 1919.

——. *The Diary of Virginia Woolf*. 5 vols. Ed. Anne Olivier Bell and Andrew McNeillie. London: Hogarth, 1977-1984.

——. *The Essays of Virginia Woolf*. (of 6) vols. London: Hogarth, 1986-1994.

——. *The Letters of Virginia Woolf*. 6 vols. London: Hogarth, 1975-1980.

——. *The Voyage Out*. London: Duckworth, 1915.

——. *To the Lighthouse*. London: Hogarth, 1927

"'Myself'—it was impossible": Queering History in *Between the Acts*

Erica Delsandro

> One becomes aware that we are spectators and also passive participants in a pageant.—"The Moment: Summer's Night."

> *Come hither to our festival* (she continued)
> *This is a pageant, all may see*
> *Drawn from our island history.*
> *England am I...*
> —*Between the Acts*

In 1940, as the history that would become World War II is exploding around her, Virginia Woolf is occupied with death: she and Leonard are contemplating suicide while bombs are falling on London;[1] she is finishing the biography of her deceased friend Roger Fry while beginning her own memoirs; she is attempting to end a novel (*Between the Acts*) that, being set in 1939 with war on the horizon, is already concluded by world events. Her diary on Saturday, 22 June, 1940 portrays her preoccupation with endings and her inclination to view the present moment through the potential of her death in the near future:

> I feel, if this is my last lap, oughtn't I to read Shakespeare? But cant. I feel oughtn't I to finish off P.H. [abbreviation for Pointz Hall, the working title for *Between the Acts*]: oughtn't I to finish something by way of an end? The end gives its vividness, even its gaiety & recklessness to the random daily life. This, I thought yesterday, may be my last walk.... And now dinner to cook. A role. (*D5* 298)

Distinguishing the life of thought captured in her diary from the life of domestic duties awaiting her, Woolf alludes to the performative nature of her identity; in the script of her life, there seems to be more than one role to play. One Virginia

---

[1] In her diary, Woolf articulates her and Leonard's intentions of suicide: "But though L. says he has petrol in the garage for suicide shd. [should] Hitler win, we go on" (*D5* 284).

Woolf muses upon the prospect of her own death; she considers her final walk and what she should be reading if this truly is her "last lap." The other Woolf, acknowledged at the end of this entry, is the woman who, regardless of impending death, must continue to play the roles required by family, marriage, and society. Implicit in this entry is Woolf's understanding that much of what composes her own history is a performance of identity, a product of the roles she plays.

Considering what it means to write a life as death closes in around her, she exposes the presence and function of performance. In the Fry biography, she struggles with what it means to write a life and a history. The experience of writing Fry's life colors her thoughts concerning her own: "Who was I then?" she writes of herself in "A Sketch of the Past" (65). Reflecting upon her personal history, Woolf recognizes the performance of self, how different selves compose the history of one's life, and how very *queer* it is to realize just how much of one's history is performative: "Queer, when its so tame after all, a book coming out, why one writes them? How much part does 'coming out' play in the pleasure of writing then? Each one accumulates a little of the fictitious V. W. whom I carry like a mask about the world" (*D5* 307).[2] As I will suggest, Woolf's sense of queer reaches beyond the literal meaning of this 1940 diary entry as she negotiates the relationship between performance, self, and history in *Between the Acts*.

Although world war, death, and the task of life-writing illuminate for Woolf in 1940 the presence of masks and the function of performance in history—personal and otherwise—such concerns have inflected her thoughts and writings throughout her career. Much earlier in her life, "apprenticed to the writing of history, not literature" (Westman 3), Woolf articulates the masked nature of history—revealed as queer in 1940—in her essay "Modes and Manners of the Nineteenth Century" (a review of a book with that title). In this 1910 essay, Woolf is concerned with the representation of large histories, of nations, epochs, and centuries, through the study of markers—masks—of social identity: modes

---

[2] Although Barber and I share Woolf's 1940 diary entry as a starting point, in "Lip-Reading: Woolf's Secret Encounters" Barber employs readings of Bloomsbury's relationship to male homosexuality and Sapphism, *The Years*, and *Between the Acts* in order to explore the queer presences in Woolf's life and fiction, as well as to suggest the performativity of Woolf's own writing project. My interests are clearly similar; however, this essay is more concerned with the relationship between the queer presences in *Between the Acts* and the history that marginalizes them, between the performance of scripted historical roles and the potential of unacted parts that queer presences offer. My interest lies in how *Between the Acts* proposes a queer relationship with the past and the present that includes both those privileged and those marginalized by historical narratives in order to suggest new ways of relating to the future.

and manners. However, an echo in her confession that there is a "fictitious V. W." whom she carries like a "mask about the world," is what she explains about history in this essay written thirty years earlier: "history is not a history of ourselves, but of our disguises" (*E1* 334).³ Woolf's past suggestion about the nature of history is inextricable from her thoughts about the present moment, a moment in which life and death, histories and potential futures are perhaps, like Woolf herself, on their "last lap."

In *Women, Modernism, and Performance*, Penny Farfan investigates Woolf's performative history, beginning with the Dreadnought Hoax in 1910: "Woolf's participation in the hoax suggests an interest in performance as a site of subversive potential that is borne out by the fact that when she returned to the subject . . . in her two 1940 talks, she was also in the process of completing her final novel *Between the Acts*" (90-91).⁴ Farfan interprets Woolf's representation of performance as "a liminal zone between art and life through which [Woolf] articulates her sense that literary texts are essentially cultural scripts which can operate in dominant and repressive capacities but which, by the same token, can put into play new modes of being by circulating alternative views of reality and devising new roles for social actors, who may see them in their 'unacted parts'" (9). It is the relationship between the "cultural scripts"—history—and "social actors" that Woolf, occupied with her own acted and unacted parts, was exploring in the last years of her life. Following from Farfan, I read *Between the Acts* as suggesting such "new modes of being" and "alternative views of reality" accessed through the productive modality of personal and historical performances. In this manner, 1910 is an echo in 1940: both the Dreadnought Hoax and "Modes and Manners of the Nineteenth Century" mark concerns that would continue to have a lifelong resonance for Woolf, as illustrated not only in her diary entries but also, as I will argue, in *Between the Acts*.

---

³ Westman also uses this quotation from "Mode and Manners of the Nineteenth Century" to conclude that "the art of fiction, more than the art of the historian, recreates the material circumstances of the past and the characters who inhabit them" (13).

⁴ According to *Virginia Woolf A-Z*, in February 1910, Virginia Woolf, her brother Adrian Stephen, Duncan Grant, and others posed as visiting Abyssinians in order "to perpetrate a hoax on the British Navy" (Hussey 74). So disguised, they toured the *HMS Dreadnought*, "the navy's most secret warship" (74). Hermione Lee writes of this incident in her biography, *Virginia Woolf*, suggesting that "[t]he Dreadnought Hoax's playful cheek and exhibitionism gets into [Woolf's] work indirectly" (282). Farfan proposes that Woolf's participation in the Dreadnought Hoax plays a crucial role in her writing and thinking.

Many feminist readings of Woolf's last novel, like Farfan's, have explored the emancipatory potential of performance as site for liberation and critique; similarly, many lesbian and queer readings of *Between the Acts*, like Annette Oxindine's, have sought in the novel's "outsiders" a critique of heteronormative narratives. My reading borrows from such scholarship while suggesting that *Between the Acts* provides more than a celebration of performativity and a critique of patriarchal power. What I wish to articulate is the way the novel exposes the relationship between history's exclusionary narratives and the performances both insiders and outsiders play. By revealing identity as performance, Woolf unmasks historically contingent identities, introducing what Stephen Barber recognizes as "a critically queer technology of the self" (401); however, by interrupting the performance of identity in order to reflect history's audience as its actors, history, too, is queered. My reading of *Between the Acts* explores the relationship between the queer performance of self and the history it haunts with the intent of raising the curtain on the potential of unacted parts.

In 1940, Woolf's present moment is interrupted by her past: roles played, performances acted; as in the 1910 essay, she conjures up another version of history that exposes it as a performance, acted in disguise. The question then emerges, what happens to those whom history does not script a part to perform? If history is composed of disguises, what about those who do not have the correct costume? These are the unacted parts that haunt historical narratives, and, I suggest, that are significant—and signifying specters—in Woolf's last novel. In *Between the Acts*, haunting disrupts the (hetero)normative temporalities that compose and enforce historical narratives, both national and personal. Following from developments in queer theory that seek to queer not only sexuality but history as well, I identify such temporal disruption as queer; the first section of this essay will propose a way to read the haunting of Pointz Hall as Woolf gesturing toward a history haunted by unacted parts—a queer history. Drawing attention to the queerness of identity, William Dodge interrupts the characters and the histories that are both the subject of the novel and the pageant play at the center of the narrative: personal and national histories are revealed as performances, both audience and actors find themselves in disguise. Queering history in the novel, Woolf creates a narrative space that reveals the potential of unacted parts: Miss La Trobe's version of English history reflects to its audience their implicit performance in the history dramatized on the Pointz Hall lawn stage. As the past interrupts the present, reflects and refracts the audience and actors, and suggests the possibility of a new, queer relationship with historical time, Woolf's words from 1910 are conjured in her novel's 1939 June day: "history is not a history of ourselves, but of our disguises."

Queer History and the Haunting of Pointz Hall

Between the Acts interrogates notions of historicism that dominate the construction of the past, influence the performance of the present, and, in 1940, threaten to manifest in martial action, and thereby, dictate the future. The daughter of a historian of sorts, Woolf, throughout her life, had been exposed to the power of history: on one hand, a participant, writing the avant-garde literary and social history of the first half of the twentieth century; on the other hand, as a daughter of the Victorian age and a woman of modernity, marginalized by and excluded from grand historical narratives. As a participant in and a spectator of history—her own and her nation's—as a reader of literature and a writer of fiction, Woolf recognizes the reciprocal relationship between history and the literature that both creates and disseminates it. Thus, in *Between the Acts*, Woolf disrupts history as it had been written by men like her father and suffered by men like her nephew Julian; moreover, by exposing the performance of history's audience in the production of history, she explores the history experienced by those whose lives are lived simultaneously inside and outside of history's grand narrative.[5]

Karin Westman traces Woolf's early exposure to and critique of history, as well as her life-long effort to acknowledge and engage history as performance by "reveal[ing] history as a fiction" (11). Westman's interest lies in the dialogical historiography that Woolf's essays and reviews propose, suggesting that Woolf's desire to write fiction emerges from her early writings on the nature of history and the manner in which it is represented: "Together, her reviews and journals provide the genesis of what will become her well-known revision of the literary form modeled upon the close detail and objectivity of a historical record: the novelistic realm of her Victorian predecessors and Edwardian contemporaries" (Westman 4). Most explicitly, in her essay "Mr. Bennett and Mrs. Brown," Woolf indicts "the close detail and objectivity" of historicism in the construction of modern literary character (Westman 4), suggesting that character escapes such narrative confines. In contrast to her Victorian and Edwardian predecessors, for Woolf, both history and literature share a relationship with fiction; history, as the

---

[5] Woolf's father, Leslie Stephen, was the first editor of the *Dictionary of National Biography* and wrote, among other biographies and histories, *History of English Thought in the Eighteenth Century* (1876). Julian Bell, Woolf's nephew, was killed in the Spanish Civil War. In *A Room of One's Own* and *Three Guineas*, Woolf critiques patriarchal history, both literary and national, for its exclusion of women. Her novel *Orlando*, which is based on her friend and lover Vita Sackville-West, calls into question the construction and understanding of sexuality and history's participation in this process.

narrative of our disguises, implicitly writes its characters as performers, acting one of many possible scripts.

However, the script authored by history traditionally rejects potential performances in favor of prescribed performances, privileges objectivity over subjectivity, and thus, is haunted by those parts unacted and those roles unplayed: "For what, after all is character—the way that Mrs. Brown, for instance, reacts to her surroundings—when we cease to believe what we are told about her, and begin to search out her real meaning for ourselves?" (*E3* 387). Woolf, herself in pursuit of her own version of Mrs. Brown, proposes an answer:

> In the first place, her solidity disappears; her features crumble; the house in which she has lived so long (and a very substantial house it was) topples to the ground. She becomes a will-o'-the-wisp, a dancing light, an illumination gliding up the wall and out the window [. . .] She changes the shape, shifts the accent, *of every scene in which she plays her role*. And it is from the ruins and splinters of this tumbled mansion that the Georgian writer must somehow reconstruct a habitable dwelling place. (*E3* 387, emphasis mine)

Mrs. Brown, the fictional character of the essay, is rendered a ghost, haunting the fiction—and the mansion—that attempts to historicize her, attracting the writers who hope to capture her, and thus, performing the fictionality of literature and history, the very fictionality that Woolf aspires to expose in *Between the Acts*.

In *Between the Acts*, Woolf attempts to reconstruct a habitable dwelling for modern character and modern history. At the center of the novel is Pointz Hall, an English country house that is haunted by the ghosts of histories written and unwritten, masks worn and parts unacted. Just as Woolf confesses in her diary the queerness of fictitious roles, so too does Pointz Hall reveal the queer nature of history through the roles performed by its residents and visitors on a June day in 1939, the day of the village pageant play. By staging an amateur English history pageant on the Pointz Hall lawn, Woolf portrays history as a collection of disguises: Miss La Trobe's pageant conflates history and literature with fiction and performance, and, in the last act, "Present Time. Ourselves," mirrors to its audience their participation in the performance of history and the possibility of their own unacted parts. With World War II on the horizon, in the novel and in her life, Woolf's *Between the Acts* is haunted—and enacts the potential of haunting—not in order to privilege the specters of the past, but to illustrate the reciprocity of past and present in the creation of the future.

Pointz Hall, like the novel itself, houses more than one kind of history. In Woolf's narrative, there is also a hidden history, a queer history—ambiguous, spectral, disruptive; like the house itself, at odd angles (*BTA* 7-8)—enacted by Pointz Hall's residents and visitors, and performed simultaneously and subversively through Miss La Trobe's English history pageant. The house masks a version of history different from the one provided in guidebooks and village annals. Keeping in mind John J. Su's observation that the "condition of the estate is taken to be emblematic of the nation as a whole" (553), Woolf's exposure and disruption of history at Pointz Hall through Miss La Trobe's pageant speaks to pastoral conceptions of nation and national history. By locating the performance on the lawn of Pointz Hall, Woolf is both validating the allegorical position of the country house as well revealing its dark secrets and, in 1939, its precarious position. Just as the two portraits in the dining room represent two versions of art—"The lady was a picture, bought by Oliver because he liked the picture; the man an ancestor. He had a name" (*BTA* 36)—so, too, does Pointz Hall participate in, and become the stage for, two versions of history. One version is represented by the ancestor: named, narrated, "a talk producer" (*BTA* 36). The other history present at Pointz Hall, like the portrait of the lady, is mysterious, unidentifiable, haunting.

Similarly, the larder, before the Reformation, was a chapel, in which a carved arch provides an entrance not only to the cellar, but to a supernatural history:

> If you tapped—one gentleman had a hammer—there was a hollow sound; a reverberation; undoubtedly, he said, a concealed passage where somebody had hid. So it might be. But Mrs. Sands wished they wouldn't come into her kitchen telling stories with the girls about. It put ideas into their silly heads. They heard dead men rolling barrels. They saw a white lady walking under the trees. No one would cross the terrace after dark. If a cat sneezed, "There's the ghost!" (*BTA* 32-3)

It is the ghost of the unwritten histories—disguises unrecognized, roles unscripted—that haunt not only Pointz Hall, but also the audience, the pageant, and the present of Virginia Woolf's *Between the Acts*. For Woolf, history is like the pond at Pointz Hall in which "the lady had drowned herself": one could be rendered a historical ghost, because, like the seemingly tranquil lily pond, history possesses "that deep centre [. . .] that black heart" (*BTA* 44).[6] In this manner, haunting becomes the means by which unwritten histories influence and interact with the present; the history of disguises that Woolf notes in 1910 and the queer-

---

[6] The lady who drowned herself is but one of many ghosts alluded to in *Between the Acts*; the "ghosts" of Pointz Hall are reminders of silenced voices, lives denied, and histories untold: "But, the servants insisted, they must have a ghost; the ghost must be a lady's; who had drowned herself for love" (*BTA* 44). In "Making History Unrepeatable in Virginia Woolf's *Between the Acts*," Catherine Wiley links the "ghosting" of women with

ness of masks she identifies in 1940 both haunt the 1939 of the novel: enacting the performance of history and exposing it as quite queer.

Many scholars of queer theory have explored the associations of marginal and unacknowledged identities with the figure of the ghost, the construction of fantasy, and the trope of metaphor. Terry Castle, Sue Ellen Case, Bonnie Zimmerman, and Marilyn Farwell all address the unacknowledged presence of non-heterosexual, non-normative identities in such haunting forms.[7] Like the ghost Mrs. Sands fears will frighten the maids of Pointz Hall, these marginal identities are always present: disguised, concealed or hiding; excluded, ignored, or repressed; on the margins and between the lines. The work of queer theory has encouraged reading between the lines of texts not simply to locate these marginal, unacknowledged identities, but moreover to facilitate the very disruption of normative identity categories. In this way, the presence of the queer in literature, history, and culture has come to signify more than "trangressive" sexuality: queering has emerged as the means by which the power of signification and the very idea of identity are interrogated, disrupted, and continuously refigured. By haunting the normative construction of identity—the texts and narratives that propagate and prescribe it—queer theory intends not to erase and deny identity but to expose it as a performance and thereby encourage the multiplicity of difference that can emerge from recognizing the potential of unacted parts.

In *Between the Acts*, through the characters William Dodge and Miss La Trobe, Woolf engages in a kind of proto-queering. These characters exist on the margins of English country house literature and the history in which this literature participates. Yet, through and between the acts of the pageant play, these two characters haunt the historical narrative that appears to govern not only the perception of the past, the experience of the present, and the potential of the future, but also the creation of identity. By exploring the way in which Dodge and Miss La Trobe, through their presence, performance, and interactions, interrupt and disrupt the June day at Pointz Hall, I suggest that history, like Miss La Trobe's pageant, has the potential to be as disruptive as it is unifying. As historical narratives are queered in and between the acts, identity, as reflected into the present by history's mirror, is revealed fractured and fragmented, a performance—like

---

the presence and power of patriarchal forms of representation: "The feminine, like communal history, tends to be hidden on another side or behind the mirror of representation . . . The disappearing woman as the essence of (or excuse for) patriarchal aesthetics has long provided the backdrop for feminist theories of representation" (5).

[7] Terry Castle's *The Apparitional Lesbian*, Sue Ellen Case's "Tracking the Vampire," Bonnie Zimmerman's "Lesbians Like This and That," and Marilyn Farwell's "The Lesbian Narrative: 'The Pursuit of the Inedible by the Unspeakable'" associate the figure of the lesbian in literature (and film) with the liminal, the metaphoric, and the spectral.

Miss La Trobe's version of history—acted on culture's stage. Like the fantasy of the ghost from the larder and untold lives of those who used only the back staircase,[8] Pointz Hall and *Between the Acts* are haunted by history's ghost: queer history. Queer history not only illuminates the unspoken, unwritten histories—the many possible performances, the many possible disguises—but also, queer history queers the very temporalities that separate the past from the present and, most importantly in 1939, the future.

In this manner, *Between the Acts* illustrates the contemporary project of critical queering. No longer exclusively concerned with sexuality, queer theory seeks to expose and question the boundaries and binaries established by history: "the project of queering . . . insists on queering historicism, with all its concomitant notions of ontology, teleology, and authenticity" (Goldberg 1610). In "Queering History," Jonathan Goldberg and Madhavi Menon articulate a project of "unhistoricism" that takes into account not only the sexual difference associated with queering, but also attempts "to challenge the notion of a determinate and knowable identity, past and present" (1609). For Goldberg and Menon, queering is as much about historical identity as it is about sexual identity:

> Paying attention to the question of sexuality *as a question* involves violating the notion that history is the discourse of answers, a discourse whose commitment to determinate signification . . . provides false closure, blocking access to the multiplicity of the past and to the possibilities of different futures. (1609)

The past's multiplicity and the possibility of different futures are at stake in Woolf's *Between the Acts* as Dodge and Miss La Trobe haunt the discourse of answers supplied by the historical narrative in which Pointz Hall and its residents and visitors participate. In this manner, the temporalities that define the present moment and the historically-contingent identities that exist within it interact, portraying history and identity *as questions*, questions very much on Woolf's own mind in 1940 as she contemplates not only the conclusion of her novel but the end of her life as well. Surrounded by the determinacy of endings, Woolf's proto-queering provides a way to access the potential of a different future.

"Queerness can never define an identity," writes Lee Edelman, "it can only ever disturb one" (17). A contemporary echo of Woolf's 1940 diary confession about the queer masks of identity, Edelman's characterization of queerness

---

[8] Throughout the novel there are moments in which the history of Pointz Hall and its previous residents are alluded to; most often these snapshots of Pointz Hall's past suggest the lives of the aristocracy and the serving class that lived together within: "Still, on going up the principal staircase—there was another, a mere ladder at the back for the servants—there was a portrait" (*BTA* 7). The portrait is rumored to be an "ancestress of sorts" and the butler "had been a soldier" (*BTA* 7).

speaks to the disruption of history and its attendant narratives that emerge in Woolf's *Between the Acts*. According to Edelman, queer theory should refuse, just as Dodge and Miss La Trobe refuse, "every substantiation of identity, which is always oppositionally defined, and, by extension, of history as linear narrative . . . in which meaning succeeds in revealing itself—*as itself*—through time" (4). In this manner, Woolf's queer characters participate in the project of "unhistoricism" that queering, according to Goldberg and Menon, advocates: "the idea of unhistoricism that we propose . . . calls for acts of queering that would suspend the assurance that the only modes of knowing the past are either those that regard the past as wholly other or those that can assimilate it to a present assumed identical to itself" (1616).[9] The performance of history on the Pointz Hall lawn stage and its reception by the audience explore these two modes of knowing the past, and thus, the present and future. In what emerge as acts of queering, Dodge, Miss La Trobe, and implicitly Woolf, reflect the question of identity—sexual, national, and historical—*as a question* to history's audience. Thus, Woolf's "prophecy" in her early essay "Modes and Manners of the Nineteenth Century" comes to fruition: "[H]istory is not a history of ourselves, but of our disguises. The poets and novelists are the only people from whom we cannot hide" (*E1* 334). In *Between the Acts*, as in her 1940 diary entry, Woolf not only acknowledges the masks of identity and the queer pleasure of "coming out," but also, by interrupting of the present moment and by reflecting history to the audience at Pointz Hall, Woolf queers history and unmasks historically determinate identities.

Seekers After Hidden Faces

"Could he say 'I'm William'? He wished to" (*BTA* 70); the very act of queering manifests in the character William Dodge whose name, never remembered by any of the characters, is an indictment of identity, and whose history, unspeakable, haunts his present actions and his interactions with his Pointz Hall hosts.[10] Upon first introduction, Dodge appears to Isa a gentleman: "He was of course a gentleman; witness socks and trousers; brainy—tie spotted, waistcoat undone; urban, professional, that is putty coloured, unwholesome; very nervous, exhibiting a twitch at this sudden introduction" (*BTA* 38). But Isa's impressions,

---

[9] Although not queering history or the novel, David McWhirter's essay, "*Between the Acts* and the Tragicomedy of History," explores the versions of historicity present in *Between the Acts* and suggests that the most "persistent characteristic" of the novel is "historical dialogical inclusiveness" (800).

[10] Barber's essay provides a queer reading of William Dodge and Miss La Trobe that investigates the connection between Woolf's own queer friends (specifically Lytton Strachey) and her appreciation and employment of "transgressive" sexualities.

themselves ambiguous—Can a gentleman be unwholesome? Does her "of course" indicate sarcasm?—are only reinforced by the contradiction between Mrs. Manresa's presentation of him as an artist and his immediate correction: "'I'm a clerk in an office'" (*BTA* 38). Isa, whose initial impression of Dodge is continuously revised throughout the novel, feels "antagonised, yet curious" (*BTA* 38); Isa, who fears the historical contingency of her own identity—"Sir Richard's daughter; and niece of two old ladies at Wimbledon who were so proud, being O'Neils, of their descent from the Kings of Ireland" (*BTA* 16)—perceives in Dodge one who also seeks after hidden faces.[11] Stephen Barber explains Isa's impulse not only to know Dodge, but also, to align herself with him: "Each character that comes across Dodge attempts to either fix him or to figure him out, in order, respectively, 'to know' so as to drive him into oblivion [like Giles] or to encounter him secretly so as to admit ethical singularity" (423).

Fear and oppression connect Isa and the ambiguous Dodge. Trapped in the traditional script of femininity, marriage, and motherhood (as earlier suggested by Jane Marcus in "Liberty, Sorority, Misogyny"),[12] Isa interprets the story of violence and rape she reads in the newspaper as both a commentary on her generation as well as an analog to the history of women, herself included. A newspaper story that begins as fantastic and evolves into romance, becomes "so real that on the mahogany door panels [in the Pointz Hall library] she saw the Arch in Whitehall; through the Arch the barrack room; in the barrack room the bed, and on the bed the girl was screaming and hitting him about the face, when the door (for in fact it was a door) opened" (*BTA* 20).[13] Since "for her generation the newspaper was a book," Isa reads between the lines of the newsprint the sobering answer to her question, "What remedy was there for her at her age—the

---

[11] In the greenhouse during an interval, Isa and Dodge "talked as if they had known each other all their lives"; Isa validates their immediate communion by posing the question: "Weren't they, though, conspirators, seekers after hidden faces?" (*BTA* 114).

[12] Rachel Blau DuPlessis also explores the consequences of social scripts explaining that "these scripts of heterosexual romance, romantic thralldom, and a telos in marriage are also social forms expressed at once as individual desires and in a collective code of action including law" (2). For DuPlessis, the romance plot, as a narrative and a social pattern, "muffles the main female character, represses quest, valorizes heterosexual as opposed to homosexual ties, incorporates individuals within couples as a sign of their personal narrative success" (5).

[13] Isa picks up the *Times* and reads: "'A horse with a green tail. . .' which was fantastic. Next, 'The guard at Whitehall. . .' which was romantic and then, building word upon word, she read: 'The troopers told her the horse had a green tail; but she found it was just an ordinary horse. And they dragged her up to the barrack room where she was thrown upon a bed. Then one of the troopers removed part of her clothing, and she screamed and hit him about the face. . .'" (*BTA* 20).

age of the century, thirty-nine—in books?" (*BTA* 19). Looking for a remedy as much for her age as for herself, Isa is disappointed and discouraged by what the library, "the nicest room in the house" (*BTA* 19), offers: screams unheard, stories unwritten, potential denied. As Stephen Barber inquires, "what remedy, indeed, when books *script* the family romance within which Isa is held captive or feels confined?" (430, emphasis mine). Trapped in this domestic history of Pointz Hall, in the history of the English country house novel—"Every summer for seven summers now, Isa had heard the same words; about the hammer and the nails; the pageant and the weather. Every year, they said, would it be wet or fine; and every year it was—one or the other" (*BTA* 22)—Isa looks for hidden faces to aid in her escape.

Recognizing in Dodge a fellow conspirator, Isa already knows the answer to the question, "'Why's he afraid?'": "A poor specimen he was afraid to stick up for his own beliefs—just as she was afraid, of her husband. Didn't she write poetry in a book bound like an account book lest Giles might suspect?" (*BTA* 50). Although, as the daughter of Sir Richard, Isa can claim a place in the pageantry of Pointz Hall, she deplores the part she is expected to act; perhaps herself a Gothic heroine instead of the angel of the hearth, "she loathed the domestic, the possessive; the maternal" (*BTA* 19).[14] Dodge notices Isa's discontented performance; as her adulterous thoughts are interrupted by the entrance of her son, Dodge watches her face change, "as if she had got out of one dress and put on another" (*BTA* 105).[15] Thus, her own history is revealed as that of disguises as Isa performs the roles of mother and wife in a script that lineage and domesticity have apparently authored for her. Similarly, Dodge is both disguised and exposed in his interactions with Isa as she marks his attire as a mask. Dressed as a gentleman, Dodge is neither simply the clerk he claims nor the artist Mrs.

---

[14] John Paul Riquelme writes that the Gothic can be "understood as a discourse that brings to the fore the dark side of modernity. As narrative, it is the black sheep of the Anglo-American novel, which has generally been taken to concern marriage and the contexts that make marriage possible" (585). Although Riqulme does not address *Between the Acts*, much of what he suggests about the relationship between the Gothic and modernity can be seen at work in Woolf's final novel, a novel that is both working within and against an English country house novel tradition. Woolf's use of Gothic elements in *Between the Acts* and the novel's subject matter—national history, family relations, the pastoral country house, the disruption of normative heterosexuality—suggest that an investigation of Gothic allusions and elements in *Between the Acts* is worth pursuing.

[15] Isa muses upon the possibility of an extra-marital affair as a means of escape from the romance script in which she feels trapped. In Rupert Haines, the gentleman farmer (exactly the occupation Giles felt obligated to reject), Isa imagines she recognizes a hidden face: "But in his ravaged face she always felt mystery; and in his silence, passion" (*BTA* 5). It is Haines that Isa seeks in the Barn during the interval (*BTA* 103).

Manresa introduces him as: both are merely roles scripted for him by others. Just as Isa searches for a remedy for the plight of her age—herself and her sex—Dodge seeks not only for hidden faces but for moments of interruption when the performance of history and its attendant conventions pause long enough for him to name himself and claim his place: "'I'm William,' he interrupted" (*BTA* 72).

During one of the play's intervals, Dodge is led by Mrs. Swithin through the empty house as she narrates the family history, not very different from that of the nation's: "'The nursery,' said Mrs. Swithin. Words raised themselves and became symbolical. 'The cradle of our race,' she seemed to say" (*BTA* 71). However, away from the audience assembling, haunting the empty house, they become ghosts of English country house history; Dodge and Mrs. Swithin become an audience unto themselves, watching the social pageant in which they struggle to participate assemble on the lawn below: "But they, looking down from the window, were truants, detached. Together they leant half out the window" (*BTA* 72). Interrupting Mrs. Swithin, Dodge reveals himself—"'I'm William'"—and in interrupting, allows Mrs. Swithin to reveal her own hidden face: "At that she smiled a ravishing girl's smile, as if the wind had warmed the wintry blue in her eyes to amber . . . She touched her bony forehead upon which a blue vein wriggled like a blue worm. But her eyes in their caves of bone were still lambent. He saw her eyes only" (*BTA* 73). Revealed, exposed, Dodge, seizing upon the promise and potential of interruption, wishes to

> kneel before her, to kiss her hand, and to say: "At school they held me under a bucket of dirty water, Mrs. Swithin; when I looked up, the world was dirty, Mrs. Swithin; so I married; but my child's not my child, Mrs. Swithin. I'm a half-man, Mrs. Swithin; a flickering, mind-divided little snake in the grass, Mrs. Swithin; as Giles saw; but you've healed me. . ." So he wished to say . . . . (*BTA* 73)

Dodge's unspoken identity haunts the history of his life; as Isa detected, a gentleman, but perhaps "unwholesome," Dodge performs the roles of husband and father and office clerk, yet his unacted part, as Giles saw, is that of a homosexual:

> A toady; a lickspittle; not a down-right plain man of his senses; but a teaser and twitcher; a fingerer of sensations; not a man to have straightforward love for a woman—his head was close to Isa's head—but simply a —— At this word, which he could not speak in public, he pursed his lips. (*BTA* 60)

"Isabella guessed the word that Giles had not spoken" (*BTA* 61); she herself, conspiring against the script history has given her, questions the refusal of history to let Dodge play his part: "Well, was it wrong if he was that word? Why judge each other? Do we know each other? Not here, not now" (*BTA* 61). Isa's sober understanding—"not here, not now"—echoes Dodge's retreat from confession: "So he wished to say; but said nothing" (*BTA* 73). Saying nothing, Dodge lets the interruption of truancy, conspiracy, and confession pass. Once more, he and Mrs. Swithin turn to look down upon the lawn of Pointz Hall, but this time the cross hanging from Mrs. Swithin's neck is struck by the sun and Dodge is struck by history's pervasiveness, its silent language of exclusionary symbols and powerful institutions: "How could she weight herself down by that sleek symbol? How stamp herself, so volatile, so vagrant, with that image?" (*BTA* 73). Normative history meets identity creation as Mrs. Swithin's cross leaves an indelible mark on her, authors the script she performs, and refuses the interruption Dodge had desired. As if on cue, "'Is it time,' said Mrs Swithin, 'to go and join—'" (*BTA* 73); she catches sight of the Reverend Streatfield below among the assembling audience: "they were truants no more" (*BTA* 73).

Thus, the moment of shared truancy ends. Moreover, the specter of Dodge's unuttered confession—"I'm a half-man . . . a mind-divided little snake in the grass"—unable even to haunt the empty house, is crushed by the progression of politics, the evolution of contemporary history, and the patriarchal structures manifesting in those, like Giles, who perform its power. Trapped in the very historical—and literary—narrative that positions him as privileged, Giles "was enraged" (*BTA* 46); expected to perform his part, Giles brokers stocks in London instead of ploughing a field: "Given his choice, he would have chosen to farm. But he was not given his choice. So one thing led to another; and the conglomeration of things pressed you flat" (*BTA* 47). Pressed flat by the power of history, changing his costume from urban professional to country house gentleman—"And he came into the dining-room looking like a cricketer, in flannels, wearing a blue coat with brass buttons" (*BTA* 46)—Giles is enraged and consequently, desires to press flat anyone who does not wear the correct costume, who does not disguise well enough their unacted part.

Contemptuous of the pageant, the people, and the press of history which he is both a spectator of and a participant in, Giles enacts his rage on his way to the barn:

> There, couched in the grass, curled in an olive green ring, was a snake. Dead? No, choked with a toad in its mouth. The snake was unable to swallow; the toad was unable to die . . . It was birth the wrong way round—a monstrous inversion. So, raising his foot, he stamped on them. The mass crushed and slithered. The white canvas on his tennis shoes was bloodstained and sticky. But it was action. Action relieved him. (*BTA* 99)

It is not simply a snake and a toad that are killed under the violent press of Giles's white, canvas tennis shoe. Rather, Giles stamps out the possibility of Dodge's confession—"a mind-divided little snake in the grass"—and denies what he envisions as the potential consequence of such a revelation: "It was birth the wrong way round—a monstrous inversion." Written in the books that fill the library shelves—poetry, history, literature—and documented in the newspaper— the girl's unheard screams—history's reproduction does not permit the likes of Dodge, an ambiguous half-man whose child is not his own; unable and unwilling to claim its own bastard child, unable to disguise his unacted part, history appears to deny Dodge a name, and consequently, an identity. Also denied the identity of his choosing, but the privileged son of history nonetheless, Giles is relieved by the only action available to him: violence, oppression, subjugation.

However, what Giles does not see is what the snake and the toad— together—represent: "The snake was unable to swallow; the toad was unable to die" (*BTA* 99). In the present moment with war casting its shadow over Pointz Hall, Giles's history is inextricable from that of Dodge's; both are trapped, like the toad and the snake, unable to live, unable to die. Violence is one way to solve the stasis—"action relieved him." By crushing what he perceives as a monstrous coupling, Giles denies the connection between himself and Dodge. However, the blood that stains Giles's sneakers is also his own. Both Giles and Dodge wear the disguises history has provided for them; both perform roles in a script that they would like to rewrite. But for Dodge, whose queerness represents the potential of Goldberg and Menon's unhistoricism, stamping out the present moment is not an adequate answer, especially when the future looks so bleak. In fact, for Dodge, who haunts history, the present is the only answer to the question of new and different futures, or rather, to the future *as a question*. Is it any surprise, then, that to Mrs Swithin's statement, "We've only the present," Dodge, replies "Isn't that enough?" (*BTA* 82).

Hidden Faces Revealed

Despite Giles's murderous act representing the violence of history—and the bleak future on the horizon—that makes ghosts out of that which it deems monstrous, the snake's blood leaves its stain and Dodge remains among the audience. As a queer presence in the novel, Dodge enacts Eve Kosofsky Sedgwick's assertion that "something about the queer is inextinguishable" (xii).[16] Thus, although

---

[16] Sedgwick's etymology of queer emphasizes the term's interminability: "Queer is a continuing moment, movement, motive—recurrent, eddying, *troublant*. The word 'queer' itself means *across* . . . Keenly, it is relational, strange" (xii).

Dodge's history remains unspoken, it haunts Pointz Hall, its residents and visitors, and also the scenes of Miss La Trobe's pageant play. The unlikely director of history's pageantry, she herself is hidden behind the bushes, "an outcast" (*BTA* 211) without lineage, nationality, or personal history: "Very little was actually known about her . . . perhaps, then, she wasn't altogether a lady?" (*BTA* 58).[17] A village outcast and, presumably, a sexual deviant—"She bought a four-roomed cottage and shared it with an actress" (*BTA* 58)—"La Trobe was invisible," the queer voice of the text, itself evading identification, admits (*BTA* 191).[18] The tension between those named and those rendered nameless, those who speak and those whose voice is unrecognizable, between those within history and those that are relegated to haunt it, is at the center of queer. As a site where identity is disrupted, queer both necessitates recognition as it concomitantly refuses the terms by which recognition is granted. The queer emerges in history to interrupt it, disturb it, and thus, present the possibility of new names, new histories, and a new understanding of identity. Queer, as suggested by Stephen Barber in reference to Dodge, emerges as "a living interruption" (424).

Miss La Trobe's presence in the novel, and especially her unlikely role as the pageant's director, is an interruption in the performance of privileged history. By interrupting history's inculcation of the present moment into its script, Miss La Trobe interrupts not only history, but the formation of identity and the construction of meaning; by interrupting the pageantry of history with the present moment, Miss La Trobe exposes the queerness that always haunts the process of identity creation. Although history is her pageant's subject, so, too, is identity, and consequently, Miss La Trobe queers not only history, but also the identities

---

[17] Miss La Trobe does have a history, but like Dodge's personal history, hers is relatively unknown, and what is known, is the stuff of village rumors: "But where did she spring from? With that name she wasn't presumably pure English. From the Channel Islands perhaps? Only her eyes and something about her always made Mrs. Bingham suspect that she had Russian blood in her . . . Outwardly she was swarthy, sturdy and thick-set; strode about the fields in a smock frock; sometimes with a cigarette in her mouth; often with a whip in her hand; and used rather strong language—perhaps, then, she wasn't all together a lady?" (*BTA* 57-58).

[18] It is worth noting that in queering the manner in which English history is represented, Woolf also queers her own medium of representation, the novel. The ambiguous, elusive, narrative voice is one example of the way she disrupts the novel, its history, its identity, arguably, in a move toward the postmodern. Kristina Busse, in her psychoanalytically inflected reading of *Between the Acts*, addresses what I would anachronistically recognize as Woolf's queering of the novel: "As a result, the novel as a whole performs the same function as the play does within the text: it disrupts the reader's attempt to construct the text and its characters as past and other as it short-circuits the safely maintained distance between text and self" (95).

that compose it, exposing the performance of identity within the creation of personal and national history. Although having once shared her bed with an actress (*BTA* 211), queering history is not simply about unspoken and marginalized sexual identity; instead and moreover, it is about "challenging the methodological orthodoxy by which past and present are constrained and straitened . . ., resisting the strictures of knowability itself" (Goldberg 1609). As Judith Butler explains, the queer is "in the present," and as such, queering is "a site of collective contestation, the point of departure for a set of historical reflections and futural imaginings, it will have to remain that which is . . . never fully owned" (228).

As the peril of national politics threatens to explode upon the villagers, their histories, and attendant presents, Miss La Trobe provides a point of departure for historical reflections and imagined futures by exposing the potential of the present to disrupt roles performed and encourage parts unacted. The "methodological orthodoxy" of history and literature is revealed as inadequate to accommodate futural imaginings that foresee beyond a horizon penetrated by war planes: "the aeroplanes interrupted" (*BTA* 200). In a novel that has not only the actors but also the audience "disguised" in costumes, historical methodological orthodoxy is itself queered; on the June day in 1939, history is rendered amateur performance and with war looming, the future looks grim.

Interrupting history's performance to reveal it as such—both in Miss La Trobe's play and on the June day in 1939—is the present moment. Having watched English history as illustrated by Chaucer, Restoration comedy, and Victorian melodrama, the audience anticipates the grand finale. In this manner, "they were all caught and caged; prisoners; watching a spectacle" (*BTA* 176); unaware that, as Woolf writes in her story "The Moment: A Summer's Night," they are "spectators and also passive participants in a pageant" (*M* 4). As the audience awaits the last act, "Present Time. Ourselves," they inquire incredulously, "But what could she know about ourselves?" (*BTA* 179). The text articulates the audience's silent anxiety: "The Elizabethans, yes; the Victorians, perhaps; but ourselves; sitting here on a June day in 1939—it was ridiculous. 'Myself'—it was impossible. Other people, perhaps. . . [. . .] but she won't get me—no, not me" (*BTA* 179). The performance of history begins to be revealed at the moment when the audience is asked to participate, unaware that the day's pageantry has been indicting their implicit participation all along. Just as Budge the publican can perform the part of Victorian constable, "so disguised that even cronies who drank with him nightly failed to recognize him" (*BTA* 160), so, too, is the audience yet unaware of their own participation despite the fact that their sons, daughters, and neighbors have been revealing history's performance all afternoon through their queer costumes and fictitious roles. Identity becomes disguise and name nothing but a mask as the impossibility of "myself" emerges.

Miss La Trobe's intention—"She wanted to expose them, as it were, to douche them, with present-time reality" (*BTA* 179)—makes the audience fidget, uncertain of their role, of the parts they have been, and could be, performing.

However, in the critical project of queering, the present moment and its identities, as Butler suggests, are "never fully owned." Accordingly, when Miss La Trobe transforms her audience into actors, no one wants to accept their role, be it the one that they have been bequeathed by history or the one they are performing in the present. Before Miss La Trobe "douche[s] them" "with present-time reality," she first represents to her audience the historical script with which they are familiar and of which they wish to consider themselves participants. On the stage appears a ladder and a wall, and from "the limited means at her disposal," Miss La Trobe constructs the history of English civilization:

> That was a ladder. And that (a cloth roughly painted) was a wall. And that a man with a hod on his back. Mr. Page the reporter, licking his pencil, noted: "With the very limited means at her disposal, Miss La Trobe conveyed to the audience Civilization (the wall) in ruins; rebuilt (witness man with hod) by human effort; witness also woman handing bricks. Any fool could grasp that. Now issued black man in fuzzy wig; coffee-coloured ditto in silver turban; they signify presumably the League of . . . " (*BTA* 182)

Miss La Trobe presents the audience with their crowning achievement: civilization in ruins, rebuilt, and a world brought together through the League of Nations. The audience—"any fool"—understands her meaning. The confusion of the Victorian age is forgotten as the audience anticipates the performance of the roles they have played in the script dictated by the vision of history that supports the monarchy, the British Empire, and now, the restoration of "civilization": "A burst of applause greeted this flattering tribute to ourselves" (*BTA* 182).

Applause, however, does not mark the end of history and its pageantry for Miss La Trobe; she is not finished with the present moment. Instead of portraying the present moment as part of history already written, Miss La Trobe—herself, like Dodge, an outcast, a seeker after hidden faces—intends to interrupt history's present. The novel embodies not only the audience's collective voice, but also the nation's, in an attempt to create a present moment congruent with the performance of history in which they hope to have played their part: "Yes, they [the swallows] seemed to foretell what after all the *Times* was saying yesterday. Homes will be built. Each flat with its refrigerator, in the crannied wall. Each of us a free man; plates washed by machinery; not an aeroplane to vex us; all liberated; made whole . . . " (*BTA* 183). Considering that homes will soon be destroyed by aeroplanes and man's freedom assaulted by tyranny and war, the irony of the novel anticipates the interruption staged by Miss La Trobe. The applause that greeted the League of Nations is disrupted:

> The tune changed; snapped; broke; jagged. Foxtrot, was it? Jazz? Anyhow, the rhythm kicked, reared, snapped short . . . What a cackle, a cacophony! Nothing ended. So abrupt. And corrupt. Such an outrage; such an insult; And not plain. Very up to date all the same . . .
> Look! Out they come, from the bushes—the riff-raff. Children? Imps—elves—demons. Holding what? Tin cans? Bedroom candlesticks? Old jars? My dear, that's the cheval glass from the Rectory! And the mirror I lent her. My mother's. Cracked. What's the notion? Anything that's bright enough to reflect, presumably, ourselves? (*BTA* 183)

Instead of the applause that greeted the restoration of civilization, this similarly crude representation is met with disbelief, anger, and shame. As the makeshift mirrors reflect the audience from the stage, the spectators see themselves on stage, positioned as actors. However, unprepared for this queer disruption, the audience is caught without the appropriate masks and disguises, and thus, are encouraged to question what the appropriate performance actually is. Unwilling to recognize themselves as playing a part in the historical performance that has led to this June day in 1939, they murmur incredulously: "Ourselves? But that's cruel. To snap us as we are, before we've had time to *assume*. . . And only, too, in *parts*. . . That's what's so distorting and upsetting and utterly unfair" (*BTA* 184, emphasis mine).

"'Myself'—it was impossible," the voice of the audience foreshadows the unexpected truth validated by the mirrors' fragmented reflections: "Ourselves? But that's cruel" (*BTA* 179). The impossibility, however, resides not in the performance of "myself" in history's pageant but in the very notion of "myself" as singular and historically contingent. Revealed by Miss La Trobe's makeshift hall of mirrors, identity—"myself"—is a performance composed of *parts*, roles *assumed*. "At the same time as the pieces of reflecting glass expose the characters' fragmented selves," Kristina Busse suggests in her exploration of mirroring, subjectivity, and history, also shattered are "the carefully maintained and cautiously safeguard[ed] constructions of history" (89). And as if to completely erase the lines between performance and identity, and consequently, history and the present, the pageant's actors emerge from the bushes, costumed, reciting lines, performing their roles, among the uproar, "which by this time had passed quite beyond control" (*BTA* 184). But perhaps "reality [is] too strong" (*BTA* 179), or at least, "the cheval glass . . . too heavy" (*BTA* 185) because

> [h]e stopped. So did they all—hand glasses, tin cans, scraps of scullery glass, harness room glass, and heavily embossed silver mirrors—all stopped. And the audience saw themselves, not whole by any means, but at any rate, sitting still.

> The hands of the clock had stopped at the present moment. It was now. Ourselves. (*BTA* 185-86)

Like the pageant itself, not singular, but a collection of acts; like the history that is not of ourselves, but our disguises, the present moment is composed of fragments of performance, reflections of disguises, scraps of the lines history has directed its actors to recite.[19] However, the audience, subject to Miss La Trobe's queer version of history, is forced to see beyond the disguises, read between the lines, and perform between the acts.

"'Myself'—it was impossible;" the voice from the bushes, "megaphonic, anonymous, loud-speaking" explains the truth behind the impossibility: "*Liars most of us. Thieves too . . . Look at ourselves, ladies and gentlemen! Then at the wall, which we call, perhaps miscall, civilization, to be built by* (here the mirrors flicked and flashed) *orts, scraps and fragments like ourselves?*" (*BTA* 187-88). Even the identity of civilization is called into question by the voice from the bushes, interrupting the play's conclusion. Misidentified, civilization and the myselves that compose it are reflected as fragments, rendered performance, stripped of identity, history, and thus, a future as well; all that the audience is given is the present moment, in all its queerness.

Just as Woolf queers history and her own identity in her essays and diary by revealing them as being about disguises and masks, so, too, does Miss La Trobe queer history by reflecting to her audience their complicity in the performance of identity. As if in anticipation of critical queering, Miss La Trobe and accordingly, Woolf, present the audience not with the meaning they continuously desire—"'What did it mean?'" (*BTA* 213)—but instead, with questions:

> Does this mean that one puts on a mask or persona, that there is a "one" who precedes the "putting on" . . . Or, does this miming, this impersonating precede and form the "one," operating as its formative precondition rather than its indispensable artifice? (Butler 230)

Thus, Woolf realizes the intention written in her diary in 1940 concerning the then nascent novel, *Between the Acts*: "but 'I' rejected: 'We' substituted: to whom at the end shall there be invocation? 'We'. . .composed of different things. . .we all life, all art, all waifs and strays" (*D5* 135). In *Between the Acts*, "I" is not simply rejected but, moreover, interrogated: the "I" of identity and its atten-

---

[19] Mrs. Manresa is the only audience member seemingly unruffled by Miss La Trobe's mirror trick: "All evaded or shaded themselves—save Mrs. Manresa who, facing herself in the glass, used it as a glass; had out her mirror; powdered her nose; and moved one curl, disturbed by the breeze, to its place" (*BTA* 186).

dant role as author, be it of history, of the novel, or of the self, is disrupted and disturbed. And the "We" that takes its place is a very queer one.

"Composed of many different things," Woolf's "We" is not that of civilization as met by the audience's applause, but instead the "We" of liars and thieves, of orts, scraps, and fragments reflected in mirrors: distorted, upset, and interrupted. According to Woolf's diary, it is this very incongruous "We" that is "all life, all art." In queering history, Woolf does not deny history, does not deny the presence of "I"; on the contrary, by interrupting history's "I" she opens the space for a "We" that is composed of different parts, "waifs and strays," the haunting and the haunted, orts, scraps, and fragments:

> Like quicksilver sliding, filings magnetized, the distracted united. The tune began; the first note meant a second; the second a third. Then down beneath *a force was born in opposition*; then another. On different levels they diverged. On different levels ourselves went forward; flower gathering some on the surface; others descending to wrestle with the meaning; but all comprehending; all enlisted. (*BTA* 189, emphasis mine).

For Woolf, "We" does not erase difference. In fact, the very potential of "We" exists in that it is "[a] force born in opposition," a queer presence, a queer present, not stopping the flow of history, but interrupting it, and thus allowing the curtain to rise once again, the performance to begin again, because "[s]urely it was time someone invented a new plot, or that the author came out of the bushes. . . " (*BTA* 215).

The author is not, however, always hiding in the bushes. Authorship—historical, national, literary, personal—implies Woolf, emerges from within as illustrated by the conclusion of Miss La Trobe's pageant. "'Myself'—it was impossible" is an echo sounding over the "orts, scraps, and fragments" that compose Miss La Trobe's history pageant, when finally, the audience is forced to acknowledge their role as authors of the history in which they are both spectators and participants (*BTA* 179). Thus, by the end of the pageant and the novel, it is not simply the ghosts of the past that haunt the present moment, but moreover, as temporalities are queered between the acts, it is the ghosts of unrealized futures—unacted parts—that are conjured in the novel's 1939 and Woolf's 1940. In *Between the Acts*, Woolf suggests that by queering history and the identities that compose it the future does not have to be a script already authored by history's "I." Rather, as in her diary entries from the last year of her life, Woolf proposes that by recognizing history as a performance and acknowledging the many parts unacted, the future is revealed as potential with "We" writing the scripts.

Consequently, *Between the Acts* ends not with a conclusion but with the possibility of a new performance engendered by the last lines of the novel: "Then the curtain rose. They spoke" (*BTA* 219). Thus, queering history in *Between the Acts* proposes not the impossibility of history, literature, and self, but rather, the possibility of engaging in a queer relationship with historical time, literary narratives, and personal identity. With the rise of Woolf's metaphorical curtain on the last page of the novel, I suggest a move from merely thinking queerly about the past to thinking in queer terms about the present and the future.

I'd like to thank Marina MacKay, Margaret Cronin, and my anonymous reviewers for their close and critical reading of this essay.

Works Cited

Barber, Stephen. "Lip-Reading: Woolf's Secret Encounters." *Novel Gazing*. Ed. Eve Kosofsky Sedgwick. Durham, NC: Duke UP, 1997. 401-43.

Busse, Kristina. "Reflecting the Subject in History: The Return of the Real in *Between the Acts*." *Woolf Studies Annual* 7 (2001): 75-101.

Butler, Judith. "Critically Queer." *Bodies That Matter*. New York: Routledge, 1993.

Case, Sue-Ellen. "Tracking the Vampire." *Writing the Body*. Ed. Katie Conboy, Nadia Medina and Sarah Stanbury. New York: Columbia UP, 1997. 380-400.

Castle, Terry. *The Apparitional Lesbian: Female Homosexuality and Modern Culture*. New York: Columbia UP, 1993.

DuPlessis, Rachel Blau. *Writing Beyond the Ending*. Bloomington: Indiana UP, 1985.

Edelman, Lee. *No Future: Queer Theory and the Death Drive*. Durham: Duke UP, 2004.

Farfan, Penny. *Women, Modernism, and Performance*. Cambridge: Cambridge UP, 2004.

Farwell, Marilyn R. "The Lesbian Narrative: 'The Pursuit of the Inedible by the Unspeakable.'" *Professions of Desire*. Ed. George Haggerty and Bonnie Zimmerman. New York: MLA, 1995. 156-68.

Goldberg, Jonathan and Madhavi Menon. "Queering History." *PMLA* 120.5 (2005): 1608-17.

Hussey, Mark. *Virginia Woolf A-Z*. New York: Oxford UP, 1995.

Lee, Hermione. *Virginia Woolf.* New York: Vintage Books, 1999.
Marcus, Jane. "Liberty, Sorority, Misogyny." *The Representation of Women in Fiction.* Eds. Carolyn G. Heilbrun and Margaret R. Higonnet. Baltimore: The Johns Hopkins UP, 1981. 60-97.
McWhirter, David. "The Novel, the Play, and the Book: *Between the Acts* and the Tragicomedy of History." *ELH* 60.3 (1993): 787-812.
Oxindine, Annette. "Outing the Outsiders: Woolf's Exploration of Homophobia in *Between the Acts*." *Woolf Studies Annual* 5 (1999): 115-31.
Riquelme, John Paul. "Toward a History of Gothic and Modernism: Dark Modernity from Bram Stoker to Samuel Beckett." *MFS* 46.3 (2000): 585-605.
Sedgwick, Eve Kosofsky. *Tendencies.* Durham: Duke UP, 1993.
Su, John J. "Refiguring National Character: The Remains of the British Estate Novel." *MFS* 48.3 (2002): 552-80.
Westman, Karin. "The Character in the House: Virginia Woolf in Dialogue with History's Audience." *Clio* 28.1 (1998): 1-27.
Wiley, Catherine. "Making History Unrepeatable in Virginia Woolf's *Between the Acts*." *Clio* 5.1 (1995): 3-14.
Woolf, Virginia. *Between the Acts.* 1941. San Diego: Harcourt, 1969.
——. *The Diary of Virginia Woolf, Volume Five.* New York: Harcourt, 1984.
——. "Modes and Manners of the Nineteenth Century." *The Essays of Virginia Woolf, Volume I.* Ed. Andrew McNeillie. New York: Harcourt, 1986.
——. "Mr. Bennett and Mrs. Brown." *The Essays of Virginia Woolf, Volume III.* Ed. Andrew McNeillie. New York: Harcourt, 1988.
——. *A Room of One's Own.* 1929. San Diego: Harcourt, 1989.
——. "A Sketch of the Past." *Moments of Being.* Ed. Jeanne Schulkind. New York: Harcourt, 1985.
Zimmerman, Bonnie. "Lesbians Like This and That." *New Lesbian Criticism.* Ed. Sally Munt.

Geometries of Space and Time: The Cubist London of *Mrs. Dalloway*

Jennie-Rebecca Falcetta

Virginia Woolf's affectionate portrait, *Roger Fry: A Biography* (1940), refers again and again to Fry's sense of the connections and formal likenesses among painting, music, and literature, particularly in the contemporary art world. In their intellectual discussions, Woolf recounts, "The arts of painting and writing lay close together, and Roger Fry was always making raids across the boundaries. . . . many of his theories held good for both arts. Design, rhythm, texture—there they were again—in Flaubert as in Cézanne" (*RF* 240). Because Fry brought a unique mixture of critic's eye and painter's sense to bear on his evaluations of her fiction, Woolf sought and valued his opinion. In one instance of "making raids across the boundaries," Fry was spurred to an act of interartistic comparison that is especially relevant to a reading of Woolf's fiction. In a 1919 review of French art at London's Mansard Gallery, Fry addresses the Cubist project of "introduc[ing] at some point a complete break of connection between ordinary vision and the constructed pictorial vision"; describing in particular a painting by Cubist Léopold Survage, Fry exclaims, "how much of modern literature is approximating to the same kind of relationship of ideas as Survage's pictures give us!"[1] ("Modern French Art" 341). The "modern literature" Fry had in mind was none other than the work of Virginia Woolf.

To test his theories of Cubism's possibilities for literature, Fry performed an exercise of *ekphrasis* on Survage's 1911 painting *Ville* (Fig. 1). His "narrative" emphasized in particular the spatial relations of the pictorial elements:

> Houses, always houses, yellow fronts and pink fronts jostle one another this way and that way, crowd into every corner and climb into the sky; but however close they get together the leaves of trees push into their interstices. . . . Between house and leaves there move the shapes of men; more transient than either, they scarcely leave a mark . . . . ("Modern French Art" 341-342)

---

[1] For the sake of clarity, I use the capitalized "Cubism" and "Cubist" to refer to practitioners of the movement, its principles and techniques, and the visual art works produced in that mode; "cubism" or "cubist" with a small "c" designates broader philosophical and aesthetic principles related to the movement and the non-Cubist works and writers to which they may be applied.

Fig. 1. Leopold Survage, *Ville*, 1911
© 2007 Artists Rights Society (ARS), New York / ADAGP, Paris

Fry pinpoints the dynamism of the visual field and the interplay of textures and planes. Even the human elements are evaluated by spatial and dimensional characteristics. Following his description Fry reflects, "I see, now that I have done it, that it was meant for Mrs. Virginia Woolf—*that Survage is almost precisely the same thing in paint that Mrs. Woolf is in prose.* Only I like intensely such sequences of ideas presented to me in Mrs. Virginia Woolf's prose, and as yet I have a rather strong distaste for Survage's visual statements" ("Modern French Art" 342; my emphasis). Upon reading the review, Woolf appears to have been neither insulted nor spurred to reflection, merely amused.[2] In Fry's view, Woolf's cubistic style—still gestating but detectable in such elements as the snail's eye view of color, space, and time in "Kew Gardens" (1919)—trumps a mediocre painting making use of a similar technique.[3]

Fry's early connection of Woolf's prose to Cubism is prescient, anticipating as it does the wealth of studies analyzing Woolf's fiction in relation to visual art.[4] His analogy not only broaches the complex subject of translating the dynamics and effects of one expressive medium into another, it raises the equally crucial concern of humanity's relation to the modern city. How might that unstable relationship be translated into the material of art? How can the subject of humans negotiating the metropolis influence the shape of a narrative or the structure of a painting? In *Mrs. Dalloway* (1925), Woolf depicts urban reality as it is perceived and experienced: an ephemeral and piecemeal admixture of sense and memory. In order to surmount the formal challenges presented by the novel's themes—the experience of lived time, the phenomenon of memory, and the complex dynamics of the modern city—Woolf formulated her aesthetic response in part by

---

[2] Woolf wrote to Fry, "I enjoyed immensely finding my name in your article. Also I thought your translation, what you call a parody, most charming" (*L2* 385).

[3] Léopold Survage (1879-1968), a Russian-born painter who eventually emigrated to Paris, was himself interested in the interrelation of art forms. Not only did he design costumes and sets for Diaghilev's Ballets Russes, he completed a series of abstract water colors entitled *Coloured Rhythm,* "which he planned to animate by means of film, using colour and spatial movement to evoke sensation as an analogy to music" (Daniel Robbins, "Survage, Léopold." Grove Art Online. Oxford University Press, [19 December 2006], http://www.groveart.com/).

[4] In addition to the scholarship used in my study, the following broader treatments have provided a useful background to this aspect of Woolf's creativity: Ian Blyth, "Virginia Woolf and Jacques Raverat" *Virginia Woolf Bulletin* 6 (Jan. 2001) 31-35; Jane Dunn, *A Very Close Conspiracy: Virginia Woolf and Vanessa Bell* (Boston: Little, Brown, 1990); Christine Froula, *Virginia Woolf and the Bloomsbury Avant-Garde* (New York: Columbia UP, 2005); Jane Goldman, *The Feminist Aesthetics of Virginia Woolf* (Cambridge UP, 1998); and *The Multiple Muses of Virginia Woolf,* ed. Diane Filby Gillespie (Columbia: U of Missouri P, 1993).

borrowing from Cubist principles and by materializing the formal possibilities suggested by Fry in his Mansard Gallery review.

The cubist lynchpin of *Mrs. Dalloway* is London as it was in June, 1923. The city appears in pieces and fragments as its streets and buildings, sounds and crowds catalyze the characters' internal monologues. Woolf renders her characters' experiences as plural realities of the same geographical space, moment in time, event, or phenomenon, thus asserting the presence of dynamic, simultaneous perspectives. Like the Cubist painters, Woolf's cubist fiction maintains the integrity of the thing represented (in this case, the living city), revealing its qualities and essence instead of a fixed homogenous view. Her achievement in *Mrs. Dalloway* reveals her apprehension of Cubism's inherent epistemology, as articulated by poet and proponent of Cubism Guillaume Apollinaire: "One does not have to be a cultivated person to realize that a chair, for example, never ceases to have four legs, a seat, and a back, no matter how we may look at it" (219). Virginia Woolf enacts this same truth in the construction of her fiction: her characters never cease to have pasts, memories, consciousnesses, sense impressions, and private thoughts, no matter how they may appear to others. As she herself attested in September 1924, in the thick of completing *Mrs. Dalloway*, "All this confirms me in thinking that we're splinters & mosaics; not, as they used to hold, immaculate, monolithic, consistent wholes" (*D2* 314). Humanity's perception of itself had altered, and Woolf realized that a novel about the remembered past and the subjective present required a form comprehending individual lived time and memory in its very architecture. In Cubism Woolf found a useful blueprint.

The Potentiality of Cubism

Cubism marked the most radical shift in visual language since Giotto "discovered" linear perspective in the early 14th century. Only now, instead of rendering objects in space as viewed from a particular perspective, with proportional distances, foreshortening, and dimension, the Cubists rendered objects in a mode which took into account more than one viewpoint. As Apollinaire wrote, the Cubists favored "conceived reality" over "the reality of the vision" (219). As dynamic as its treatment of space, Cubism was an evolving project: it achieved a greater degree of abstraction and universality the further away it moved from an early piece like Picasso's *Demoiselles d'Avignon* (1907). Although Cubist works may abstract their forms from forms in nature, the movement differs from later schools like Abstract Expressionism in that Cubism is *never* non-representational. In Cubism's Analytical mode, objects and subjects maintain some of their representational status, even as they are abstracted. The function of the canvas alters: "It is no longer the representation of a segment of nature, but an architectonic formula expressing an abstract order" (Haftmann 1: 99).

Thus in a painting like Picasso's *Reservoir, Horta de Ebro* (1909), the buildings remain recognizable (Fig. 2). The formal treatment exaggerates the geometry while simultaneously offering views not accessible from a single vantage point. What appears in the painting is not the reservoir but a universalized abstraction of the reservoir's form. Synthetic Cubism, which developed around 1912, achieved the inverse of the Analytic approach: the construction of representation from forms of pure abstraction. This type of painterly practice led to the "invention" of collage, in which the introduction of an actual fragment of paper or fabric onto the canvas "produced an effect of shock on the viewer, surprised to discover a completely realistic passage in an otherwise non-naturalistic picture" (Haftmann 1: 116).

Examining the implications of a Cubist way of seeing, John Berger asserts, "The Cubists created the possibility of art revealing processes instead of static entities. The content of their art consists of various modes of interaction: the interaction between different aspects of the same event, between empty space and filled space, between structure and movement, between the seer and the thing seen" (153). To a novelist like Woolf in search of a new fictional architecture, Cubism offered specific plastic possibilities. My analysis explores Woolf's translation of essential cubist principles from painted canvas to fictional form in order to produce *Mrs. Dalloway*—a novel she described as "a study of insanity & suicide: the world seen by the sane & the insane side by side" (*D2* 207). Cubism allowed Woolf her "sides."

In its depiction of multiple subjective Londons, *Mrs. Dalloway* exhibits qualities attributed by Robert Hughes to Cubist paintings: "As description of a fixed form, they are useless. But as a report on multiple meanings, on process, they are exquisite and inexhaustible: the world is set forth as a field of shifting relationships that includes the onlooker" (32). The terms "process" and "relationship" clearly seconding Berger's summation of Cubism's innovation, Hughes also emphasizes the dynamism of perception and the viewer's complicity in constructing the view—principles which translate readily into the realm of fiction. In *Mrs. Dalloway*, I argue, Woolf puts to work Cubist ideas about structure, continuously locating, dislocating and relocating her characters within this "field of shifting relationships." She deliberately populates the novel with characters who are not only socially Other—shell-shocked Septimus, Rezia the foreigner, Maisie Johnson the Scot—but also Other in the city, unsure of how to negotiate the urban space. Their experiences of dislocation within the English capital stand in high contrast to Clarissa Dalloway's intimate, personalized relationship with the city. Furthermore, the reader must accommodate and synthesize the multiple

Fig. 2. Pablo Picasso, *Reservoir, Horta de Ebro,* 1909
© 2007 Estate of Pablo Picasso / Artists Rights Society (ARS), New York

unstable views to participate in the creation of *Mrs. Dalloway*'s narrative discourse.

Although *Orlando: A Biography* and not *Mrs. Dalloway* occasioned his comments, Raymond Williams offers a useful summary of Woolf's treatment of the urban environment. In her fiction, "the discontinuity, the atomism of the city were aesthetically experienced, as a problem of perception which raised questions of identity—and which was characteristically resolved on arrival in the country" (241). In *Mrs. Dalloway,* however, inscribed within London city limits, the characters return to the country only in memory. For Clarissa, the country is Bourton, site of "the most exquisite moment of her whole life," Sally Seton's kiss (*MD* 35); for Rezia, her home in Milan, a city, yes, but not the impersonal, grey metropolis she finds London to be. Septimus's country is the Italian front which robbed him of his beloved Evans. For him, the pastoral can never be antidote to the urban, for his "problem of perception" lies far beyond mere "questions of identity." Woolf skillfully appropriates Cubism's ability to problematize received notions of perception, keeping her characters and their city in creative instability.

A Woolf Among the Painters

Roger Fry may have been the first to connect Woolf's experimental prose to painterly technique, but he has hardly been the only one to do so. In fact, Fry's theories have become implicated in the project of analyzing Woolf's relation to visual art. In 1946, just five years after Woolf's suicide, John Hawley Roberts examined the unity of *Mrs. Dalloway* in light of Fry's remarks on Cézanne. Roberts contends that "The reader's response to the whole [of the novel] is very much like that of one who standing before a painting begins to see, as Fry would see, how this mass necessarily balances that, how this line repeats, with a difference, that one, how a high-light here inevitably answers a shadow there, how, in other words, the meaning of the picture lies in our discovery of the fact that the forms agree" (839).

Nearly forty years later, David Dowling's 1985 study *Bloomsbury Aesthetics and the Novels of Forster and Woolf* cites the sense of "divorce" between the literary and visual arts Woolf felt early on, adding that "two important biographical accidents helped to bridge this gulf in Woolf's career: her close friendship and subsequent aesthetic education with Roger Fry, and her affection and sympathy for the work of her sister Vanessa" (96). By contrast, Diane Filby Gillespie's *The Sisters' Arts* aims "to shift the emphasis in the ongoing discussion of Virginia Woolf and the visual arts from Roger Fry to Vanessa Bell" (2). In my view, both Fry and Bell heightened Woolf's awareness of the possibilities for fictional form latent in Cubist abstraction, but each contributed quite differently to her development. While Fry may have had a more cerebral influence and Bell a more intuitive, experiential one, I do not mean to imply any gender essentialism. Bell's and Fry's influences on Woolf resulted from their respective functions in Woolf's life as sister and trusted friend. By exploring new territories of figuration and representation in her paintings and drawings, Vanessa showed Virginia how art might originate from private interior life, especially formative experiences like the early death of their mother Julia. "Because the sisters shared values and a view of reality," writes Gillespie, "they often found themselves stimulated by each other's work or capable of creating parallel work. Just as Woolf was tempted to produce verbal versions of some of her sister's paintings . . . . so Vanessa found pictures forming when she read Virginia's stories" (*Sisters'* 10).

If Vanessa Bell modeled formal experimentation for Woolf, Roger Fry equipped her with the critical vocabulary for discussing it. Fry introduced her to terms like "psychological volumes," a concept he drew from the work of French philosopher Charles Mauron, a personal acquaintance of Fry and Forster (he was the dedicatee of Forster's *Aspects of the Novel*). Detecting in the literature of some of his contemporaries a three-dimensionality of consciousness akin to the plastic mass of visual art mediums, Mauron helped to pioneer psychological literary criticism. Ever fascinated by the possibility of equivalences—or at least of analogues—between art forms, Fry seized upon Mauron's concept and employed it as a tool "to explore those kinds of visual art which approximate to literature" (Dowling 31)—an echo of Fry's observation about modern literature in the Mansard Gallery review.

Other studies corroborate and extend Dowling's examination of Fry and Woolf, particularly the sense that Woolf's novelistic goals required the development of an aesthetic theory that was primarily visual and plastic. Yet few investigate the possible influence of visual art on *Mrs. Dalloway* and none pursues the novel's cubist dimensions.[5] In fact, responding to Wendy Steiner's use

---

[5] In *The Pictorial in Modernist Fiction*, Deborah Schnitzer connects *Jacob's Room* to the "ocular realism" of Impressionism, and the more mature narrative of *To the Lighthouse* to the "conceptual realism" of the Post-Impressionists. Even as she suggests the progressive nature of Woolf's appropriation of art, Schnitzer stops just short of linking her to the pivotal innovations of Cubism; of the writers she examines, only Gertrude Stein fits her paradigm of cubist "total representation" in narrative (207). Panthea Reid, calling *Mrs. Dalloway* "a painterly novel," mentions it in conjunction with both the paintings of Bell, Fry, and Duncan Grant and the innovations of the Cubists, but does not develop these connections with any specificity (279). For Goldman, who focuses her penetrating examination of Woolf and visual aesthetics on Woolf's other writings, *Mrs. Dalloway* escapes mention.

of "cubism" as a period concept, Marianna Torgovnick remarks early in her introduction to *Visual Arts, Pictorialism and the Novel* that none of the writers in her study (James, Lawrence, and Woolf) "makes Steiner's list of cubist writers" but concedes, "each, moreover, *might* be fitted into the cubist framework, though I see little to be gained by that maneuver" (9, Torgovnick's emphasis). However obliquely, Torgovnick appears to have thrown down the gauntlet, and this reading takes up the challenge by way of questioning why *Mrs. Dalloway* is so often treated as an exception to Woolf's engagement with visual art. Andelys Wood gestures toward an explanation when she reviews the "too limiting" critical tendency to focus on *either* time *or* space in the novel without acknowledging Woolf's frequent distortion of the relations between the two (26). By bringing Cubism's temporal-spatial engagement to bear on Woolf's urban novel, my analysis offers an analogy to pictorial representation in line with the productive visual art readings of her other work.

If literary critics generally hesitate to connect Woolf to Cubist innovations, critics of visual art seem more able to make the leap. As we have seen, it was a Cubist cityscape that inspired Roger Fry's comparison of Survage and Woolf. More recently, no less a historian of Cubism than the late Robert Rosenblum has traced the movement's translatability into other forms of art. Writing in 1959, Rosenblum heard Cubism in Stravinsky's *Le Sacre du Printemps*, with its tonality "destructive of a traditional sense of fluid sequence." In literature, Rosenblum looked not to the poetic experiments of Gertrude Stein for the realization of Cubist principles, but to the urban narratives of Joyce and Woolf, both, as he points out, "born within a year of Picasso and Braque." In *Ulysses* and *Mrs. Dalloway*, "the narrative sequence is limited in time to the events of one day; and, as in a Cubist painting, these events are recomposed in a complexity of multiple experiences and interpretations that evoke [sic] the simultaneous and contradictory fabric of reality itself" (43). Cubist fragmentation, multiplicity, and simultaneity may have originated with painted canvas, but in Rosenblum's estimation, they need not remain only there.

One literary critic who explicitly entertains the possibility of Woolf's appropriation of cubist effects is Jack F. Stewart. In an astute, well-researched, and generously illustrated application of Cubist principles to *Between the Acts*, Stewart proposes that "a new economy and compactness closely related to Cubist structures" allows "objective reality [to be] split and reassembled in patterns that no longer depend upon unified narrative perspective" (68). He does suggest, however, that Woolf did not apply her understanding of Cubism until this last novel, in which "Cubist esthetics contribute to the general ferment of ideas that made her late stylistic changes possible" (87). While not refuting the particulars of Stewart's reading, I would argue that *Between the Acts* was neither the first nor the only time Cubism's inherent epistemological shift furnished Woolf with a paradigm for representing abstractions like consciousness or history. After all, the documentary evidence of Woolf's exposure to Cubism Stewart provides at the start of his article dates mainly from the 1910s, including Vanessa Bell's meeting with Picasso in 1914 and his visit to London five years later.[6]

Reading Woolf's work in visual art terms has a long and rich history (and by all indications, a healthy future) and a firm grounding in historical particulars, but what of Woolf's own cubist sensibility? In 1925, the same year *Mrs. Dalloway* appeared, Woolf published an essay entitled "Pictures" in the *Nation and Athenaeum*. This brief but dense essay reveals Woolf's sense that painting was the dominant mode of the age, tempered by a note of playful skepticism toward painters. "Pictures" also provides insight into her sense of an art gallery's usefulness to verbal artists: "They are not there to understand the problems of the painter's art. They are after something that may be helpful to themselves. . . . Free to go their own way, to pick and choose at their will, they find modern pictures, they say, very helpful, very stimulating" (142). This grazing method, applied to individual paintings, yields useful fragments and tidbits: nourishing color or "somebody's room, nose, or hands" (143). The foraging writer also finds in the "silent painters"—Cézanne, Sickert, Mrs. Bell, and Picasso—something beyond mere words, which "as we gaze . . . begin to raise their feeble limbs in the pale border-land of no man's language, to sink down again in despair" (142). That this quartet of painters represents a spectrum of color use, a range of forms, and varying levels of abstraction suggests that Woolf herself benefited from the visual elements of different painting schools. That she never directly applies the label "Cubism" to her writing does not preclude her digestion and deployment of the movement's structural and epistemological principles.

The Novelist As Architect

In a 1923 diary entry Woolf clearly articulates her intended architecture for *Mrs. Dalloway* in terms that emphasize spatiality:

> I should say a good deal about The Hours [the novel's working title], & my discovery; how I dig out beautiful caves behind my characters; I think that gives exactly what I want; humanity, humour, depth. The idea is that the caves shall connect, & each comes to daylight at the present moment. (*D2* 263)

To lend her characters dimension, incorporate their remembered pasts, and link their existential situations, Woolf lights upon a decidedly spatial solution, artic-

---

[6] See Stewart 66-67 for more particulars of the Bloomsbury-Cubism relation.

ulated in revealingly visual terms. When these caves of consciousness connect around shared objects or events (as in the explicit link between Clarissa and Septimus), it is analogous to the Cubist method of depicting objects experienced simultaneously or sequentially by more than one beholder.

Furthermore, the phrase "beautiful caves" encapsulates Woolf's need for a form as gorgeous as it was structural, and purchasers of the original Hogarth Press edition would have caught a glimmer of this ordered loveliness on the book's cover. Vanessa Bell's *Mrs. Dalloway* design is the most austere of the covers she produced for Virginia's work, with large black and white shapes alleviated by occasional strokes of a cool yellow (Fig. 3).[7] The lettering of the title and author's name, larger and more fluid in other of Bell's designs, here appears boxy, as if cut out or stenciled, and is confined to the top third of the cover. The bottom third contains an open fan rhyming in shape with the bouquet of flowers beside it, twin emblems of female class privilege. The central part of the design features a wide band of white with five black ovals, the largest located in the middle, and the two on the end half hidden by an undulating shape around the border, suggestive of a curtain ruffle. The exact nature of this form is difficult to determine: it could be an edifice with windows or archways; it could be a bridge; it could be a grove of trees with spaces between. Or, it could be Woolf's "beautiful caves," all come to daylight at the same time. The cover design relies heavily on structural abstraction, as well as on key Cubist principles. The picture plane is flattened, a hallmark of Bell's style, one she shared with Cézanne and Matisse. In contrast to those French masters, however, color plays a minimal role in Bell's image, as in the drab canvases of high Analytical Cubism. Although not Cubist in the strictest sense, the cover illustration heralds the importance of abstracted structural form to the novel's texture and substance.

To realize the novel's architecture, of which London was the cornerstone, "[Woolf's] business was to select, arrange and present the London she experienced in the 1920s. Civilised or not, there it must be" (Dowling 137). The terms "select, arrange, and present" indicate deliberate composition of formal and spatial relationships within a frame. Dowling's succinct idea also underscores the centrality to the novel of both "lived" London and "real" London. The narrator renounces investment in a single, stabilized depiction of the city in order to accommodate the characters' subjective experiences of it; in the gap between these Londons and "London," the universal signifier, lurks a tension. Cubism

---

[7] See chapter five of Diane Filby Gillespie's *Sisters' Arts*, "Still Lifes in Words and Paint," for a discussion of Bell's book designs, particularly for her sister's texts (224-266). In an extended endnote Gillespie inventories the critical treatment of Bell's designs for Woolf and implies that the topic has suffered severe neglect (332-33 *n*21).

Fig. 3. Vanessa Bell, *Mrs. Dalloway* cover design. Hogarth Press, 1925 © Vanessa Bell Estate, courtesy Henrietta Garnett.

attempted to address, if not resolve, that tension by simultaneously presenting the fragments, without privileging any one over the other, to render the whole. Just as Cubist canvases maintain "the attachment between the picture surface and the material reality" (Schnitzer 185), Woolf's fidelity to the physical actualities of London stabilizes the narrative in the midst of multiple subjective representations. Emphasizing topographical specificity—Bond Street, Mayfair, Regent's Park, the Serpentine—*Mrs. Dalloway* maintains the integrity and recognizability of these landmarks while simultaneously fracturing the picture plane, as it were, in its depiction of the urban environment. The reader of *Mrs. Dalloway* may find herself in the dense thicket of a character's consciousness and memory, but she always knows the coordinates of her location in the city.

Not surprisingly, critical attempts to "map" Mrs. Dalloway have revealed a highly patterned, almost mathematical, geometry undergirding the narrative, lending support to a cubist analysis. In Susan M. Squier's reading, Clarissa's Bond Street flower purchase, Septimus's walk down the same street to Regent's Park, and the short trip of Peter Walsh from the Dalloways' house to Regent's Park, function as three legs of a triangle (95). Charting the main characters' movements within 21 episodes, Avrom Fleishman maps circular trajectories which for him embody the novel's recursive treatment of time and point up Woolf's evocation of death's inevitability. The overlap which occurs as the figures traverse the same streets and parks, I would add, constitutes a cubist narrative infrastructure, a geometry of place. Superimposing the "leaden circles" of Big Ben's regular chime over the triangles and circles of physical movement, Woolf appears to follow Cézanne's famous admonition to Émile Bernard, taken to the extreme by the Cubists: "treat nature by the cylinder, the sphere, the cone" (Cézanne 19). Woolf, however, treats time and subjectivity—greater abstractions by far than Cézanne's material "nature"—and thus requires an architecture more precise, actualized, and multivalent than the precepts of Post-Impressionist painting could anticipate.

Woolf invests the novel's larger physical symbols, experienced uniquely by different characters, with concepts and metonymies similar to those taken up by the Cubist painters. Thus Big Ben stands in for time, an analogue to the simultaneous composite view.[8] While a Cubist painting might allude to specific material trappings to suggest social status or function (e.g. newspapers and absinthe glasses to evoke café society) Woolf uses the Prime Minister's car; the skywrit-

---

[8] In Christine Froula's reading of *Mrs. Dalloway* as a postwar elegy, the repetition of Big Ben and the novel's other motifs are implicated in the work of mourning (89). See her chapter four.

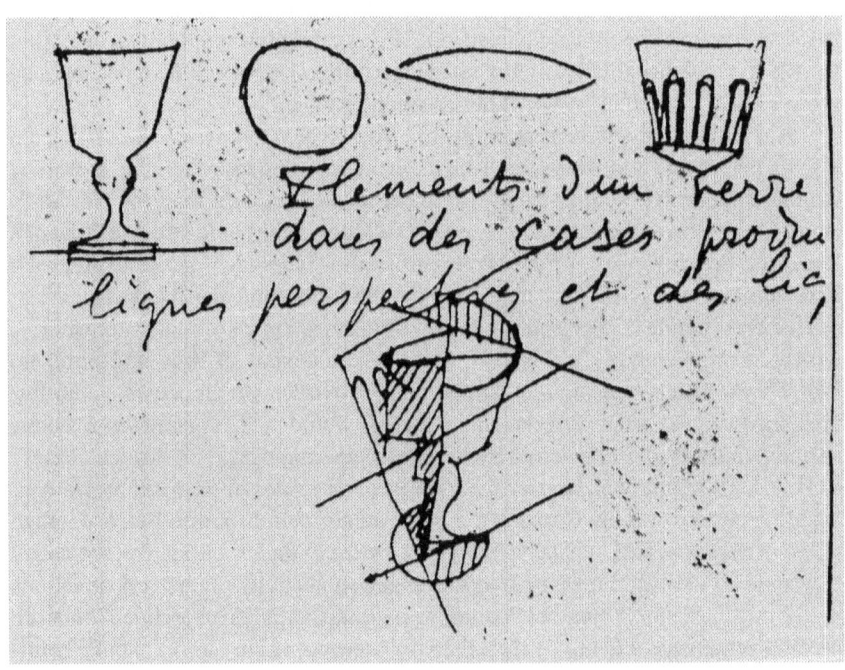

Fig. 4. Andre Lhote's composite sketch of a glass, 1952.
© 2007 Artists Rights Society (ARS), New York / ADAGP, Paris

ing signifies both modernity and the arbitrariness of language, akin to newsprint collaged or letters painted onto a Cubist canvas.[9] One can even trace the cubist structuring elements of *Mrs. Dalloway* through the lived experience of the characters, down into the specifics of syntax and fragment, literary parallels to the passages and brushstrokes of painterly language.

Time Reconsidered

In Cubist painting, "[T]he premise that the canvas represents one atemporal moment of vision by a perceiver standing in a fixed position is exploded by the multiple views of a single object simultaneously on the picture plane" (Steiner 180). In this more accurate record of an object's totality, the viewer must extrapolate the object's form from the tangle of perspectives presented. This activity requires both awareness of and adjustment in the viewer's perception: she must acknowledge the limitation of a fixed view in time and space and accept the opening up of many views—and thus many times—enacted by a Cubist painting.

Consider this example of a visual-narrative parallel. A 1952 sketch by Andre Lhote shows discrete elements of a goblet: the outline of the form; the top view, a circle; the indentations and texture of the glasswork; the lip of the glass looking like a slit, as one approaches to drink. Beneath the parts, he drew a composite whole, a unified Cubist image (Fig. 4). Similarly, Woolf collapses time by allowing her characters to travel a greater distance than actually possible in the time allotted,[10] and by keeping other times and places constantly in play on the field of London, 1923. Peter Walsh's London perambulations, complicated by memories of his youth with Clarissa and his recent experience in India, illustrate this narrative tendency. After noticing Septimus and Rezia in Regent's Park, Peter returns to the present after reminiscing about his sad past with Clarissa and thinking it "awful." In response, his consciousness constructs the moment as a series

---

[9] For a helpful general overview of collage elements in Woolf, see Mary Ann Caws, "Framing, Centering, Explicating; Virginia Woolf's Collage," *New York Literary Forum* 10-11 (1983): 51-78. Caws defines a "successful 'literary' collage" as a text in which "elements of another style, period, or substance can be imported into and then imposed on the already existing matrix, the entire product then exposed and explicated as a two-layered structure" (52). A prominent example of this importation, the repetition of "Fear no more the heat o' the sun" throughout *Mrs. Dalloway*, also functions as a key connective between Clarissa and Septimus.

[10] Andelys Wood's "Walking the Web: The Lost London of *Mrs. Dalloway*" documents specific time-place inconsistencies. Wood reads Woolf's inaccuracies as a deliberate technique to keep the reader equally conscious of place and time and as "clues to meaning in a London that no longer exists, some of which had already vanished by 1925 when the novel was published" (30).

of contributing factors, multiple perspectives cemented to one another by the repeated and conditional "still": "Still, the sun was hot. Still, one got over things. Still, life had a way of adding day to day. Still, he thought, yawning and beginning to take notice—Regent's Park had changed very little since he was a boy, except for the squirrels—still, presumably there were compensations" *(MD* 64-65). Peter experiences the Regent's Park moment cubistically, as a simultaneous composite of time, memory, and sensory perception.

According to Cubism's early advocates Apollinaire and Salmon, "Cubist art was conceptual, not only perceptual . . .that is, it drew upon memory as well as upon objects actually viewed by the eyes" (Chipp 194). If time and memory become "conceptual" subjects of the painting, then the inclusion of such abstract elements demands a new style of rendering. If anything, the verbal nature of fiction allows it to treat greater stretches of time than painting and thus to accommodate memory more adroitly. The novel's treatment of Regent's Park constitutes a composite view in which time functions as a primary component of perception. Of Woolf's subjective handling of location, Miroslav Beker writes, "Regent's Park is never described, its place in the structure of the novel is never adjectival, subsidiary, a frame around a character, but rather it is verbal, fully functional in revealing the characters of those who are found there" (384). Eschewing any external view of the park, Woolf's narrative renders it instead as variously constituted by each of its visitors. Cast in cubist terms, Regent's Park works similarly to both Analytic and Synthetic Cubism, which, according to Stephen Scobie, "In their different ways . . . play along this border of legibility: reducing or fragmenting the sign, dispersing its elements across the grid of the picture surface, setting its attributes in new and paradoxical relationships to each other, deconstructing but never abandoning its codes of representation" (86-87). Woolf's treatment of the park tests the limits of signification in quite the same way. Considering that she often compared her novels to "canvases" (*D2* 323; *D3* 176; *D5* 336), and bearing in mind her emphasis on compositional form in *Mrs. Dalloway*, it follows that Woolf deliberately lays out a composite of Regent's Park by accommodating competing views.

And the various "Regent's Parks" play this out. Young Maisie Johnson, "only up from Edinburgh two days ago," passes the Warren Smiths in the park, thinks them "queer" and speculates about the manufacture of memory:

> should she be very old she would still remember and make it jangle again among her memories how she had walked through Regent's Park on a fine summer morning fifty years ago. For she was only nineteen and had got her way at last, to come to London; and now how queer it was . . . now all these people (for she had returned to the Broad Walk), the stone basins, the prim flowers, the old

men and women, invalids most of them in Bath chairs—all seemed, after Edinburgh, so queer. (*MD* 26)

Maisie's perception, a catalogue of both people and landscape, animals and plants, is marked by the "queerness" of her new environment, a fact Cubism's rupturing tendency can contain. As she has no past with Regent's Park, Maisie's temporal sense must necessarily point future-ward. Peter Walsh's movement through the Park, however, walks the reader around to the other side of time-perception, while staying within the same geographical space. Peter's initial sensory apprehension of the Park in the present links almost simultaneously to his memory, and the narrative combines statement, affirmation and memory to convey all: "There was Regent's Park. Yes. As a child he had walked in Regent's Park" (*MD* 55).

Peter's revisited memories exemplify Wendy Steiner's general claim that "The cubist interaction with the past makes a simultaneity of it, a system whose elements are altered not in substance but in context" (191). Individual memory is the by-path Woolf employs most often to inventory her characters' mental lives, but it is not the only one. If personal history is an inevitable influence on perception, shared public history is exponentially so. The novel's specifics of time and place occasion meditations on the Great War, which bruised the collective English consciousness. Steiner aptly summarizes Cubism's potential as a historical lens:

> Cubism thus tells us to think of history in a new way, not as a plotted narrative moving toward a resolution, but as a cubist painting whose elements maintain their heterogeneity—objects, people; things, signs; the banal, the dramatic; the contemporaneous, the anachronous—in an aestheticized structure of interrelations. (191)

In applying Steiner's concept to the postwar London of *Mrs. Dalloway*, we note that war, while ended, remains ever present. Its having been (and having been so scarring and horrifying) is incorporated into the integrity of everything seen and experienced. Of "life, London, this morning in June" it is inextricably a part, imparting an inescapable sadness and producing an exquisite sense of relief. The dynamic of war, even war ended, embeds itself into the fabric of the novel. Thus, even on her way to the flower shop, under a washed blue June sky, Clarissa cannot help but think of "Lady Bexborough who opened a bazaar, they said, with the telegram in her hand, John, her favourite, killed" and others for whom the war is not over (*MD* 5). In this moment, Clarissa's relief cannot be separated from her perception of her surroundings.

As the novel's embodiment of the war conflict, Septimus bears psychological wounds—still open and raw. For him the elements of his environment do not, as Steiner puts it, "maintain their heterogeneity." He conflates topographies—Regent's Park with the trenches. He sees Evans everywhere—behind a tree, in a man (Peter Walsh) walking toward him. The signs of the skywriting, the royal seal, his own urgent scribblings, do not signify to him as they ought. While it is true that he is Clarissa's double, he is also her foil. As Sue Roe points out, "the radical difference between them is that Clarissa, though her thoughts transcend the spatial relations which define her, may always return to those spaces, while Septimus can never return" (180). By nature ruptured, a cubist narrative can accommodate the mental fracturing caused by Septimus' experience with trench warfare—a task never required of a novel before 1914.

Dynamics of the Present Moment

The past indeed complicates the present, but the present harbors its own complexity. Woolf confirms this truth via another mode of temporal representation: the depiction of synchronously lived moments of multiple characters, which constitute a clear deployment of cubist narrative strategy. One such passage provides a multidimensional view of the noon hour:

> It was precisely twelve o'clock; twelve by Big Ben; whose stroke was wafted over the northern part of London; blent with that of other clocks, mixed in a thin ethereal way with the clouds and wisps of smoke, and died up there among the seagulls—twelve o'clock struck as Clarissa Dalloway laid her green dress on the bed, and the Warren Smiths walked down Harley Street. Twelve was the hour of their appointment. Probably, Rezia thought, that was Sir William Bradshaw's house with the grey motor car in front of it. The leaden circles dissolved in the air. (*MD* 94)

This relatively brief paragraph, less about consciousness than about ironic difference, enacts skillfully what Erich Auerbach has called "polyphonic treatment" (34). The various sectors of central London connect through the shared sound of Big Ben's chime, and the narrative gains height by following the sound upward. Constructing the moment of noon cubistically, the paragraph sets the banality of Clarissa's dress-mending (metonymy for her party) alongside Septimus's need to consult a doctor for his precarious mental health. The implicit class contrasts combine to form a multisided social picture: compare Clarissa's pampered domesticity and the Bradshaws' automobile with the Warren Smiths, who live in rented rooms, travel London on foot, and work menial jobs. Also, juxtaposing the three families—Dalloways, Bradshaws, and Warren Smiths—prefigures the overlapping relational geometry by which Clarissa will hear of Septimus's suicide at her party.

Here the narrative voice itself is cubist, shifting from a third person reportage into Rezia's consciousness and back out again with the repeated line, "The leaden circles dissolved in the air." The phrase has chimed before; it will resound before the narrative is out. Its familiarity and solidity ground the reader amidst the narrative flux. Repetition within the novel replicates the recursive nature of memory and functions as a marker to help the reader impose order on what might otherwise feel like a chaotic narrative. Big Ben is the central repeated motif and the one shared by the greatest number of characters, all of whom live out their day within earshot of its booming chime. The striking of the great clock is a particularly multivalent grounding device: it represents time, it foreshadows death.

Big Ben sounds first at the opening of the novel, when the narrative eye is trained upon Clarissa; present in the description are the "leaden circles" but also the sinister evocation of time's ineluctable progression: "First a warning, musical; then the hour, irrevocable" (*MD* 4). Throughout the day, the clock sound penetrates and punctuates the inner monologues of its hearers: the 11:30 chime "stuck out between them with extraordinary vigour" at the awkward meeting between Peter and Elizabeth in Clarissa's drawing room (*MD* 48); the half-one chime gives rise to Richard Dalloway's annoyance with luncheon parties (*MD* 117); sedated after her husband's suicide, Rezia hears the "sensible sound" of the six o'clock chime as the only ordered thing in her traumatized consciousness (*MD* 150).[11] The final striking occurs at the party as Clarissa ponders Septimus' death and watches the old woman in the window opposite (*MD* 186). Big Ben is time translated into sound, its "leaden circles" the geometry of the hours.

The Subject in the City

Evaluating various cubist readings of literature, Wendy Steiner expresses concern that such studies "almost never make explicit the basis of a given comparison—why perspective is parallel to point of view, for example" (179).[12] Steiner cautions us against the lack of rigorous theoretical underpinning in order to avoid "an impressionism that is embarrassing to read" (178), yet in *Mrs. Dalloway* generally and in the skywriting scene in particular, perspective as seen from an exact location in space (in combination with other, more individuated factors) determines narrative point of view. Occurring shortly after the passing of the car, the skywriting is an especially significant event because of its semiotic

---

[11] The British Library holograph edition identifies the 6:00 chime Rezia hears as St. Pancras (Wood 30).

[12] Marianna Torgovnick echoes Steiner's claim in the outlining of her own methodology (10).

nature. In this instance, Woolf deploys a group of characters, many of whom do not reappear, to construct a microcosm of London life and to emphasize class distinctions. Quite literally standing around a circumscribed space and looking up, the characters offer varying interpretations of the same event, and physical perspective *does* correlate with point of view.

At its first appearance, "the sound of an aeroplane bored ominously into the ears of the crowd"—an understandable reaction in a city traumatized by the German bombing raids of the Great War (*MD* 20). Over the course of this scene, airspace is reclaimed for the use of commerce, and thus redeemed—at least until the next war. Sarah Bletchley and Emily Coates, "the poor mothers of Pimlico"; Mr. Bowley, who lived in the Albany; a nursemaid or two; and Septimus and Rezia all share in this moment, but read the skywriting differently:

> But what letters? A C was it? an E, then an L? . . . a K, an E, a Y perhaps?
> "Glaxo," said Mrs. Coates, in a strained, awe-stricken voice . . . .
> "Kreemo," murmured Mrs. Bletchley, like a sleepwalker. . . .
> "That's an E," said Mrs. Bletchley— . . .
> "It's toffee," murmured Mr. Bowley— . . .
> So, thought Septimus, they are signalling to me. (*MD* 20-21)

Like the Cubist painters, who incorporated fragments of abstracted text into their canvases (e.g. the "JOU" often used by Picasso to denote, among other things, *Le Journal* newspaper), Woolf abstracts bits from the advertisement to point up the relatively arbitrary nature of the letters as signs. These Ts, Os, Fs, presumably suggesting a banal consumer product, cut language down to its basic phonemic level. In the sky as in a Picasso, "the incompleteness of the words is also important," as Stephen Scobie writes. The outlines of letters are the brushstrokes of language, calling attention to the structural bones of speech and reading by exposing and orphaning them to our own interpretation. A set of non-words "*invites* the viewer [reader] to guess its complete form," and yet, "the word fragments insist on their own incompletion" since "they refuse any reading as iconic signs, as exact resemblances" (97, Scobie's emphasis). When we cannot decipher the signified, we become that much more aware of the properties of the sign.

One can also read the scene as an ironic modernist reworking of the *topos* of heavenly revelation: instead of angels singing "Gloria in excelsis Deo, et in terra pax," modern London receives a vaporous and inscrutable message—which is ultimately an advertisement—dispensed by an aeroplane. Thus, the episode concludes with the aircraft flying over an unnamed man poised to enter St. Paul's Cathedral, contemplating going before "a cross, the symbol of something which has soared beyond seeking and questing and knocking of words together and has become all spirit disembodied, ghostly" (*MD* 28). But the reader never knows for certain if the man goes inside. Instead, the scene ends with a final glimpse of the aeroplane "curving up and up, straight up, like something mounting in ecstasy, in pure delight, out from behind poured white smoke looping, writing a T, an O, an F" (*MD* 28-29)—the language here hinting at both sexuality and religion. Furthermore, the prominence of the aeroplane suggests that the cross of its wings has supplanted the Christian cross as a symbol of transcendence.

And yet, for Clarissa at least, the city offers the possibility of transcendence. More than the other characters, she obliterates any subject-object division between herself and London. Early in the narrative, spurred to thought by the passing of the Piccadilly omnibuses, Clarissa revels in the inscrutableness of being, refusing to "say of anyone in the world now that they were this or were that," and allowing herself a multiple and simultaneous apprehension of life (*MD* 8). Later, as Peter Walsh recalls her atop a city bus, his memory suggests that London and Clarissa construct one another mutually:

> . . . she felt herself everywhere; not "here, here, here"; and she tapped the back of the seat; but everywhere. She waved her hand, going up Shaftesbury Avenue. She was all that. So that to know her, or anyone, one must seek out the people who completed them; even the places. (*MD* 152-153)

While aspects of London merely suggest identity or spur memory for the other characters, Clarissa seems most completed by her urban surroundings, most liable "to confuse inner and outer, self and other" and to "[possess] a spiritual vision of human relatedness and endurance firmly grounded in the daily creativity of the city around her" (Squier 98).

In a sense, then, Clarissa *is* London—or, at least, *her* London. In a single lived day, the city serves her as locus of memory, of community, of death, of possibility and future—of "what she loved; life; London; this moment of June" (*MD* 4). As for Peter Walsh, "Never had he seen London look so enchanting—the softness of the distances; the richness; the greenness; the civilisation, after India" (*MD* 71). Even Septimus Warren Smith, with his questionable sanity, embraces the trees, birds, and sounds of the city, which "All taken together meant the birth of a new religion" (*MD* 23). The continuity of ecstatic identification within the novel prefigures and prepares for the complex and seemingly contradictory climax of death-in-life at the party scene.

Ironic Isolation

Virginia Woolf understood that modern urban life comprehended both Wendy Steiner's "aestheticized structure of interrelations" and Raymond

Williams's "aesthetically experienced atomism." Despite their opposition, these binaries both can be—indeed, *are*—aestheticized. The flux between the two poles is in a sense the subject of the novel, the "supreme mystery" pondered by Clarissa: "here was one room; there another. Did religion solve that, or love?" (*MD* 127). The novel does not answer the question either, but a problem so crucial to human experience needs to be asked anew in the language of its age. A narrative that makes use of cubism can depict relationships within a field (the watchers of the skywriting) and the atomization present even between a married couple (Richard Dalloway's inability to speak his love for his wife even as he hands her a bouquet of white and red roses). Assisted by Woolf's cubist prose, the death of Septimus accommodates both opposing elements.

The novelistic trajectory of the Warren Smiths, each isolated within their troubled marriage, culminates when Septimus hurls himself out the window to his death. While the reader experiences the suicide firsthand through the narrative, more pathos lies in oblique, secondhand experiences than in the direct account. Peter Walsh hears the ambulance rushing too late to the scene of Septimus's self-destruction—ironically unaware of the connection between the arguing couple he had noticed earlier in Regent's Park and the ambulance he thinks of as "one of the triumphs of civilisation," an indicator of "the communal spirit of London" (*MD* 151). Peter's narrated monologue here supports Dorrit Cohn's claim regarding the mode's ironic power: "Precisely because they cast the language of a subjective mind into the grammar of objective narration," narrated monologues "throw into ironic relief all false notes struck by a figural mind" (Cohn 117). Peter's ignorance of his encounter with the tragic couple simultaneously undercuts and reinforces the concepts of civilization and community which he ponders, revealing their less attractive facets of denial and exclusion.

This irony of not knowing that one knows is balanced by Clarissa's feeling of connectedness to Septimus, whom she did not know or ever see. When Sir William Bradshaw, Septimus' doctor and witness to his suicide, appears at Clarissa's party and shares the news of the tragedy, her initial reaction illustrates the complex variety contained by one moment. She exclaims, "Oh! . . . In the middle of my party, here's death" and moves to an empty room to be alone (*MD* 183). Viewing the mutual corroboration of the two main characters as vital to the book's success, Josephine O'Brien Schaefer writes, "without the presence of Septimus, Clarissa's emotions might seem minor and trivial" (86). Indeed, she echoes Woolf's original assertion that "Septimus and Mrs Dalloway should be entirely dependent on one another" *(L*3 189).[13] If this dependence is thematic,

---

[13] For discussions of the complementary relationship between Clarissa and Septimus, see Fleishman (1975), Squier (1985), Roe (2000), and Matz (2001).

reinforcing the novel's meditations on memory and death, it is equally structural, providing two complementary views of shared urban space in postwar London.

Attempting to puzzle out the inscrutability of death, Clarissa surveys its many sides. She tries to conjure the visceral experience of a voluntary jump and violent fall to one's end, and meditates on the purity and "defiance" of death. In the end, rooted in life as she is, Clarissa relates death to what she knows:

> She had once thrown a shilling into the Serpentine, never anything more. But he had flung it away. They went on living (she would have to go back; the rooms were still crowded; people kept on coming). They (all day she had been thinking of Bourton, of Peter, of Sally), they would grow old. . . . Death was an attempt to communicate; people feeling the impossibility of reaching the centre, which, mystically, evaded them; closeness drew apart; rapture faded, one was alone. There was an embrace in death. (*MD* 184)

If, as we have seen, Clarissa sees little boundary between herself and her city, her conception of not-being would naturally incorporate some element of London. Throwing something of value into the depths—a coin into a lake—is the best comparison she can muster. And yet, try as she might to imagine dying, Clarissa can keep neither the present moment nor memory from breaking into her thoughts, indicated syntactically by intrusive parentheses. Here is the novel's most poignant brand of cubism at work: a composite of disparate physical spaces, present time, past time, and imagined sensation, working in concert to construct from the facets and fragments of death its ultimately impenetrable whole. This passage underscores the isolation which death certifies, while allowing a Clarissa to experience a kind of imaginative sympathy, however unconsummated.

Clarissa's metaphysical moment, a result of Septimus's suicide, demonstrates the fact that her London of June, 1923, is not his—nor does that divide become more traversable by her understanding of his fate. In fact, Clarissa's is not the same London from minute to minute, from leaden circle to leaden circle, reminding one that Raymond Williams observed of Leopold Bloom's Dublin "in a way, there is no longer a city, there is only a man walking through it" (243). Even were we to alter Williams's claim to reflect "a woman walking through it," the single perceiver, Clarissa, cannot hold all the Londons of her experience (let alone the London of another's) in her consciousness at once. But the novel *can*: its cubist aesthetic integrates several subjective Londons into a whole, expressing in Woolf's glittering prose the idea that at any given moment, the crowd of minds walking in, around, and through a city in one sense *are* that city.[14]

---

[14] I wish to acknowledge a debt to Jerry Phillips, who provided the original context for the production of this essay. Margaret Higonnet has read and responded to this piece

Works Cited

Apollinaire, Guillaume. "The Beginnings of Cubism." *Theories of Modern Art.* Edited by Herschel B. Chipp. Berkeley: U of California P, 1968. 216-219

Auerbach, Erich. "The Brown Stocking." *Virginia Woolf.* Ed. Rachel Bowlby. London: Longman, 1992. 20-45

Beker, Miroslav. "London as a Principle of Structure in *Mrs. Dalloway*" *Modern Fiction Studies* 18 (1972): 375-385.

Berger, John. *The Look of Things*, ed. Nikos Stangos. New York: Viking, 1971.

Blyth, Ian. "Virginia Woolf and Jacques Raverat." *Virginia Woolf Bulletin* 6 (Jan. 2001): 31-35

Caws, Mary Ann. "Framing, Centering, Explicating; Virginia Woolf's Collage." *New York Literary Forum* 10-11 (1983): 51-78

Cézanne, Paul. "Excerpts from the Letters." *Theories of Modern Art.* Edited by Herschel B. Chipp. Berkeley: U of California P, 1968. 16-23

Chipp, Herschel B., ed. "Cubism: An Introduction." *Theories of Modern Art.* Berkeley: U of California P, 1968. 193-199.

Cohn, Dorrit. *Transparent Minds: Narrative Modes for Presenting Consciousness in Fiction.* Princeton: Princeton UP, 1978.

Dowling, David. *Bloomsbury Aesthetics and the Novels of Forster and Woolf.* New York: St. Martin's, 1985.

Dunn, Jane. *A Very Close Conspiracy: Virginia Woolf and Vanessa Bell.* Boston: Little, Brown, 1990.

Fleishman, Avrom. *Virginia Woolf: A Critical Reading.* Baltimore and London: Johns Hopkins UP, 1975.

Froula, Christine. *Virginia Woolf and the Bloomsbury Avant-Garde.* New York: Columbia UP, 2005.

Fry, Roger. "Modern French Art at the Mansard Gallery." *The Roger Fry Reader.* Ed. Christopher Reed. Chicago: U of Chicago P, 1996. 339-342.

---

at all stages of its development, offering unflagging guidance and thoughtful feedback at every turn. Thank you to the readers at *Woolf Studies Annual* for insightful revision suggestions and to Anthony Falcetta for technical assistance with the illustrations. I am grateful for a fellowship awarded by the University of Connecticut Humanities Institute which facilitated the completion and revision of this article. Lastly, thanks to Emily Hinnov for her consistent friendship and support in matters Woolfian and beyond. It is a great pleasure to have my work appear in this volume alongside her scholarship.

Gillespie, Diane Filby, ed. *The Multiple Muses of Virginia Woolf.* Columbia: U of Missouri P, 1993.

——. *The Sisters' Arts: The Writing and Painting of Virginia Woolf and Vanessa Bell.* Syracuse: Syracuse UP, 1988.

Goldman, Jane. *The Feminist Aesthetics of Virginia Woolf.* Cambridge: Cambridge UP, 1998.

Haftmann, Werner. *Painting in the Twentieth Century.* Vol. 1. London: Lund Humphries, 1965.

Hughes, Robert. *The Shock of the New.* New York: Knopf, 1980.

Matz, Jesse. *Literary Impressionism and Modernist Aesthetics.* Cambridge: Cambridge UP, 2001.

Reid, Panthea. *Art and Affection: A Life of Virginia Woolf.* Oxford and New York: Oxford UP, 1996.

Roberts, John Hawley. "'Vision and Design' in Virginia Woolf." *PMLA* 61 (1946): 835-847.

Roe, Sue. "The Impact of Post-Impressionism." *The Cambridge Companion to Virginia Woolf.* Ed. Sue Roe and Susan Sellers. Cambridge: Cambridge UP, 2000. 164-190.

Rosenblum, Robert. *Cubism and Twentieth-Century Art.* New York: Harry N. Abrams, 1976.

Schaefer, Josephine O'Brien. *The Three-Fold Nature of Reality in the Novels of Virginia Woolf.* The Hague: Mouton, 1965.

Schnitzer, Deborah. *The Pictorial in Modernist Fiction.* Ann Arbor: UMI, 1988.

Scobie, Stephen. *Earthquakes and Explorations: Language and Painting from Cubism to Concrete Poetry.* Toronto: U of Toronto P, 1997.

Squier, Susan M. *Virginia Woolf and London: The Sexual Politics of the City.* Chapel Hill: U of North Carolina P, 1985.

Steiner, Wendy. *The Colors of Rhetoric: Problems in the Relation Between Modern Literature and Painting.* Chicago: U of Chicago P, 1982.

Stewart, Jack F. "Cubist Elements in *Between the Acts*." *Mosaic* 18/2 (1985): 65-89.

Torgovnick, Marianna. *The Visual Arts, Pictorialism, and the Novel: James, Lawrence, and Woolf.* Princeton: Princeton UP, 1985.

Williams, Raymond. *The Country and the City.* Oxford: Oxford UP, 1973.

Wood, Andelys. "Walking the Web in the Lost London of *Mrs. Dalloway*." *Mosaic* 36/2 (2003): 19-32.

Woolf, Virginia. *The Diary of Virginia Woolf.* Ed. Anne Olivier Bell and Andrew

McNeillie. 5 vols. New York: HBJ, 1984.
—. *The Letters of Virginia Woolf*. Eds. Nigel Nicolson and Joanne Trautmann. 6 vols. New York: HBJ, 1975-1980.
—. *Mrs. Dalloway*. 1925. Introduction by Maureen Howard. New York: HBJ, 1992.
—. "Pictures." *The Moment and Other Essays*. London: Hogarth Press, 1947. 140-144.
—. *Roger Fry: A Biography*. London: Hogarth Press, 1940.

Taking Note: Text and Context in Virginia Woolf's "Mr. Bennett and Mrs. Brown"

Eve Sorum

Virginia Woolf's essay "Mr. Bennett and Mrs. Brown" now stands as one of her most well known aesthetic statements.[1] In it she argues that the contemporary world demands a new form of fiction—one that strives to capture the essence of the modern character, even though this necessitates inventing a new form of writing. The essay appears in such groupings as the *Collected Essays* volumes, Andrew McNeillie's *The Essays of Virginia Woolf*, and anthologies like *The Virginia Woolf Reader*.[2] All three of these contexts introduce Woolf as a fully canonized author, and the essay becomes, therefore, a part of her copious oeuvre and is representative of one aspect of her equally plentiful talent. These settings influence our reading of the piece, most prominently through their emphasis on its generic affiliations (especially in the *Collected Essays* and the McNeillie collection, but also in the *Reader*, in which selections are grouped according to genre). Mitchell Leaska's preface to the *Reader* offers additional direction, for he describes "Mr. Bennett and Mrs. Brown" as "one of her consistently controversial shorter essays" (viii). The commentary preceding the piece further highlights the polemics: after an admirable description of the essay's publication history, which describes its original function as a defense against Arnold Bennett's critique of Woolf's fiction, Leaska names it a "kind of literary manifesto" and an obloquy against the "novels of the earlier generation" (192). The *Virginia Woolf Reader* proves an apt title, for Leaska—as do all editors—provides us with his own reading of the text.

Though Leaska, an expert on Woolf who seems aware of his weighty editorial responsibility to designate "best work," may be an ideal guide, his direction unavoidably obscures the control Woolf asserted over her text and its interpreta-

---

[1] See Lee, "Virginia Woolf's Essays," 94; Cuddy-Keane, 190; and Majumdar and McLaurin, 16-17. Many thanks to John Fulton, Paul Sorum, George Bornstein, Mark Hussey, and the anonymous reviewer for their helpful comments on various drafts.

[2] The essay's publication trajectory after Woolf's death is as follows: *The Captain's Death Bed and Other Essays* (1950), collected and edited by Leonard Woolf; *Virginia Woolf: Selections from Her Essays* (1966); *Collected Essays*, Volume I (1966); *The Essays of Virginia Woolf*, Volume 3 (1988); *The Virginia Woolf Reader* (1984); and, finally, Rachel Bowlby's 1992 collection, *A Woman's Essays*. All information comes from Kirkpatrick and this list does not include translations or foreign editions.

tion.³ An exploration of the different editions of the essay published in Woolf's lifetime illuminates a network of alternative interpretive codes unavailable to the present day reader. As George Bornstein illustrates in "How to Read a Page: Modernism and Material Textuality," the bibliographic codes—the "semantic features of material instantiations" (30) that include the organ of publication, time of publication, placement in the publication, surrounding graphics, and layout—determine the work's meaning as fully as the linguistic codes. Therefore, the context informs interpretation as much as the words on the page.

In the versions printed during Woolf's lifetime, beginning with the *Criterion* publication, the essay includes a note stating: "A paper read to the Heretics, Cambridge, on May 18, 1924." Though Leaska diligently lists this oral event in his commentary preceding the essay, his notation conveys little of the note's impact and none of its interpretive pressure. Yet Woolf's decision (and the acquiescence of other editors, even in its *New York Herald Tribune* edition) to leave the note in all publications following the speech indicates that it performs an essential role and cannot be omitted without altering the essay.⁴ In fact, the note, as a vital textual feature, profoundly influences interpretation, especially in relation to contexts that politicize, historicize, or aestheticize the text. Concomitantly, the different contexts of publication also transform the meaning and function of the note, as well as of the whole essay. My inquiry will trace the manifestations in Woolf's lifetime of "Mr. Bennett and Mrs. Brown" in order to reveal the contextual and textual ways in which Woolf and the organs in which she published directed interpretation and dealt with the text as an aesthetic object enmeshed in history. The note will prove an integral, though not isolated example of the importance of reading text *and* context, as I analyze the bibliographic and linguistic changes in the essay's publication trajectory: from a brief defense in the *Nation & Athenaeum*, to a speech for the Heretics society, to an appearance in the *Criterion*, to pamphlet form with the Hogarth Press, to a reprint in the *New York Herald Tribune*, and finally as the leading essay in the 1928 Doubleday compilation of *The Hogarth Essays*.⁵

---

³ Brenda Silver makes a similar argument in relation to manuscript editing, pointing out that with Woolf's work, "feminist editors began to perceive and reveal the trenchant, frequently scathing, cultural criticism beneath the surface of the seemingly flawless, apolitical, aestheticized work of art" (195).

⁴ Of course, as Silver argues, Woolf did not seem concerned with "a stable text. She knowingly sent out different versions, different texts" (196). Yet her use of the note in all of the essays following the speech suggests that this was an element that was an integral part of the text.

⁵ I focus on the *Nation & Athenaeum* "Mr. Bennett and Mrs. Brown" rather than the *New York Evening Post* publication because the former is a British organ. As such, Woolf

Woolf's writing demands attention to the bibliographic codes especially because of her privileged position as co-owner and operator of the Hogarth Press, and her resulting awareness of the editorial decisions involved in every act of publication. The press arose as an unlikely hobby—Woolf needed a diverting project (or so her husband, Leonard, thought) to take her away from the too consuming task of writing (Willis 4). Woolf had experimented with bookbinding as a young woman, and her decisions already foreshadowed her dislike of Victorian styles in her dismissal of "the high art style for the practical and workmanlike binding" (Willis 7). The press provided mental relief on another level—no longer would Woolf have to subject her writing and her psyche to the opinions of outside editors and publishers. She writes in a 1917 letter to her friend and fellow-writer David Garnett that "it is very amusing to try with these short things, and the greatest mercy to be able to do what one likes—no editors, or publishers, and only people to read who more or less like that sort of thing" (*L2* 167). Woolf's apparent delight in the restriction of her audience hints at her acute perception of the reader's role and the way that a perceived audience can influence literary decisions.[6] Writing for a supposedly appreciative group allowed her to break out of more realist styles and venture into experimental territory. The liberation that this control over herself and, less directly, over her audience gave Woolf led to a burst of creative activity that resulted in the literary experimentation she is known for today. The fruit of her preliminary outpouring of energy was *Jacob's Room*, the first novel published by the Hogarth Press. The appearance of this book spurred Woolf's confidence, and she "began increasingly to take an aggressive public stance in her essays, denouncing Victorian and Edwardian fiction and formulating her own aesthetic" (Willis 61).

Yet once a book was published, Woolf had to face the criticism of her readers, and Arnold Bennett's response to *Jacob's Room* challenged Woolf's newly found voice. Bennett's essay, a short critique antagonistically titled "Is the Novel Decaying?" appeared in *Cassell's Weekly* (March 1923). He entered the debate

---

was more likely to have had some control over or awareness of the presentation of her piece (an awareness enabled, of course, by Leonard Woolf's position as literary editor). Moreover, with the essay acting as a response to Arnold Bennett's critique, Woolf's originally projected audience can be assumed to be readers who would have encountered Bennett's piece, which was also published in a British journal, *Cassell's Weekly*.

[6] In "Readin', Writin', and Revisin'," Beth Rigel Daugherty explores Woolf's awareness of audience by looking at the publication history of the essay "How Should One Read a Book?" Daugherty examines how Woolf changed the tone and linguistic codes in order to appeal to the intended audiences: first, the student body at the Hayes Court School (Jan. 1926); second, the readers of *The Yale Review* (Oct. 1926); and third, the readers of the second *Common Reader* (1932).

about the existence of "young novelists with promise of first-rate importance" (160), using *Jacob's Room* to illustrate the major deficiency of young writers—unrealistic characters.[7] Though he acknowledged that future grand masters may be "writing to-day [sic] without any general appreciation" (162), Bennett still claimed that young writers like Woolf were too "obsessed by details of originality and cleverness" (162) to create true characters, the "foundation of good fiction" (161). As Daugherty has shown, Bennett's critique of *Jacob's Room* followed his publication of the book *Our Women: Chapters on the Sex-Discord* (1920), which questioned women's ability to write great literature and which had already provoked Woolf to defend herself and other women writers.[8] Bennett's criticism of Woolf's novel can be seen as part of an ongoing debate with Woolf about women, literature, and literary merit.

Bennett's review inspired the original version of "Mr. Bennett and Mrs. Brown," published first in the literary review section of the *New York Evening Post* (November 1923), then in the *Nation & Athenaeum* (of which Leonard Woolf had become the literary editor) on December 1 of the same year. On February 2nd the same piece came out in the Boston based *Littell's Living Age*, a magazine that compiled and reprinted articles from an assortment of British and American magazines. Woolf's original response, only a third of the length of the later version, turned the tables on Bennett's criticism by adopting his own position that character is the most important element of the novel, but identifying the Edwardians—naming Galsworthy, Wells, and Bennett himself—as the culprits in the novel's decline. As Samuel Hynes has noted, the essay at this point is more a retaliation against Bennett's critique than it is a seminal statement about the function of modern fiction (Hynes 38), though I would argue that the essential elements of her call for a new method of character creation are already in place. The Edwardian writers, Woolf argues, had never captured "Mrs. Brown," the elusive character that all writers should chase. The title of her essay cleverly conveys this critique, for it sets up a connection between Mr. Bennett and Mrs. Brown, fictionalizing Bennett and actualizing Brown. Edwardian writers have failed to create convincing characters, Woolf contends, because they only write about the extrinsic details—work, class, and societal relations. She patronizingly excuses their inattention to the actual characters because they occupy the unfor-

---

[7] All references to Bennett's essay will cite page numbers from his 1926 collected essays, *Things That Have Interested Me*.

[8] See Daugherty's discussion in "Mr. Bennett and Mrs. Woolf." She takes issue with Samuel Hynes's reading of the quarrel behind "Mr. Bennett and Mrs. Brown" as a dispute about class, instead persuasively arguing that Woolf was responding to a difference "about women's intellectual and artistic abilities" (269).

tunate role of successors to the overwhelmingly rich Victorian novelistic tradition. As Daugherty argues, Woolf's piece thereby emphasizes the dialogue between writers of different generations, usually characterized, Woolf writes, by "the respectful hostility which is the only healthy relation between old and young" (342).[9]

Woolf's focus on relations between writers highlights a perhaps accidental relationship established between her essay and the one preceding it in the *Nation & Athenaeum*. Immediately before "Mr. Bennett and Mrs. Brown" comes A. A. Milne's spoof about a leaflet produced by the National Unionist Association promoting economic protectionism. The characters in the original leaflet and in his parody are Mrs. Jones and Mrs. Brown, and we are left with the curious juxtaposition of Milne's very serious, completely one-sided Unionist Mrs. Brown, and Woolf's ephemeral Brown, who pops into her essay a paragraph from the end as the character that every writer must chase. This adds an interesting twist to Hynes's contention that Woolf's inclusion of the Mrs. Brown figure seems an "afterthought" (38). Did, in fact, Woolf name her character "Mrs. Brown" because of prior knowledge about the preceding piece? While it seems unlikely in light of the essay's original publication two weeks earlier in the *New York Evening Post*, the coincidence is suggestive.

In any case, the dialogue between generations of writers translates into a dialogue between literature and society in the *Nation & Athenaeum* context, as the character of fiction blurs with the characters of political and national debates. The serial's introductory section on "Events of the Week" details the political battles between the Unionist, Liberal, and Labour parties, and the list of articles preceding Woolf's essay—on such topics as Baldwin and Poincaré and trade "facts and figures"—further emphasizes the day's debates over free trade and protectionist practices. Woolf criticizes the Edwardians for their single-minded concern with social injustice, which turned their novels into vehicles for reform. In the context of this periodical, however, Woolf's own argument begins to be endowed with historical, and therefore political, significance. Instead of positing a simple move away from the social responsibilities of literature, Woolf describes the task of the Georgian writer to reconstruct character from the ruins of the previous generations in order to create "a man or woman whom we know" (343). The project of the writer thereby depends on understanding contemporary

---

[9] I agree with Daugherty's identification of this generational dispute as an essential element in Woolf's critique of Bennett. She reads Woolf's response to Bennett over the course of a number of years, beginning in 1917 with Woolf's praise for Bennett's essay on the 1910 Post-Impressionist exhibition and moving towards her critique of his writing and his position on women (270-75).

society and its influence on men and women. In light of the surrounding articles and the general political focus of the *Nation & Athenaeum*, "Mr. Bennett and Mrs. Brown" seems to be as much about social and historical transformations as it is about aesthetic choices.

The essay next surfaces, significantly expanded, as a speech called "Character in Fiction" that Woolf gave to the Heretics Society of Cambridge in May 1924. The society (referred to simply as the Heretics) formed in 1909 as an undergraduate group that promoted freethinking and religious discussions not based on Biblical authority. While similar to Cambridge's long standing secret society, the "Apostles," the Heretics were as interested in scientific as in philosophical debate.[10] Nonetheless, a number of writers, many of whom were in Woolf's group of friends and acquaintances (T.S. Eliot, Edith Sitwell, E.M. Forster, and Lytton Strachey) lectured to the Heretics.[11] The text of the speech provided the basis for Woolf's further revisions of the essay.

Soon after giving the speech, Woolf published the lengthened piece in *The Criterion* (July 1924), a literary magazine begun by Eliot in 1922. As might be expected, the text in the post-speech version had become more informal in tone than what was published in the *Nation & Athenaeum*. The most interesting transformations, however, appear in the way that Woolf positions herself as author, and in the addition of the story that illustrates her point about the creation of character.[12] Arnold Bennett no longer seems the instigator of the dialogue, but simply a foil for Woolf's explication of character. Though she has identified herself as an author in the first lines—"It seems to me possible, perhaps desirable, that I may be the only person in this room who has committed the folly of writing, trying to write, or failing to write, a novel" (420)—she does not refer to her own novels.[13] Arnold Bennett's review of *Jacob's Room* fades into the background because of the elapsed time, the new space, and the absence of references. Yet Woolf also highlights her own position as a contemporary novelist through that first self-deprecating sentence, and thereby invisibly aligns

---

[10] See Deacon 89-93 for a brief discussion of the Heretics.

[11] This information on the Heretics comes from rather meager references in Chaney, 203, and Rosenbaum, 184. See also McNeillie's brief remarks on the Heretics in his introduction to the transcription of the talk (*E3* 501-2).

[12] Majumdar and McLaurin speculate that the responses to Woolf's first version of "Mr. Bennett and Mrs. Brown," written by J. D. Beresford (December 29, 1923) and Logan Pearsall Smith (February 2, 1924) and published in the *Nation and Athenaeum*, may have led to some of the changes that Woolf made in her expanded version of the essay (16, 124).

[13] My references to the post-speech published essay use the page numbers of "Character in Fiction" in McNeillie's edition of the *Essays*.

herself with her list of "Georgian" writers—"Mr. Forster, Mr. Lawrence, Mr. Strachey, Mr. Joyce, and Mr. Eliot" (421). The aesthetic and the personal responses merge most fully in the addition of Mrs. Brown's story, which demonstrates Woolf's virtuosity at character creation at the same time as it reveals the shortcomings of the Edwardians' attempts. Unlike the character in the first version of the essay, Mrs. Brown (though with her gender first unspecified) enters the introductory paragraph in this version and becomes the vehicle through which Woolf can make her point about fiction writing in general and her own in particular.

Woolf's changes in pronouns alter the experience of the text as much as do the additions. In the first version she uses the conservative "we," eliding her own opinion into a larger, unspecified perspective. This move provides the armor needed for a defense by claiming allies and deflecting attention away from the personal nature of the response. Yet it also erodes some of the essay's power by not acknowledging the "I" behind the opinions. The post-speech version strongly reclaims that authorial identity with its repeated use of "I." We see on the linguistic level the embodiment of the author—a rhetorical manifestation of the actual embodiment that occurs when giving a speech. Knowledge of that context transforms Woolf from a ghostly name to a flesh-and-blood person, while also directing attention to the implied listening audience.[14] In the final portion of the piece Woolf names the audience as vital participants in the construction of an appropriately modern novel. She alternates between first and second-person pronouns as the essay progresses, aligning herself with the audience—"now let *us* examine what Mr. Bennett went on to say"—before making sweeping assertions—"And there *I* cannot agree" (427, my italics). She carries the audience along so successfully that in her final lines she can ask them to help the Georgian writer's cause by insisting "that writers shall come down off their plinths and pedestals, and describe beautifully if possible, truthfully at any rate, our Mrs.

---

[14] The implied audience, identified as the Heretics by the note (as I will discuss in more detail later), has been subject to different interpretations by earlier critics, probably in large part because of the lack of information about who the Heretics were. Hynes and Daugherty (who, presumably, based her claims on Hynes's discussion) both assume that they were a group at the women's college of Girton. This leads Daugherty to discuss in her essay on "The Whole Contention Between Mr. Bennett and Mrs. Woolf, Revisited" the implications of this audience on the essay. She reads the presence of a female audience as the reason behind Woolf's new use of the first-person pronoun (279). In light of our knowledge now about the make-up of the Heretics, I interpret this change in pronouns differently later in this essay. (I am indebted to my anonymous reviewer for drawing my attention to this issue in Hynes's and Daugherty's work.)

Brown" (436). The audience *must* be on the same side as the writer, Woolf suggests, after having already elegantly positioned them next to her.[15]

This rhetorical maneuvering of the audience/author relationship brings up a change between the text of the speech "Character in Fiction" and that of the published essay—a change that is small, yet striking in its implications. While Woolf's revisions to her speech generally involved the tightening of her points, the refinement of her thesis, and the strengthening of her assertions, her removal of two names from her list of Georgian writers begs inquiry.[16] In the *speech* to the Heretics, Woolf lists the Georgian writers as "Mr Joyce, Mr Lawrence, Mr Forster, Mr Strachey, Mr Eliot, Miss Sitwell, Miss Richardson" (*E3* 503). In the *published* essay, however, she omits Edith Sitwell and Dorothy Richardson from the list. Why did Woolf make such a change, especially in light of what Daugherty has identified as the feminist slant of the essay? The change carries her away from the original argument with Bennett over women's ability to write good literature, which preceded the debate over character, and perhaps it can be seen as an attempt to avoid revisiting that issue. Woolf counters this elision, however, in the additions made in the following paragraph, which describe the changes in human character that occurred "on or about December 1910" (421). In the speech Woolf attributed the shift in human relations to Freud and to a "vaguer force. . .called the Spirit of the Age" (*E3* 504), but in the essay she is more specific, citing changes in the role of servants, in readers' interpretations of the women in Greek tragedies, and in the evaluation of the relationship between husbands and wives—examples that underscore women's new opportunities and

---

[15] An interesting comparison can be made with *A Room of One's Own*, another text that emerged from (in this case) two speeches Woolf made at Newnham and Girton colleges. In *A Room of One's Own* Woolf similarly aligns herself with her audience with her informal tone and her positioning of herself, the speaker, as a character ("call me Mary Beton, Mary Seton, Mary Carmichael or by any name you please" (5) in the text.

[16] An example of her increased assertiveness can be seen in the difference between the opening lines of the second paragraphs in the two texts. In the speech Woolf has written, "I do not think that I am the only writer who has had this experience. Most novelists, if you asked them, would say I think that they are haunted in precisely the same way" (*E3* 502). In the published version Woolf has condensed those two sentences into the succinct and declarative "Most novelists have the same experience" (420)—a sentence that omits the "I think" that weakens the authority of her first claims. While other such changes take place over the course of the essay, Woolf does add one self-deprecating aside in the published version that was not in the speech. She excuses her use of the first person (which would not need to be excused in a talk, we assume), saying, "I do not want to attribute to the world at large the opinions of one solitary, ill-informed, and misguided individual" (421). Woolf's extreme self-deprecation verges on the ironic, but the sentence effectively positions her as an outsider, perhaps both deflecting criticism and asserting the originality of her stance.

their past repressions.[17] If she erases the names of contemporary women writers from the essay, she brings in issues of women's role in society at large.

This insertion of arguably feminist issues into the essay underscores another difference between the *Nation & Athenaeum* version and the post-speech essay—Woolf's increased politicization of the text. In both versions she suggests that a rupture in human character, occurring in 1910, made the old tools of character creation obsolete. In the first version the change takes place on purely literary territory (what happens when we stop believing in the Mrs. Brown the Edwardians have given us?), but in the speech Woolf focuses on the destruction of identity and security in the world at large. The "prevailing sound of the Georgian age" (434) is heard "in poems and novels and biographies, *even in newspaper articles and essays*, the sound of breaking and falling, crashing and destruction" (433-4, my italics). The problem of character creation in novels reflects, Woolf suggests, the conflict of the age—a time when structures of life are crumbling even on the most basic level of identity and class relations.[18] And this leads, Woolf continues, to a breakdown in the relationship between writer and reader: "At the present moment we are suffering, not from decay, but from having no code of manners which writers and readers accept as a prelude to the more exciting intercourse of friendship" (434). Thus the historical and political relevance of the essay, emphasized by the *context* in the first version, is illuminated by the *text* in the speech.

A final, and perhaps the most striking, linguistic change from the essay's first published version, is the title change. No longer "Mr. Bennett and Mrs. Brown," Woolf now presents the essay as "Character in Fiction," the title that she gave to the speech as well. Keeping this title alters the import and impact of the essay, for it decontextualizes and depoliticizes, separating it from both its original form and its original emphasis on the dialogue between Edwardian and Georgian writers. This choice reflects the immediate context of publication. The table of contents of the July 1924 issue reveals *The Criterion*'s primary function as a literary journal that publishes works by some of the most influential con-

---

[17] See Daugherty's "The Whole Contention Between Mr. Bennett and Mrs. Woolf, Revisited" (281) for an analysis of the feminist elements of this passage.

[18] Contemporary critics both supported and took issue with these claims about shifts in the fabric of being. J. D. Beresford agreed, arguing that "taking the average English man or woman, we shall find them more aware of their own diversity, more introspective, and hence more complicated, than would be the corresponding specimens picked out from a sample of early Victorians" (123). "Simon Pure," a pseudonym for the novelist Frank Swinnerton, attacked Woolf's assumption that human nature has changed, instead saying that it "is Mrs Woolf who has become self conscious" (132).

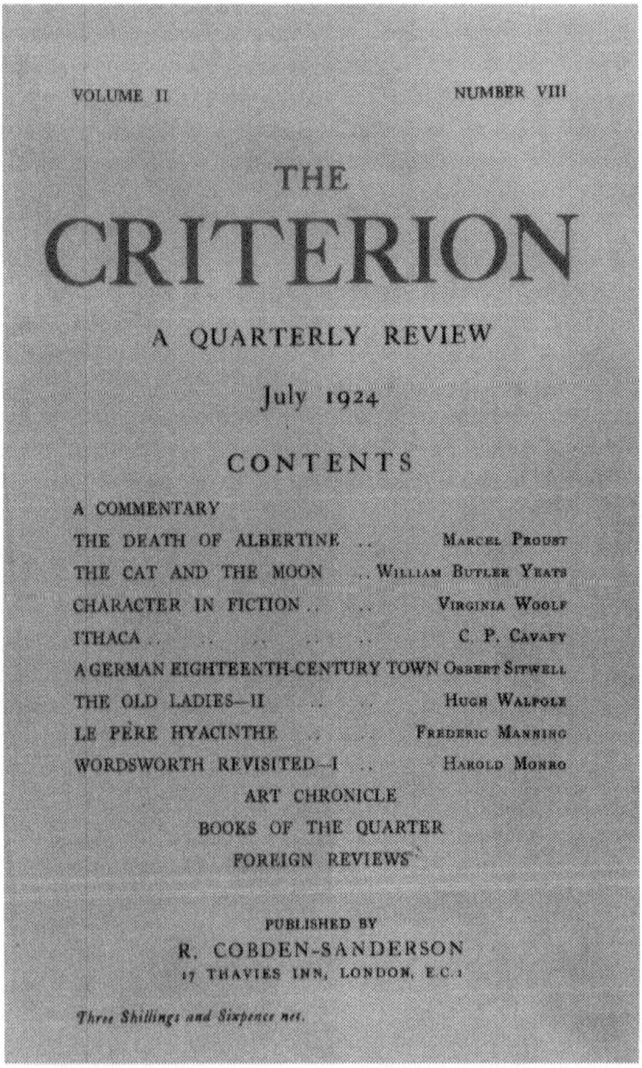

VOLUME II NUMBER VIII

THE

CRITERION

A QUARTERLY REVIEW

July 1924

CONTENTS

PUBLISHED BY

R. COBDEN-SANDERSON

17 THAVIES INN, LONDON, E.C.1

Three Shillings and Sixpence net.

Figure 1: Table of contents from *The Criterion*, July 1924. Courtesy of Widener Library, Harvard College Library P.142.7.

temporary writers. (Figure 1) Contributors include Proust, Yeats, Cavafy, and Walpole, all writing stories or poetry. The title "Character in Fiction" allows Woolf's piece to act as commentary on the surrounding contributions, while "Mr. Bennett and Mrs. Brown" would have seemingly closed off those connections and emphasized its role as an angry response to one particular writer. Of course, the text of the essay still includes the previously examined historically and politically located transformation of human character, but the new title foregrounds the literary nature of the critique, as opposed to its immediate historical (and personal) relevance.

These changes in the text reflect, therefore, the changing context of the essay. Importantly, the linguistic code remains the same in all its further publications, indicating that the text achieved a state that Woolf wanted to perpetuate.[19] Yet, more than simply reprinting the text of the speech, Woolf decided that its identity as a speech to the Heretics needed to be emphasized through the previously quoted note: "A paper read to the Heretics, Cambridge, on May 18, 1924"(Figure 2). Through a textual element the essay became forever connected to that particular historical event and moment.

If the title appears to restrict the relevance of the essay to literature and the contents of the journal, the inclusion of the note gestures to another audience—equally elite, but outside the small circle of fellow writers.[20] Most mundanely, the note allows Woolf to print the essay in its speech format, keeping the informality of tone and the address to an audience. Yet, in her other essays that are based on speeches, Woolf rarely includes *in the text* a note on a piece's origin, even when she keeps the speech text intact.[21] For example, when publishing *A*

---

[19] A few typos were corrected in the Hogarth Press publication. See "Character in Fiction" in McNeillie's edition for the specific changes.

[20] Rosenberg and Dubino's comment about Woolf and the essay form seems pertinent: "The essay. . .is a structure that takes its lead from the idea, essence, or being that comes before" (12). The introductory note is an essential part of this idea that defines and explains this essay.

[21] Daugherty identifies the essays that were originally lectures as "Mr. Bennett and Mrs. Brown," "How Should One Read a Book?," "The Narrow Bridge of Art," *A Room of One's Own*, "Professions for Women," and "The Leaning Tower" ("Taking a Leaf," 34). Of the four essays that I have not discussed above, three *do not* have notes about their origins in the publications that appeared during Woolf's lifetime. No note about the speech is attached to "How Should One Read a Book?" in its publication as part of the 1932 *Second Common Reader*. (I have been unable to view a copy of the October 1926 *Yale Review*, where it also appeared.) A version of "The Narrow Bridge of Art" was published during Woolf's lifetime as "Poetry, Fiction and the Future" in the *New York Herald Tribune* (14 and 21 August 1927); no note was included anywhere in the article. "Professions for Women" was only published posthumously (in *The Death of the Moth*

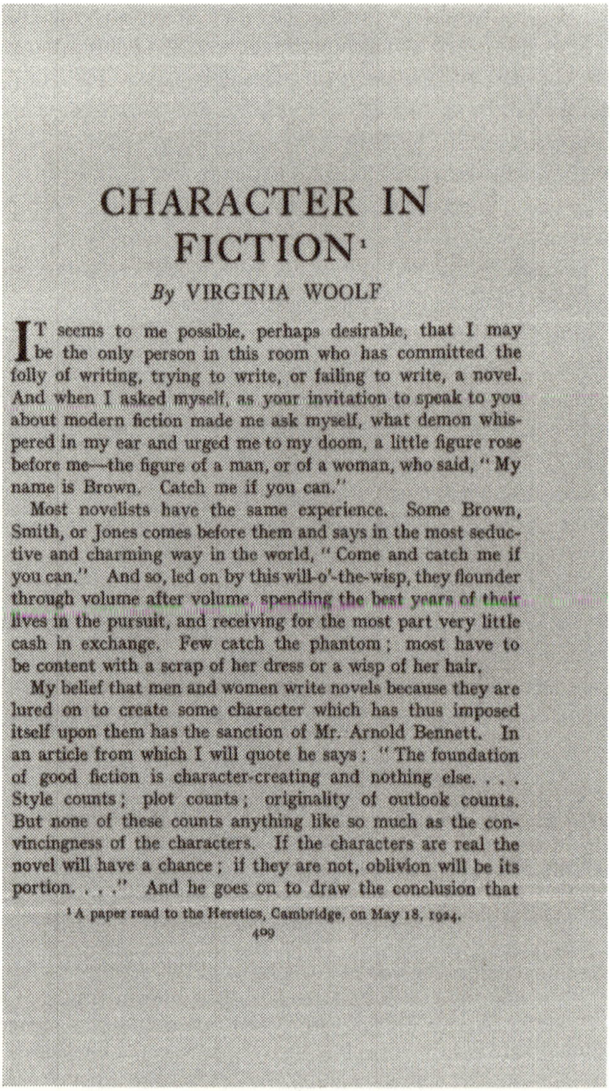

CHARACTER IN FICTION[1]

By VIRGINIA WOOLF

IT seems to me possible, perhaps desirable, that I may be the only person in this room who has committed the folly of writing, trying to write, or failing to write, a novel. And when I asked myself, as your invitation to speak to you about modern fiction made me ask myself, what demon whispered in my ear and urged me to my doom, a little figure rose before me—the figure of a man, or of a woman, who said, "My name is Brown. Catch me if you can."

Most novelists have the same experience. Some Brown, Smith, or Jones comes before them and says in the most seductive and charming way in the world, " Come and catch me if you can." And so, led on by this will-o'-the-wisp, they flounder through volume after volume, spending the best years of their lives in the pursuit, and receiving for the most part very little cash in exchange. Few catch the phantom; most have to be content with a scrap of her dress or a wisp of her hair.

My belief that men and women write novels because they are lured on to create some character which has thus imposed itself upon them has the sanction of Mr. Arnold Bennett. In an article from which I will quote he says : " The foundation of good fiction is character-creating and nothing else. . . . Style counts ; plot counts ; originality of outlook counts. But none of these counts anything like so much as the convincingness of the characters. If the characters are real the novel will have a chance ; if they are not, oblivion will be its portion. . . ." And he goes on to draw the conclusion that

[1] A paper read to the Heretics, Cambridge, on May 18, 1924.

409

Figure 2: First page of "Character in Fiction" in *The Criterion*, July 1924. This is the first published version of the essay to include the note about the Heretics. Courtesy of Widener Library, Harvard College Library P.142.7.

Room of One's Own, which emerged from two speeches, Woolf places a note on its origins in the Hogarth Press publication (1929), but on the page facing the publication information, separated from the text by three pages. The note's content also weakens the connection between the speech and the written essay, for it states: "This essay is based upon two papers read to the Arts Society at Newnham and the Odtaa at Girton in October 1928. The papers were too long to be read in full, and have since been altered and expanded." Though it mentions the essay's conception, it differentiates between the speeches and the published version, and therefore does not function with the same interpretive force as the Heretics note.[22]

The "Character in Fiction" note not only explains the style of the piece, but also locates it in the contemporary moment, thereby providing another interpretive layer for the reader to negotiate. In this way the note works against the abstraction of the title, fixing the speech as a response to a specific situation and audience.[23] It therefore identifies the essay, for readers who know of the Heretics society, as a piece that would appeal to a "freethinking" group, specifically one that identified itself as opposed to traditional forms of authority and analysis, even while operating within the intellectual establishment of the university. The paper thus positions itself as breaking from previous traditions and engaging in a particularly modern project, if for a relatively small audience of educated readers. Yet even for those unfamiliar with the group (as are most readers today, and probably many during her lifetime) the name alone—"The Heretics"—creates a similar image of the essay, if not one more radical. Thus, before even entering into the text, the note resolves some of the tendencies towards aestheticization promoted by the title and the surrounding pieces.

A few months later, Woolf published the essay herself as the first of the Hogarth Essay series. In this new context the piece reappears as *Mr. Bennett and Mrs. Brown*. The return to the original title reconnects the essay with its original

---

(1942); the included note is therefore Leonard Woolf's editorial addition. "The Leaning Tower" was published before Woolf's death in the Hogarth Press *Folios of New Writing* (Autumn 1940), and it did include a note that states: "A paper read to the Workers' Educational Association, Brighton, May 1940." (See Kirkpatrick for the publication trajectories of these essays.)

[22] For a reading of the other notes in *A Room of One's Own*—notes of explanation and erudition—see John Whittier-Ferguson's chapter on Woolf in *Framing Pieces*. Whittier-Ferguson argues that Woolf's use of notes in this essay "signal her awareness. . .that she writes always as part of a community of writers, and that every sentence of hers is framed in innumerable ways by the culture from which it springs" (81).

[23] Indeed, Eliot wrote to Woolf after receiving her essay that it was a "most important piece of historical criticism" (quoted in Lee, *Virginia Woolf*, 439).

form in the *Nation & Athenaeum*, and thus with the critique of Mr. Bennett. Yet the title performs a second function more pertinent for the reader. As *Mr. Bennett and Mrs. Brown*, the essay appears not as a literary critique, perhaps only interesting to writers and intellectuals, but as a story about two characters—Bennett and Brown. The title invites a larger audience into the piece, a necessary invitation because, for the first time, the essay was appearing in a single edition and not in the context of a periodical or newspaper. Though Woolf may have written to David Garnett early on in the history of the Hogarth Press to celebrate the small size of the audience, over the years the hobby had become a business, and the Woolfs became increasingly involved in selling their publications to a wider reading public. The financial success of the Press was becoming a matter of pride, as the 1923 press flyer illustrates:

> Of these [the nineteen publications] not one, we are glad to state, has failed to justify, even in a pecuniary sense, the faith we put in it. In each case both author and Press have found themselves in pocket and not out of pocket by their venture. When we remind you of the aims which we had in view in starting the Press, you will agree, I think, that these results are highly encouraging. (qtd. in Willis, 63)

Though 1924 saw fewer profits with a larger number of published books, the Press was entering a phase of increased productivity and the more readers that bought *Mr. Bennett and Mrs. Brown*, the better.

The cover of the Hogarth Press edition contributed to this welcoming atmosphere. Vanessa Bell, Virginia Woolf's sister who had designed the covers of multiple Hogarth books, provided a woodcut for the jacket illustration (Figure 3). The picture depicts a woman with her arms cradled like a Madonna and resting on an open book. The tilt of her head and the crescent line of her eyes makes her look almost asleep, and certainly relaxed. This drowsing Madonna of books renders the act of reading completely non-threatening, especially for the woman reader. The cover thereby invites all readers in for an informal and pleasurable experience, even as it also points to the central role played by women in producing modernist texts.[24]

Yet, as the first of the Hogarth Essays Series, *Mr. Bennett and Mrs. Brown* presented itself as more than an enjoyable read. In the month following its publication the press put out three other essays in the series: Roger Fry's *The Artist and Psycho-Analysis*, Theodora Bosanquet's *Henry James at Work*, and T. S.

---

[24] See Jayne Marek's *Women Editing Modernism* for a discussion of the role that women played in shaping modernist literary production.

Figure 3: Cover of the 1924 Hogarth Press edition of *Mr. Bennett and Mrs. Brown*. Illustration by Vanessa Bell. Courtesy of Widener Library, Harvard College Library Quad-828.B17 9W.

Eliot's *Homage to John Dryden* (Willis 108). As the first representative of the series, Woolf's essay foreshadowed the rigorously critical nature of the following contributions. After 1924, the Woolfs focused increasingly on nonfiction—literary and aesthetic theory, psychoanalysis, foreign affairs, economics, biography, and travel.[25] Part of this emphasis stemmed from the institution of different series—"The Hogarth Essays," the "Lectures on Literature," "Lectures on War and Peace," and "Day to Day Pamphlets"—which, as Mary Gaither argues, "were conceived of as a way, deliberately, to bring before the public significant ideas in literature, art, politics, and criticism" (22). Hogarth Press publications represented the forefront of modern intellectual thought and often entailed a definitive break from the mores and theories of the preceding generation. Thus Woolf's essay once again became firmly ensconced in a context that promoted its political and historical relevance. The note served a textual function similar to that of the Hogarth Press context. It rattled the ahistoric and fictional tone established by the title and the jacket design with its abrupt tug back into the contemporary moment and its small signal (via the reference to the Heretics) that this essay will critique established boundaries.

Almost a year later the essay made its American debut in the "Books" section of the *New York Herald Tribune*. "Mr. Bennett and Mrs. Brown" appeared in two parts (on August 23 and 30, 1925), complete with the note in the first installment, as well as with a brief statement under Woolf's name advertising the publication of *Mrs. Dalloway* and *The Common Reader* earlier that year. Though this edition reveals no profound changes in the linguistic code, the bibliographic context, like the note, positions the essay in both the literary and the extra-literary world. The placement of "Mr. Bennett and Mrs. Brown" in a newspaper connects it, albeit mechanically, to current events. The "Books" section calls itself "A Weekly Review of *Contemporary* Literature" (my italics)—asserting its role as the arbiter of the *present* state of literature. The picture occupying the prominent central space of the first page on August 23rd contributes to this mod-

---

[25] The Woolfs did not only publish the stories and poems of their circle, including such influential works as T. S. Eliot's *Poems*, *The Waste Land*, and essays; stories and essays by E. M. Forster; poems and essays by Robert Graves; works by Katherine Mansfield, Gertrude Stein, and John Maynard Keynes; and (of course) their own writing. They also brought out translations of Russian literature and a series on psychoanalysis, establishing new intellectual territory in England. In 1922 they began publishing translations of Freud's writing, and then took over the publication of the International Psycho-Analytic Library (IPL) in 1924, becoming the "sole English publishers of Freud's work in translation" (Willis 297).

Figure 4: Illustration of Carl Van Vechten next to the first installment of "Mr. Bennett and Mrs. Brown" in *The New York Herald Tribune* "Books" section, August 23, 1925.

ern tone, even though it accompanies the other front-page article (Figure 4). It displays a caricature of Carl Van Vechten, the author reviewed in the piece, dressed in shirt and tie and glowering into the distance. The background shows a bleak city scene of contemporary office buildings. Such an image of modern life rubs off onto "Mr. Bennett and Mrs. Brown," so that when Woolf claims near the bottom of the page that "about December 1910, human character changed," the frightening visage in the picture immediately presents itself as just such a particularly modern being.

In contrast, another element of the bibliographic code in the *New York Herald Tribune* (and one that Woolf likely had no control over) forced readers to dwell on the literary debate between the Georgians and the Edwardians. The first installment of the essay was divided in the middle of Woolf's critique of Wells, Galsworthy, and Bennett, ending with the line: "Their books, then, were incomplete as books, and required that the reader should finish them, actively and practically, for himself." The following Sunday, August 30th, the essay resumed with her statement: "Perhaps we can make this [the attitude of the Edwardians toward character] clearer if we take the liberty of imagining a little party in the railway carriage—Mr. Wells, Mr. Galsworthy, Mr. Bennett are travelling to Waterloo with Mrs. Brown." While the linguistic code is unchanged, aside from the editorial insertion that clarifies the demonstrative pronoun "this," the division emphasizes Woolf's critique of the Edwardians. The problems with these three writers, as articulated by Woolf in the first installment, would linger in the minds of readers during the intervening week, and then would be revisited in the first paragraphs of the second part.

"Mr. Bennett and Mrs. Brown" last appeared during Woolf's lifetime (aside from a second impression of the Hogarth Press edition) in a 1928 Doubleday collection published in the United States and titled *The Hogarth Essays*. In it the Doubleday editors compiled eleven of the essays from the Hogarth Series (both First and Second) that they viewed as particularly important and influential. "Mr. Bennett and Mrs. Brown" claims the place of honor as the first essay in the book, effectively setting the stage for the following pieces. Though this placement might simply appear as a logical reflection of the chronology of publication, an examination of the table of contents reveals no adherence to a chronological organizing system. Indeed, the second essay is number eight of the Second series, the third is number twelve of the First, the fourth is number six of the First, and so on. The choice of "Mr. Bennett and Mrs. Brown" as the leading piece must have had a non-chronological logic. The publisher's note in the beginning of the book suggests the underlying system, for it terms Leonard and Virginia Woolf as "representative figures" of this group of modern writers:

> *The Hogarth Essays*, The Hogarth Press, and Leonard and Virginia Woolf, in so far as they are respectively their characteristic expression, common publishing organ, and representative figures, stand for certain writers who have enough in common, in technique and interests, to be called a group. To those who have not yet encountered the work of this group and taken its measure for themselves, we may venture the introductory opinion that when critics come to look at the intellectual movements of our time they will rank the collective work of these writers as among the most significant of the period, and consider it, in its course and effect, among the more notable of the currents caused by groups that have appeared in English life and letters. (v-vi)

The publishers specifically set up their book as the harbinger of a new intellectual movement. Woolf's essay expresses this movement on three levels: as a member of the Hogarth Essay series and *The Hogarth Essays*, as the first essay printed by the "common publishing organ," and as a piece by one of the movement's "representative figures." The publisher also brings back an important aspect of "Mr. Bennett and Mrs. Brown" missing from the bibliographic code in publications since the *Nation & Athenaeum* edition—its prominent role in the ongoing debate about the state of modern fiction. The essay's content, which remained the same, had continued this theme throughout its publication history, but it lost its bibliographic resonance as its publication context changed. In *The Hogarth Essays,* Woolf's piece again acts not only as the introduction into this modern literary discourse, but also as a declaration around which discussions revolve. The publisher places the essay on "The Prospects of Literature" by Logan Pearsall Smith immediately after "Mr. Bennett and Mrs. Brown." Smith's essay directly responds to some of Woolf's claims about the state of modern writing, thus making her piece the center of a dialogue, just as it had been when first written.

Context and text all prove influential in determining the import of "Mr. Bennett and Mrs. Brown." Especially in Woolf's case, because of her involvement in the material production of books, reading outside the traditionally defined text seems imperative for editors and critics. Examining the contexts and the changing bibliographic codes of "Mr. Bennett and Mrs. Brown" reveals the essay's historical and political significance and message—its role as a literary-political manifesto that calls into question the materialistic vision of the previous generation and, therefore, uncovers more truthfully contemporary experience. Taking note of these issues in Woolf's essay means taking the note as an integral part of the whole.

Works Cited

Bennett, Arnold. "Is the Novel Decaying?" *Things That Have Interested Me, Third Series*. New York: George H. Doran Company, 1926. 160-163.

Beresford, J. D. "The Successors of Charles Dickens." *Nation & Athenaeum*, Dec. 29, 1923: 487-8. Rpt. in *Virginia Woolf: The Critical Heritage*. Ed. Majumdar and McLaurin. 120-123.

Bornstein, George. "How to Read a Page: Modernism and Material Textuality." *Studies in the Literary Imagination* 32.1 (Spring 1999): 29-58.

Bowlby, Rachel, ed. *A Woman's Essays: Selected Essays I*, by Virginia Woolf. London: Penguin, 1992.

Chaney, Graham. *A Literary History of Cambridge*. New York: Cambridge University Press, 1985.

Cuddy-Keane, Melba. *Virginia Woolf, the Intellectual, and the Public Sphere*. New York: Cambridge University Press, 2003.

Daugherty, Beth Rigel. "Readin', Writin', and Revisin': Virginia Woolf's 'How Should One Read a Book?'" *Virginia Woolf and the Essay*. Ed. Beth Carole Rosenberg and Jeanne Dubino. New York: St. Martin's Press, 1997. 159-176.

———. "Taking a Leaf from Virginia Woolf's Book: Empowering the Student." *Virginia Woolf Miscellanies: Proceedings of the First Annual Conference on Virginia Woolf*. Ed. Mark Hussey and Vara Neverow-Turk. New York: Pace University Press, 1992. 31-40.

———. "The Whole Contention Between Mr. Bennett and Mrs. Woolf, Revisited." *Virginia Woolf: Centennial Essays*. Ed. Elaine K. Ginsberg and Laura Moss Gottlieb. Troy, New York: The Whitson Publishing Company, 1983. 269-294.

Deacon, Richard. *The Cambridge Apostles: A History of Cambridge University's Elite Intellectual Secret Society*. London: Robert Royce Ltd., 1985.

Gaither, Mary E. "The Hogarth Press: 1917-1938." *A Checklist of the Hogarth Press, 1917-1938*. Ed. J. Howard Woolmer. Andes, New York: Woolmer/Brotherson LTD, 1976.

Hynes, Samuel. "The Whole Contention between Mr. Bennett and Mrs. Woolf." *NOVEL: A Forum on Fiction* 1.1 (1967): 34-44.

Kirkpatrick, B. J. and Stuart N. Clarke. *A Bibliography of Virginia Woolf*. 4th ed. New York: Oxford University Press, 1997.

Lee, Hermione. *Virginia Woolf*. 1996. New York: Vintage Books, 1999.

———. "Virginia Woolf's Essays." *The Cambridge Companion to Virginia Woolf.* Eds. Sue Roe and Susan Sellers. New York: Cambridge University Press, 2000. 91-108.

Majumdar, Robin and Allen McLaurin, eds. *Virginia Woolf: The Critical Heritage.* Boston: Routledge & Kegan Paul, 1975.

Marek, Jayne. *Women Editing Modernism: "Little" Magazines and Literary Publishing.* Lexington: University of Kentucky Press, 1995.

McNeillie, Andrew, ed. *The Essays of Virginia Woolf, Volume Three, 1919-1924*, by Virginia Woolf. New York: Harcourt Brace Jovanovich, 1988.

Pure, Simon [Frank Swinnerton]. Review of "Character in Fiction." *Bookman* October 1924: 193-195. Rpt. in *Virginia Woolf: The Critical Heritage.* Ed. Majumdar and McLaurin.130-132.

Rosenbaum, S. P. *Aspects of Bloomsbury.* New York: St. Martin's Press, 1998.

Rosenberg, Beth Carole and Jeanne Dubino. Introduction. *Virginia Woolf and the Essay.* Ed. Rosenberg and Dubino. New York: St. Martin's Press, 1997. 1-24.

Silver, Brenda. "Textual Criticism as Feminist Practice: Or, Who's Afraid of Virginia Woolf Part II." *Representing Modernist Texts: Editing as Interpretation.* Ed. George Bornstein. Ann Arbor: University of Michigan Press, 1991. 193-222.

Whittier-Ferguson, John. *Framing Pieces: Designs of the Gloss in Joyce, Woolf, and Pound.* New York: Oxford University Press, 1996.

Willis, J. H. *Leonard and Virginia Woolf as Publishers: The Hogarth Press, 1917-41.*Charlottesville: University Press of Virginia, 1992.

Woolf, Virginia. *The Captain's Death Bed and Other Essays.* New York: Harcourt, Brace & Company, 1950.

———. "Character in Fiction." [Transcription of the speech to the Heretics.] *The Essays of Virginia Woolf: Volume Three, 1919-1924.* Ed. Andrew McNeillie. 501-517.

———. "Character in Fiction." *The Criterion* July 1924: 409-430.

———. "Character in Fiction." *The Essays of Virginia Woolf, Volume Three, 1919-1924.* Ed. Andrew McNeillie. 420-438.

———. *Collected Essays: Volume I.* New York: Harcourt, Brace & World, 1967.

———. *The Diary of Virginia Woolf: Volume II: 1920-1924.* Ed. Anne Olivier Bell. London: The Hogarth Press, 1978.

———. *The Essays of Virginia Woolf, Volume Three, 1919-1924.* Ed. Andrew McNeillie. NewYork: Harcourt Brace Jovanovich, 1988.

———. *The Letters of Virginia Woolf, Volume 2.* Ed. Nigel Nicolson and Joanne Trautmann. New York: Harcourt Brace Jovanovich, 1976.

——. "Mr. Bennett and Mrs. Brown." *New York Evening Post*, Nov. 17, 1923, 4: 253-4.
——. "Mr. Bennett and Mrs. Brown." *Nation & Athenaneum,* Dec. 1, 1923: 342-343.
——. *Mr. Bennett and Mrs. Brown*. London: Hogarth Press, 1924.
——. "Mr. Bennett and Mrs. Brown." *New York Herald Tribune* 23 and 30 Aug. 1925, 5: 1-3; 1-4.
——. "Mr. Bennett and Mrs. Brown." *The Hogarth Essays*. New York: Doubleday, Doran, & Company, 1928. 1-28.
——. "Mr. Bennett and Mrs. Brown." *The Essays of Virginia Woolf, Volume Three, 1919-1924*. Ed. Andrew McNeillie. 384-89.
——. *A Room of One's Own*. New York: Harcourt Brace Jovanovich, 1989.
——. *Virginia Woolf: Selections from Her Essays*. Ed. Walter James. London: Chatto and Windus, 1966.
——. *The Virginia Woolf Reader*. Ed. Mitchell Leaska. New York: Harcourt, 1984.
——. *A Writer's Diary.* Ed. Leonard Woolf. London: The Hogarth Press, 1965.
Woolmer, J. Howard. *A Checklist of the Hogarth Press, 1917-1938*. Woolmer/Brotherson LTD, 1976.

A Plot Unraveling into Ethics: Woolf, Levinas, and "Time Passes"

David Sherman

I

> *Temporalization as lapse, the loss of time, is neither an initiative of an ego, nor a movement toward some telos of action. The loss of time is not the work of a subject. . . . Time passes.*
>
> —Levinas, *Otherwise Than Being* (51-52)

> *For a long time it was thought that language had mastery over time, that it acted both as the future bond of the promise and as memory and narrative; it was thought to be prophecy and history. . . . In fact, it is only a formless rumbling, a streaming; its power resides in its dissimulation. That is why it is one with the erosion of time; it is depthless forgetting and the transparent emptiness of waiting.*
>
> —Michel Foucault, "Maurice Blanchot: The Thought From the Outside" (55)

In diary entries, Woolf describes "Time Passes," the short middle chapter of *To the Lighthouse* in which the Ramsays' uninhabited summer house ages ten years, as "this impersonal thing, which I'm dared to do by my friends, the flight of time" and "the most difficult abstract piece of writing . . . all eyeless and featureless with nothing to cling to" (*D3* 36, 76). These suggestive phrases for the chapter's dislocations from normal life help us appreciate its strange narrative qualities, its intimation of a not-quite-human voice that seems to cling to nothing in order to cling to the passing of time. Yet, as many critics have noticed in recent years, this section is not simply an exercise in abstraction or formalism; the perspective of "Time Passes" is distinct from the rest of the novel—and new to modernism—but not because it moves from particularity to generality, from contingent events to their essential forms.[1] The haunting narrative unlocatability of

---

[1] Even within the current diversity of established critical approaches to "Time Passes," there is a recurring tendency (provided, in part, by Woolf's diary terms) to read the narrative detachment of the chapter principally as an exercise in abstraction or formalism, even if such characterizations are subordinated to other arguments and critical contexts. Recently, Christine Froula has described the chapter as a turn to "formal abstractness" that gives "symbolic refuge from time and death" in a process that (in terms taken from Wilhelm Wörringer's *Abstraction and Empathy*) "abstracts the poetics of loss

its language carries a palpable stillness and silence, an almost reverential care not to wake the sleeping and dead, rather than narrative omniscience or objectivity. In this essay, I discuss the fragile stillness and delicate lyricism around the absences of "Time Passes," not as abstraction, but as the narrative poetics of alterity, the poetics of the subject's intuition of its responsibility towards others, and especially of its involvement in the deaths of others. I argue that Woolf anticipates concepts in ethical criticism and philosophy regarding the subject's response to the death of the other as the origin of time. "Time Passes" is an especially vivid example of an important strain in Woolf's writing—I also refer briefly to *Jacob's Room, Mrs. Dalloway*, and *A Room of One's Own*—in which the death of the other inaugurates the subject's temporality, and in which this temporality exceeds the subject's knowledge by virtue of its impossible ethical demand.

In other words, I argue that the narrator of "Time Passes" speaks with the ethically-inflected voice of selfhood bound to the other more than to its own being, a self for whom the fullness of autonomous identity is not a sufficient meaning of the human. For these few pages, Woolf leaves the familiar horizons of traditional Western subjectivity to narrate in the voice of its unnarratable, voiceless exteriority, rendering intelligible a void in consciousness that is hard to describe or imagine. This can be thought as something like an eclipse,[2] a shadow saturated with light that evades or pains our seeing. Locating the exteriority of self, like grasping darkness as a substantial thing, confuses familiar notions of identity and difference, giving what is other and alien a value that is not compatible with the internal economy of self. To describe "Time Passes" in terms of alterity and exteriority instead of abstraction is to suggest that its narrative tech-

---

into a formal 'crystal of intensity' with affinities to... theories of abstract art" (153, 130). Similarly, Alice van Buren Kelley claims that by abstracting experience, this narrative experiment "affirm[s] the continual existence of meaning, of pattern behind appearances, even in the face of the greatest upheaval" (105). Various others also refer, sometimes casually, to "Time Passes" as abstraction that resists different kinds of chaos. See Perry Meisel, *The Absent Father: Virginia Woolf and Walter Pater* (New Haven: Yale UP, 1980) 198; Martin Corner, "Mysticism and Atheism in *To the Lighthouse*," *Virginia Woolf's To the Lighthouse*, ed. Harold Bloom (New York: Chelsea House, 1988) 43-58; and Oddvar Holmeland, *Form as Compensation for Life: Fictive Patterns in Virginia Woolf's Novels* (Columbia, SC: Camden House, 1998) 128-29.

[2] Jane Goldman also uses this analogy for "Time Passes," but for a very different purpose: it is "a kind of eclipse since it marks the occlusion of one way of life, or one sense of subjectivity, and leads to the emergence of another. This elegiac movement may be considered in terms of gendered and contested subjectivity" (169). Goldman's reading of this eclipse—that in it "the gender of subjectivity seems to have become unfixed" (177)—elaborates in more identity-political terms my phenomenological concern with the subject's representation of its ethicality to itself.

nique animates difference as a meaningful discrepancy in being, rather than subsuming difference in identity or rendering it an object for the subject's grasp. Alterity, in this sense, differs from Wilhelm Wörringer's emphasis on modernist abstraction in that it does not provide solace to a self vulnerable to death and decay by creating a new (aesthetic) order; rather, alterity is the experience of selfhood that achieves an ethical value in its relation to others.[3] Exteriority and alterity, as this essay explores them, do not oppose subjectivity in the same way that objectivity does. "Time Passes" is not non-subjective narration because it is somehow "objective," free from idiosyncratic perspectives, but because it dislocates its idiosyncratic perspectives from a discrete mind that might contain them.[4] The voice of the chapter is the voice of a subject that is other than and outside itself; in this difference from itself, it is able to approach the difference of others without subsuming them as the same.

We might think of this otherness from self—not in abstraction or objectivity, but in difference and alterity—as an undoing of self, a dissolution of the self-same identity of consciousness in currents of language and time. Woolf puts in narrative form the impulses of a long continental philosophical tradition that questions the priority and certainty of the individual, self-possessed ego—a tradition that runs from Hegel through Foucault and Derrida, approximately, against claims by such philosophers as Descartes and Locke that the self is best understood as rationally self-interested, epistemologically and ethically autonomous, and sovereign over its private being and property. "Time Passes" is in the voice of this ideal's undoing, a narration of what, in the last chapter of *A Room of One's Own*, Woolf calls the "shapeless mist" in "the shadow of the 'I'," the restless excess in selfhood that comes in moments at which language and time cannot be reduced to one's consciousness and intentionality (*AROO* 104). In this chapter of *Room*, Woolf dramatizes such a moment: she describes how passersby in the street "all seemed separate, self-absorbed, on business of their own" until a "lull and suspension" in traffic gives "a signal pointing to a force in things which one had overlooked. It seemed to point to a river, which flowed past, invisibly,

---

[3] Wörringer, who has influenced many Woolf critics, writes that "the urge to abstraction finds its beauty in the life-denying inorganic, in the crystalline or, in general terms, in all abstract law and necessity" (4). Especially since he relates this characterization of modern art primarily to the plastic arts (3), it is important to trace the elements of "Time Passes" that are modern without a "life-denying" inorganicism.

[4] While Erich Auerbach's classic, influential insight in *Mimesis* that the novel's "exterior events have actually lost their hegemony" and "serve to release and interpret inner events" is no doubt true, the point is that there is another sense of exteriority available in Woolf's language, a sense that supersedes this subject-object dialectic altogether (538).

around the corner, down the street, and took people and eddied them along" (*AROO* 100). Sharing this current, momentarily removed from their individual self-importance, these are figures for the dissolution of the subject's identification with itself as a self. In "Time Passes," I argue, Woolf helps us understand this dissolution of the "I am" as an ethical response to another's death, a way of mourning performed by the modern subject.[5]

Woolf charges the mournful otherness of the narrative voice in "Time Passes" with the meaning of time, coupling time and exteriority as mutually unthinkable, unsubsumable enigmas: time passing is the untraceable signature of the other, especially of the other's death, in which the self is involved in ways that it cannot fully represent to itself. Time passing, in Woolf's chapter, is not time as we notice or measure it, but time that anticipates the "diachrony," "infinity," and "pure patience" of Emmanuel Levinas. These concepts help us think time without familiar subjective-objective or psychological-physical oppositions; Woolf shows time passing as neither of these.[6] Rather, she shows time as the ethical distortion and interruption of identity, the subject's dispossession of itself in its encounter with alterity. Woolf thinks time, not as the subject's object, but as its exteriority—an "exteriority which is not objective" (Levinas, "Intentionalité et métaphysique," quoted in Derrida 85).[7] By considering the

---

[5] Robin Paula Silbergleid reads Woolf's lyricism generally as "a way of dealing ethically and aesthetically with loss," focusing on "Time Passes," which "in particular demonstrates the convergence of formal and thematic losses in Woolf's work" (58). In contrast with my reading of this lyricism as an expression of self's relation to alterity, however, Silbergleid reads this lyricism as a technique that "removes the deaths of Mrs. Ramsay, Prue, and Andrew from the novel's linear flow of time" with an "omniscient point of view" (58). As I explain below, I disagree that "Time Passes" has an "omniscient" (i.e., heterodiegetic) point of view.

[6] In his historical materialist examination of this opposition, David Harvey insists that "subjective" (stream of consciousness, durée) and "objective" (clock, calendar) time are flip sides of the same coin: "Public time was becoming ever more homogenous and universal across space.... Indeed, it was only in terms of such a public sense of time that reference to private could make sense" (266-67). Shaun Gallagher makes a similar point about "objective" time as ultimately reducible to the solipsistic "theater of subjectivity" in philosophical terms: "Even objective time, to the extent that it is allowed to play its role, is something that is filtered through individual consciousness, something that appears at the end of the intentional process, a constituted noematic time" (108).

[7] Again, this is to put in a new context Auerbach's early, important observation that Woolf contrasts "the brief span of time occupied by the exterior event and the dreamlike wealth of a process which traverses a whole subjective universe" in an "elaboration of the contrast between 'exterior' and 'interior' time" (538). While this contrast is important in Woolf, I'm focusing on time as it exceeds the subject, not because it is objective or quantified (which doesn't really exceed the subject at all), but because it achieves an ethical meaning more important than the meaning of identity.

relations among time, exteriority, and the ethics of mourning in "Time Passes," we can better appreciate what ethical criticism of modernism can gain by paying attention to modernist representations of time. In other words, we can reckon with Ned Lukacher's insight that "the first step toward reversing philosophy's foreclosure of the other is to think the otherness of time" (18).[8] Following Lukacher, I hope to demonstrate that time provides modernism with a crucial poetics of the self's relation to alterity.

What does it mean to think "authentic," "primordial" time without reducing it to inner flux or stream of consciousness, to some immediacy of subjectivity or immanence of being? How can we approach time, as we most desire to know it, not as the first alibi for the subject's private interiority and ontological weight (as Bergson's durée or Heidegger's horizon of being), but as the possibility of the subject's ethical transcendence of self-sameness, as the risk of its dissolution in exteriority? We might start by reversing Augustine's famous complaint—"What then is time? Provided that no one asks me, I know" (230)—into a different kind of admission: "What then is time? I know only when another asks me, and when I can acknowledge this asking." Time as the interruption of the other, the event of alterity; for Levinas, time as the subject's non-synchrony with itself in revelation of the other's sheer diachrony, this "slippage of the earth beneath my feet" of an "irrevocable lapse" in which we acknowledge "the impossible synthesis of I and the Other" (*God, Death, and Time*, 111). In other words, time as it is at stake in Levinas's ethical philosophy is not inscribed in any isolated, individual subject, but emerges at this subject's—the traditional Western subject's—vanishing point, when it is powerless, in the face of the other, to merely inhabit itself: "the situation of the face-to-face" is "the very accomplishment of time" (*Time and the Other*, 79). This "accomplishment" of time is this inherited version of subjectivity becoming strange to itself, feeling the residue in its identity of an excessive responsibility, a responsibility for the other that exceeds the subject's self-knowledge and self-possession. For Levinas, the experience of this strange

---

[8] See also Elizabeth Grosz's meditations on time in terms of Becoming, emergence, the new, and futurity as "modalities of difference" (38). In a Deleuzean return to Bergson, Grosz approaches time as "a movement of differentiation, divergence and self-surpassing or actualisation of virtualities in the light of the contingencies that befall them" (52). While this description of time values the non-identity of the present with itself as a kind of temporal alterity, Grosz's interest in the contingency and unpredictability of the future contrasts with Levinas's interest in ethics, an interest in the alterity of time as always and inevitably leading to one non-contingent event: the revelation of God in the Other. (For a wide-ranging and creative discussion of temporal indeterminacy and emergence in narrative, complementary to Grosz's, see Gary Saul Morson's *Narrative and Freedom: The Shadows of Time* (New Haven: Yale UP, 1994).

excess registers as temporality, as the subject's diachronic sway and flow through the tenses of being.

To think of the subject's temporality as a function of its ethicality, to approach time as the phenomenological representation of responsibility for the other and implication in the death of the other, helps us understand Woolf's narrative technique in "Time Passes." Between two longer chapters taking place on single days ten years apart, "Time Passes" is a kind of connective interlude, a pause in the dramas of interiority that define the rest of the novel. With characters' interiorities held in abeyance, de-focalized by the shifting and ever-withdrawing narrator, the events of these ten years take on the strange half-light of a world made intelligible without being perceived, as if it were a memory held by someone who had never experienced it, or as if the house itself were remembering from within its own emptiness.[9] This play between presence and absence is the narrative voice of phenomena in exteriority, overheard second-hand by a subject, retaining its echo-like distance and difference from interiority:

> And now as if the cleaning and the scrubbing and the scything and the mowing had drowned it there rose that half-heard melody, that intermittent music which the ear half catches but lets fall; a bark, a bleat; irregular, intermittent, yet somehow related; the hum of an insect, the tremor of cut grass, dissevered yet somehow belonging; the jar of a dor-beetle, the squeak of a wheel, loud, low, but mysteriously related; which the ear strains to bring together and is always on the verge of harmonising, but they are never quite heard, never fully harmonised, and at last, in the evening, one after another, the sounds die out, and the harmony falters, and silence falls. (*TTL* 212)

It is a single sentence taken by its rhythms beyond itself, musically overriding its syntax into lyrical fragments. That these fragments are sonically interwoven with as much care as something by Hopkins—notice the metered repetitions of the first 15 or so words; the assonance and consonance of the second, third, and fifth lines; the cadenced shifts among short and long clauses in the sequence after the final semi-colon—complicates the passage's final statement about incoherence,

---

[9] I consider these somewhat impressionistic descriptions compatible with Ann Banfield's analytical descriptions of the narrative liminality of "Time Passes" and the interludes in *The Waves* in terms of the epistemology of the unperceived: "The unobserved thus finds in the novel a 'neutral monist' language. In between Russell's division of the sensible ("I see X") and the physical ("There is X"), Woolf explores the neutral ("Here there was X") representing a sense-datum without 'I'" (318). See also Banfield's more recent essay on the influence of Cambridge time philosophy and Post-Impressionist aesthetics on the design of *To the Lighthouse*, and especially "Time Passes," in "Time Passes: Virginia Woolf, Post-Impressionism, and Cambridge Time," *Poetics Today* 24.3 (2003) 471-516.

silence. There is an unlocatable presence embedded in the almost-related world itself, but the world pauses at the threshold of a subject's knowing, suggesting meanings and relations but not assimilating, mediating, or realizing them in the interiority and intentionality of consciousness.

We might better understand this non-interiorized perception and narration in "Time Passes" by comparing it to Woolf's earlier experiment with such narrative ambiguity in *Jacob's Room*. In this novel, narrative speech moves in and out of clear subject positions; Woolf makes an especially dramatic display of such narrative detachment by repeating the same episode in a forest, the second undoing the defined focalization of the first:

> The upper wings of the moth which Jacob held were undoubtedly marked with kidney-shaped spots of fulvous hue. But there was no crescent upon the underwing. The tree had fallen the night he caught it. There had been a volley of pistol-shots suddenly in the depths of the wood. . . .
> The tree had fallen, though it was a windless night, and the lantern, stood upon the ground, had lit up the still green leaves and the dead beech leaves. It was a dry place. A toad was there. And the red underwing had never come back, though Jacob had waited. (*JR* 17)

> . . .If you stand a lantern under a tree every insect in the forest creeps up to it—a curious assembly, since though they scramble and swing and knock their heads against the glass, they seem to have no purpose—something senseless inspires them. One gets tired of watching them, as they amble round the lantern and blindly tap as if for admittance, one large toad being the most besotted of any and shouldering his way through the rest. Ah, but what's that? A terrifying volley of pistol-shots rings out—cracks sharply; ripples spread—silence laps smooth over sound. A tree—a tree has fallen, a sort of death in the forest. After that, the wind in the trees sounds melancholy. (*JR* 25)

This explicit de-focalization[10] can be read as a subtle prefiguration of Jacob's death in the war—the tree "a sort of death," pistol sounds, mourning wind—associating death with narrative effacement. Woolf renders this effacement, this narrative non-personhood that witnesses an unwitnessed scene, as a kind of game: if nobody is in a forest, what language does nobody use to describe the sound of a falling tree? Or, in another turn of the screw: if nobody—a narrator

---

[10] While the second passage might be interpreted as a representation of Jacob's private thoughts from his own first-person perspective, unmediated by the narrator that organizes the rest of the novel, this interpretation strains against the impersonality of the framing pronouns ("you," "one"—no "I") and the extreme atypicality of such direct access to his interiority. It seems much more likely to me that this passage remains in the speech of the slyly ironic, floating narrator that precedes and follows, and that this narrator has simply done away with Jacob's presence for the moment.

with no intelligible subject position of its own and that falls between the cracks of character subject positions—narrates, what sound does it make when it tries to use the word "I"? Later in *Jacob's Room*:

> Only to prevent us from being submerged by chaos, nature and society between them have arranged a system of classification which is simplicity itself; stalls, boxes, amphitheatres, gallery. The moulds are filled nightly. There is no need to distinguish details. But the difficulty remains—one has to choose. For though I have no wish to be Queen of England—or only for a moment—I would willingly sit beside her; I would hear the Prime Minister's gossip; the countess whisper, and share her memories of halls and gardens; the massive fronts of the respectable conceal after all their secret code; or why so impermeable? And then, doffing one's own headpiece, how strange to assume for a moment some one's—any one's—to be a man of valour who has ruled the Empire; to refer while Brangäne sings to the fragments of Sophocles, or see in a flash, as the shepherd pipes his tune, bridges and aqueducts. But no—we must choose. Never was there a harsher necessity! or one which entails greater pain, more certain disaster; for wherever I seat myself, I die in exile. (*JR* 57)

This sudden and brief first-person enters the text to lament the fatal constrictions of identity, refusing fully to submit to the exigencies it describes by trying to sit somewhere beside identity, as if to overhear it without being implicated. There is no character who corresponds to this "I," but it sounds enough like a person in this moment—it suffers enough from proximity to identity—to register an elusive subjectivity. We might consider it the voice of an unconfirmed hypothesis of subjectivity, a focalization of the condition that precedes the formulated subjectivity we experience as personhood. Speaking as a potential subject, and not as a transcendent or totalized one, the narrator's authority is derived not from omniscience but from its mastery of fragmentariness, contingency, and irony.[11] Something other than consciousness as we know it is at work here, and in the passage from "Time Passes" above: these modes of consciousness are not temporalized as the coherence of identity narrating itself securely from past to future; rather, as Levinas later puts it, "this is the temporality in which the plots of being and ontology are unraveled in ethics" (*Entre-nous*, 153).[12]

---

[11] Ronald Schleifer describes Woolf's disembodied narration in a similar fashion, as one of the "disembodiments" common "at the turn of the twentieth century" that—rather than being a "transcendental disembodiment of a view from nowhere"—"are as vague as the subtle rhythms of experience, haunting not quite 'positively' the edges of things" (126). In other words, Woolf's narrators are "anonymous, but whose anonymity, like Clarissa Dalloway herself, exists in the position of dispersal rather than a transcendental future" (ibid.).

[12] Levinas occasionally describes this ethical interruption of ontology in narrative

Untangling, in his large body of work, the plot of being as it has unfolded through Western philosophy, Levinas seeks an alternative to "ontological categories" to think "the proximity of the one to the other," an alternative to thinking of the other as either an adjunct or limitation to the self's being, essence, and identity (*Otherwise Than Being*, 15). Levinas suggests that this "one" need not approach its "other" as that which it must either totally exclude from or subsume within itself; for Levinas, the subject has a capacity beyond treating the other as either "a limit or complement to the accomplishment of the adventure of essence" (ibid., 16). There is a more important adventure that gives selfhood its value and meaning: the ethical encounter with the other, in which assuming one's responsibility for the other is the defining mystery of the self. Levinas uses the "trope" of "the-one-for-the-other" to radicalize ethics beyond normative rules and invoke an originary, primordial obligation to alterity, an "allegiance of the same to the other," at the heart of being and identity (ibid., 100, 25).

This ethical alternative to ontological terms for approaching alterity is, more generally, an alternative to "the dialectic of being and nothingness in the flow of time," a way of understanding the relation between life and death without making them simple, mutual negations (*God, Death, and Time*, 14). "Time Passes" is so exemplary an instance of modern fiction because it occupies the same irreducible liminality in this dialectic, becoming a third term in the traditional opposition between homodiegetic and heterodiegetic narration, somewhere in the realm of free indirect discourse but without recognizable minds to anchor and focalize speech. In this chapter, narrative speech arrives anonymously and remains exterior, the passive voice of what Levinas calls an "atmospheric density, a plenitude of the void, ... the impersonal 'field of forces' of existing" (*Time and the Other*, 46). It is neither being nor nothingness, a narration at the outskirts of ontology that correlates to an "existing without existents," to "the fact that there is [*il y a*]," to a disembodied passivity of presence that precedes or survives actual beings (ibid., 45-6). Returning to a strain of thought about the impersonality of Being that is especially important in Heidegger (whose "*es gibt*" anticipates Levinas's "*il y a*"), he explores this "irremissibility of pure existing" when "there is neither anyone nor anything that takes this existence upon itself" (ibid., 47).

This idea of an "ambience of being" that is "behind every negation" helps us read the presence that Woolf ascribes to nothingness (ibid., 48):

> So with the lamps all put out, the moon sunk, and a thin rain drumming on the roof a downpouring of immense darkness began. Nothing, it seemed, could sur-

---

terms, e.g.: "This responsibility appears as a plot without a beginning, anarchic" (*Otherwise than Being*, 135); "One is tempted to call this plot religious. . ." (ibid., 147).

vive the flood, the profusion of darkness which, creeping in at keyholes and crevices, stole round window blinds, came into bedrooms, swallowed up here a jug and basin, there a bowl of red and yellow dahlias, there the sharp edges and firm bulk of a chest of drawers. Not only was furniture confounded; there was scarcely anything left of body or mind by which one could say, "This is he" or "This is she." Sometimes a hand was raised as if to clutch something or ward off something, or somebody groaned, or somebody laughed aloud as if sharing a joke with nothingness. (*TTL* 189-90)

No character's perspective mediates, but this is not simply omniscient, abstract, or objective narration; rather, it is as if the voice is following in the wake of subjectivity, nostalgic for being as it knows and affirms itself—for being in its self-recognition. This voice is intimately situated in the scene, but the agency resides entirely with nothingness, darkness, figures for negation. This negation is focalized as a source of experience and knowledge, personifying the void that, because it is the defining limitation of consciousness, consciousness cannot represent to itself. Yet—and this is the remarkable thing—the language quietly registers a mind present and at work: the cautious "it seemed," implying someone there to whom it seemed; the deictics associated with someone's particular perspective: "here a jug. . ., there a bowl. . ., there the sharp edges. . ."; and, in the first two sentences, the figural collapsing of darkness and rain, an analogy showing a mind's interpretive involvement in the scene and desire to communicate how it feels. It is as if Woolf's diary description of "nothing to cling to" describes our clinging, literally, to a nothingness that articulates itself.[13]

This quasi-wakefulness in the night of "Time Passes" achieves what might be called a narrative insomnia, a preternatural vigilance in the narrator that exceeds the available means of being a subject. In what condition do we find subjectivity when, without daybreak, "Night. . . succeeds to night" (*TTL* 192)? The idea of insomnia, or sleeplessness, is philosophically suggestive (and has been taken up by various modern thinkers—Kierkegaard, Nietzsche, Blanchot, Cioran): insomnia is the continuation of subjectivity by other means, a mind that has fallen out of the dialectic of waking and sleeping, being and nothingness. No longer bound by these rhythms and repetitions, insomniac consciousness makes less sense, loses its bearings, is unable to return to itself in a self-recognizing

---

[13] In his essay "The Narrative Voice (the 'he,' the neuter)," Blanchot describes a similar quality of narration (with reference to Kafka and Duras, in particular) in which, in his terms, "the speech of the tale always lets us feel that what is being told is not being told by anyone: it speaks in the neuter," in which "the other speaks" (*The Gaze of Orpheus*, 140, 141). The neuter speaks "from nowhere, suspended in the tale as a whole" and "comes from exteriority itself, the outside that is the special enigma of language in writing" (142). And so on.

embrace after an absence. Subjectivity uninterrupted by sleep is an Odysseus who never leaves home, an eventless epic; or it is a visual perspective into distance without a horizon, extended to the point of emptiness. We can think of narrative insomnia, the voice of wakefulness that stirs while characters sleep in "Time Passes," as storytelling without the limiting horizons of past, present, or future. In other words, insomniac narrative is unbound by a familiar sense of time. It warps time, creating a subjectivity that voices itself not-in-the-present-tense, non-synchronously, as time passing or even surpassing the subject.[14] As Levinas describes Blanchot's writing: "Thus is diachrony restored to time. A nocturnal time. . . . A diachrony without protention or retention, . . . the opposite of subjectivity" ("The Servant and Her Master" 155).

Woolf restores diachrony to the subject's synchrony by making a complicated perspectival move: she gives voice to this insomniac consciousness without domesticating it; she narrates from inside its exteriority. The wandering airs and random lights, the narrator's empty placeholders for focalized subjects, are refused entry to the recognizable interiorities before them:

> So some random light directing them with its pale footfall upon stair and mat, from some uncovered star, or wandering ship, or the Lighthouse even, the little airs mounted the staircase and nosed round bedroom doors. But here surely, they must cease. Whatever else may perish and disappear, what lies here is steadfast. Here one might say to those sliding lights, those fumbling airs that breathe and bend over the bed itself, here you can neither touch nor destroy. Upon which, wearily, ghostlily, as if they had feather-light fingers and the light persistency of feathers, they would look, once, on the shut eyes, and the loosely clasping fingers, and fold their garments wearily and disappear. (*TTL* 191)

Woolf grammatically frames the air and light as speculative and conditional personifications, as estranged representations of consciousness, reinforcing their rejection from the inhabited bedrooms that they approach. This estrangement from interiority—showing interiority from outside, and this outside from inside—is one way to understand insomnia. Levinas characterizes the impersonal *there is* as "a vigilance without possible recourse to sleep" or "refuge in unconsciousness," a consciousness "without the possibility of withdrawing into sleep as into a private domain" (*Time and the Other*, 48-9). This idea that the self gets tired of being itself, and that it cannot remain itself without periods of anni-

---

[14] Emile Benveniste helps us understand the fundamental violation that this speech not-in-the-present-tense represents: "there is no other criterion and no other expression by which to indicate 'the time at which one *is*' except to take it as 'the time at which one *is* speaking.' This is the eternally 'present' moment" (227). My point is simply that Woolf's narrator is somehow speaking outside of this eternally present moment.

hilation, suggests that interiority and exteriority are not separate positions, but part of the same one, and that we inhabit our subjectivity only to the extent that we can also be excluded from it. "Time Passes" is an attempt to represent this exclusion.

Woolf's narrative position within exteriority, looking at interiority from its beyond, may be approached with Levinas's elusive, often fragmented concept of diachrony (a concept in relation to which we, as his readers, necessarily feel positioned outside). We need to elaborate this idea of time emerging from the subject's relation to the other, even to risk a few spatial metaphors, before continuing. We might call diachrony the exteriority of time as we know it, the outside of the now and all of the past and future that we encompass within the now of memory and anticipation. Diachrony is unordered and unmeaning passage itself, nocturnal to the subject's daytime schemas, "refractory to all synchronization" (*Otherwise Than Being* 9). Yet it is not simply the impersonal time of physics, moving in a uni-directional line without human perspective. It is the non-synchronic dimension of time—"the instant falling out of phase with itself"—that is just as alien to physics as to metaphysics (ibid.). Levinas insists that "there must be signaled a lapse of time that does not return,. . . a transcending diachrony," a moment that cannot be accounted for in any relation among past, present and future (or, in terms of physics: before, simultaneous with, after) (ibid.).[15] The idea of diachrony is the idea of a moment "foreign to every present, every representation," a moment that "signif[ies] a past more ancient than every representable origin, a pre-original and anarchical *passed*" (ibid.). Levinas "emphasizes the powerlessness of memory over the diachrony of time" as a way to imagine a moment that never passes because it has always already passed (*God, Death, and Time* 111). This is the ethical moment prior to the moment of self-identified being, the moment of "ethical antecedence" by which the self is founded, "without reference to my identity guaranteed its right," by being given responsibility for the welfare of the other (*Entre-nous* 150). This dimension of

---

[15] The preceding phrases from Levinas are especially resonant with (and influential on) writing by Derrida and, to a lesser extent, de Man. For Derrida's thought about time relevant to Levinas's diachrony, see, for example, *Of Grammatology*, trans. Gayatri Chakravorty Spivak (Baltimore: Johns Hopkins UP, 1974) 65-73; *Writing and Difference* 79-152; *Spectres of Marx: The State of the Debt, the Work of Mourning, and the New International*, trans. Peggy Kamuf (NY: Routledge, 1994) xviii-xx, 18, 39-40); and *Given Time: I. Counterfeit Money*, trans. Peggy Kamuf (Chicago: U of Chicago P, 1992). For de Man's, see "The Rhetoric of Temporality" in *Blindness and Insight: Essays in the Rhetoric of Contemporary Criticism*. 2nd ed. rev. (Minneapolis: U of Minnesota P, 1983), and his quintessentially deconstructive statement that "As a writer, Proust is the one who knows that the hour of truth, like the hour of death, never arrives on time, since what we call time is precisely truth's inability to coincide with itself" (*Allegories of Reading*, 78).

selfhood, "the diachrony of subjectivity, is my entry into the proximity of the neighbor" (*Otherwise Than Being* 127).

It is the immemorial moment in which the self's sovereignty over the being it experiences is in question: a self whose very right to be is under interrogation by the other. *To the Lighthouse* is inaugurated with an unheard question; its first words refer to the question that precedes them: "Yes, of course, if it's fine tomorrow. . . ." Levinas thinks of the self-in-time as a response, as in-response, to the other who is always asking: "a putting in question of the one who questions. That would be temporality" (*God, Death, and Time* 110). As I will discuss more in section two of this essay, it is especially "the death of the other" that "puts me in question, as if. . . *I*, through my eventual indifference, became the accomplice; and as if, even before being doomed to it myself, *I* had to answer for this death of the other, and not leave the other alone in his death-bound solitude" (*Entrenous* 145-46).

To the Lighthouse reverberates with an unsettled interrogative current, culminating with the unanswerable deaths of Mrs. Ramsay, Prue, and Andrew. Woolf's proliferating questions are not merely preludes to answers, but what Mrs. Ramsay thinks of as "[i]nsoluble questions," escalating interruptions in narrative order and subjective coherence (*TTL* 18). While "Time Passes" is the strongest expression of this interrogative impulse, it pervades the novel; Mrs. Ramsay experiences it near the end of "The Window": "Slowly it came into her head, why is it that one wants people to marry? What was the value, the meaning of things? (Every word they said now would be true)" (*TTL* 183). The logistical and informational questions of the preceding dozens of pages deepen here into less answerable abstractions, questions veering towards the existential, towards the meaning of questioning itself.

From early on, "Time Passes" renders existence in its anonymous and unsubjected state, existence as *there-is*, as interrogation:

> Nothing stirred in the drawing room or in the dining-room or on the staircase. Only through the rusty hinges and swollen sea-moistened woodwork certain airs, detached from the body of the wind (the house was ramshackle after all) crept round corners and ventured indoors. Almost one might imagine them, as they entered the drawing-room questioning and wondering, toying with the flap of hanging wall-paper, asking, would it hang much longer, when would it fall? Then smoothly brushing the walls, they passed on musingly as if asking the red and yellow roses on the wall-paper whether they would fade, and questioning (gently, for there was time at their disposal) the torn letters in the wastepaper basket, the flowers, the books, all of which were now open to them and asking, Were they allies? Were they enemies? How long would they endure? (*TTL* 190-1)

These questions are of ambiguous source, attributed to the roaming airs but also a function of an unidentified mediating and narrating consciousness: "Almost one might imagine them...," "they passed on musingly *as if* asking..." (emphasis added). In this ambiguity, the narrative voice seems to be both asking and receiving questions at the same time. The narrative voice, an unlocatable quasi-presence, is realized increasingly as a self-questioning. In fact, we might think of the voice in "Time Passes" as a presence that has been undone by the strength of its own interrogative impulse. "But what, after all, is one night?"; "How long, she [Mrs. McNab] asked, creaking and groaning on her knees under the bed, how long shall it endure?" (*TTL*, 192, 197) If subjectivity that owns its own being is a constative state, its obverse as anonymous and insomniac existence is its interrogation.

More important, Woolf renders exteriority-as-interrogation specifically as questions about *time*; narrative insomnia and questioning correspond in questions about the meaning and possibility of endurance. Time is at issue ("would it hang much longer, when would it fall? . . . How long would they endure?") in the anonymous narrative voice and negative rhetorical form of exteriority, a function of the beyond-being that cannot be known in the terms of the subject. "Time Passes" is the novel's approach to the presence of time as an otherness to be intuited, evoked, but never fully deciphered or defined: "Almost it would appear that it is useless in such confusion to ask the night those questions as to what, and why, and wherefore, which tempt the sleeper from his bed to seek an answer" (*TTL* 193). Like Woolf, Levinas takes the interrogative as a stance toward being and identity from which to thematize time and death:

> Would not the dis-quiet of emotion be the question that, in the nearness of death, is precisely at the point of being born? An emotion in the sense of a deference toward death; in other words, an emotion as a *question* that does not contain, in the posing of the question, the elements of its own response. A question that attaches to that deeper relation [*rapport*] to the infinite, which is time (time understood as a relation to the infinite). (*God, Death, and Time* 17)

Levinas describes the subject's intimation of death as a profound experience of interrogation, a confrontation with "a pure question mark" that indicates the "original question, one without the posing of a question; a question without a thesis; a pure question that raises itself; a question that is the pure raising of a question" (*God, Death, and Time* 21, 106). For Levinas, death is not an annihilation but an absolute, unanswerable question, "the question that is necessary for this relationship with infinity, or time, to be produced" (*God, Death, and Time* 19). This description of death and time as part of the same interrogation of a subject's claim over its own being is, more precisely, the question asked us *by another*, a question that is alterity interrupting the selfhood of the self. The other asks us a contentless question by dying. In her narrative poetics, Woolf shows how this passing of the other carries the ethical enigma of passing time.

II

> *By taking part in the infinite solitude of the Other's dying. . ., the self is granted an exposure to mortality. Holding the hand of the one who dies in the present, one affirms that there is no "now" in which I could die. The self can never mourn its own death, precisely because "my death" could never occur in or as the present.*
> —Joseph Suglia (53)

"Time Passes" is not simply "abstract"—omniscient, impersonal—but de-centered, transcending localized subjectivity, not into objectivity, but by a paradoxical inhabitation of the subject's exteriority. Woolf's lyricism emanates from and contains within it a silence that articulates itself against positive speech, and brings to obscure life something like a darkness that occupies the territory outside light. The chapter briefly interrupts the free indirect discourse of various characters in the long first and third chapters with, we might say, the free indirect discourse of nothing, of absence itself. It is a narration of exteriority, I argue, that abides by diachronic time as Levinas later conceives it, time that, in its alterity, is irreducible to the subject's endless present. Diachrony—a nocturnal temporality that Woolf and Levinas associate with insomnia and radical questioning—emerges in the subject's ethical relation to others, and especially to the other at or in death. In "Time Passes," Woolf narrates the oblique, irrational involvement that the self has in the other's death, the responsibility that the self bears in mourning.[16] It is a difficult relation to represent because, strictly speaking, it is not a relation at all: the death of the other is not a term in a relation, it is not something one can make an object of knowledge or part of an intersubjective dialectic. The death of the other is an absence in being that puts the subject's own being in question, that ruptures its immanence and totality, and that thereby gives subjectivity a relation to alterity that inaugurates its ethical dimension.

As Suglia suggests above, we can imagine a subtle compensation for our non-presence at our own death with the other's exposure to our death, and with our exposure to the deaths of others; it is a kind of ontological and temporal sub-

---

[16] J. Hillis Miller suggests this idea that Woolf's narrator is shaped by its involvement in character deaths when he writes that the "narrator is without life, personality, opinions, feelings of its own, and yet is doomed to see all the lives, personalities, opinions, and feelings which it relives from the perspective of that prospective death toward which they all move, and where the narrating mind already is" (174).

stitution. It leads to a post-Heideggerian conception of the self's absolute relation to its own death, a response to Heidegger's insistence in *Being and Time* that one's relation to death is not only individual but the very source of individual identity.[17] "Da-sein," Heidegger's term for an individual human being (and loosely translated as "being-there"), finds its most defining and affirming possibility in dying; death is Da-sein's "ownmost potentiality of being" (232). This potential is necessarily "my own," it is "a matter of the being of my own Da-sein," because "[i]n dying, it becomes evident that death is ontologically constituted by mineness" (Heidegger 223). Heidegger's idea of death's individual mineness—a mineness that creates the individual's very capacity for self-possession—is also an idea of death's "nonrelational" nature, one in which "all relations to other Da-sein are dissolved" (ibid., 232). Da-sein's nonrelationality in mortality guarantees its authenticity:

> Death does not just "belong" in an undifferentiated way to one's own Da-sein, but it *lays claim* on it as something *individual*. The nonrelational character of death understood in anticipation individualizes Da-sein down to itself. . . . It reveals that the fact that any being-together-with what is taken care of and any being-with the others fails when one's ownmost potentiality-of-being is at stake. Da-sein can *authentically* be *itself* only when it makes that possible of its own accord. (Heidegger 243)

Heidegger describes the irreconcilability of authentic being-toward-death and being in the publicly shared world (the inevitable, originary social situation he calls "being-with" [*Mitsein*]). It is an idea of authenticity that excludes the presence of the other from the self's death and the self from the death of the other.

Levinas attempts to re-think Heidegger's model of mortal self-possession, or as Jonathan Strauss calls it "the coercive ideology of mortal self-identity" ("After Death" 100), in ethical terms that can help us understand Woolf's narrative approach to the deaths of three members of the Ramsay family in "Time Passes." Levinas presents the "obligation not to leave the other alone in the face of death" as that which "summons me, demands me, claims me: as if the invisible death faced by the other. . . were 'my business'" (*Entre-nous* 131, 145). Where for Heidegger death "lays claim" on the individual as its ownmost potentiality, Levinas considers "a more radical substitution for an other" involving "a respon-

---

[17] While Suglia does have Heidegger specifically in mind here, Heidegger comes at the end of a long tradition of thought about the individualizing effect of mortality; see Jonathan Strauss's discussion of this tradition in "After Death" in *diacritics* 30.3 (Fall 2000): 90-104. For an even larger discussion, see the entire issue of *diacritics* of which it is a part, which takes as its theme "Post-Mortem: The State of Death as a Modern Construct."

sibility... in bearing his misfortune or his end *as if one were guilty of causing it.* This is the ultimate nearness. *To survive as a guilty one*" (*God, Death, and Time* 39). It is this oblique answerability and non-causal guilt we carry as another dies, this "awakening and vigilance in... affective turbulence," that Levinas identifies as the condition of ethical subjectivity (*Entre-nous* 146). Ethical subjectivity is involved in the other's dying, dies with the other, learns to die from the other, "even if, at the last moment, the not-leaving-the-other-alone consists... only in answering 'Here I am' to the request that calls on me" (*Entre-nous* 131). This ethical call and claim resist explication because they are not intelligible to rational thought, they do not correspond to any knowledge in the transcendental subject: they are "as if," "at the last moment," an "affective turbulence." In their recalcitrance to the terms of verifiable knowledge, or what we might call their epistemological non-finitude, this call and claim are essentially religious. In their religiosity, they are unnarratable.

In "Time Passes," Woolf represents the unrepresentability of our "relation" to the death of the other, narrates the unnarratability of the subject's non-intentional presence at and response to this death. The chapter's focalization of exteriority, its ambiguity of narrative presence, anticipates the ambiguity of Levinasian ethics, the way the subject both cannot and must bear responsibility for the death of the other. In "Time Passes," Woolf structures the representation of the deaths of the Ramsays so that we are both present and absent at them; they occur at a narrative distance, bracketed and elliptical, but at a distance that is fraught with ethical desire.

> [Mr. Ramsay, stumbling along a passage one dark morning, stretched his arms out, but Mrs. Ramsay having died rather suddenly the night before, his arms, though stretched out, remained empty.] (*TTL* 194)

> [Prue Ramsay died that summer in some illness connected with childbirth, which was indeed a tragedy, people said, everything, they said, had promised so well.] (*TTL* 199)

> [A shell exploded. Twenty or thirty young men were blown up in France, among them Andrew Ramsay, whose death, mercifully, was instantaneous.] (*TTL* 201)

These deaths are shocking precisely because Woolf does not fully give them to us, does not deploy the representational apparatus of traditional fiction to render the illusion of readerly access to experience. She leaves them in the second-hand "they said" or "people said," in an explicit or implied narrative derivation, as if we have, in our negligence and distraction, arrived at these scenes too late. This is not to say that they happen "off stage," but that they happen without happening for or to us, without their ethical relevance to us simply *given* to us. These deaths, almost journalistically noted, cut against Suglia's ethical fantasy of the survivor patiently holding the hand of the dying, the fantasy of unambiguous contact with the other in death. It is a fantasy that we (even as readers) can intentionally will this contact, that we can clearly perceive when and how it happens, and that we can comprehend what it is—what the content of such an experience would be, what we might take and give in such an encounter—to accompany someone in death. The deaths in "Time Passes" put us in the position of *failed* ethical subjects, removed from the mortality of the other but pained by this removal. This pain is the animation of ethics itself. Woolf gives us our ethicality, not simply as our mourning for the other, but as our mourning for our own ethical limitations, our failure to enter into the mournful exteriority of living. In *The Magic Mountain*, Thomas Mann writes that "[w]hat we call mourning for our dead is perhaps not so much grief at not being able to call them back as it is grief at not being able to want to do so" (675). The way Woolf brackets and withholds these deaths signals both these griefs at once: Mrs. Ramsay, Prue, and Andrew are lost to us, but these losses risk being indifferent to the self-contained, transcendental subject that reads them.

Against Heidegger and others, Levinas argues that death is not nothingness, negation, but that there is a meaning and value in the absence of the dead. In *Mrs. Dalloway*, Peter Walsh remembers Clarissa's theory that, after death, "the unseen part of us, which spreads wide, the unseen might survive, be recovered somehow attached to this person or that, or even haunting certain places after death. . . perhaps—perhaps" (*MD* 153). One way to understand ethical subjectivity is as that which, in its inevitably late arrival to the scene of the other's death, can attend to this (uncertain) haunting, can delineate something of value and meaning in the wake of this absence. Woolf provides images of this delineation in "Time Passes":

> What people had shed and left—a pair of shoes, a shooting cap, some faded skirts and coats in wardrobes—those alone kept the human shape and in the emptiness indicated how once they were filled and animated; how once hands were busy with hooks and buttons; how once the looking-glass had held a face; had held a world hollowed out in which a figure turned, a hand flashed, the door opened, in came children rushing and tumbling; and went out again. Now, day after day, light turned, like a flower reflected in water, its sharp image on the wall opposite. Only the shadows of the trees, flourishing in the wind, made obeisance on the wall, and for a moment darkened the pool in which light reflected itself; or birds, flying, made a soft spot flutter slowly across the bedroom floor. (*TTL* 194-5)

Woolf represents an elusive way of knowing in which subjects do not perceive objects but perceive the hollowed or reflected or shadowed residues of objects, the empty spaces (shoes, cap, skirts, coats) or mirror images (in the looking-glass and water) or flitting shadows (of trees, birds) that take on an ambiguous epistemological status, an epistemology of felt absence. It is not simply memory that happens in this passage—there is no subject remembering here, *qua* subject—but a kind of perceptual haunting that registers in the delicate prose-rhythms, word repetitions, and fragmented imagery that give this passage what we might call the poetics of ethical intuition. The narrative voice summons what is gone from the remaining traces, complicating and elaborating epistemology with mourning, with a guilty response to the dead. We might call it a way of knowing the dead that no subject can perform, because there is no object for it to know, and no specific guilt to claim or atone for.

There is no object, but there is not nothing. Woolf represents the process in which the self, by achieving a proximity to the other that is not an epistemological relation, is reconfigured around the deaths it participates in besides its own. It is the self as it sacrifices itself in the death of the other. Levinas writes that

> the sacrifice for another [*autrui*] would create an other relation with the death of the other: a responsibility that would perhaps answer the question of why we can die. In the guiltiness of the survivor, the death of the other [*l'autre*] is my affair. *My* death is my *part* in the death of the other, and in my death I die the death that is my fault. (*God, Death, and Time* 39)

Levinas has us imagine our own death as the manifestation of guilt—of non-indifference, of an oblique implication—we bear in the other's dying, our belated answer to the question posed by the death of the other. For Levinas, the word "time" names the warping of the subject's contours by its irreducible exteriority, its ethical excess. The subject in diachrony cannot simply be when it is: it has always already passed, along with the other, for whom it mourns.

The narration of "Time Passes" is in the voice of this passing. It is a nocturnal passing that shadows the day that comes to eclipse it.

> In spring the garden urns, casually filled with wind-blown plants, were gay as ever. Violets came and daffodils. But the stillness and the brightness of the day were as strange as the chaos and tumult of the night, with the trees standing there, and the flowers standing there, looking before them, looking up, yet beholding nothing, eyeless, and so terrible. (*TTL* 203)

Woolf's images of what it is to lose the logic of interiority, to have a blindness in which one actually beholds nothing, are strange and beautiful because they represent the subject's exposure to an exteriority in which one substitutes one's mortality for another's. We cannot know we do this; it is not a knowledge. It happens as time happens, terrible and inevitable, a night-wind overheard in sleep.

Works Cited

Auerbach, Erich. *Mimesis*. Trans. Willard R. Trask. Princeton: Princeton UP, 1953.
Augustine. *Confessions*. Trans. Henry Chadwick. Oxford: Oxford UP, 1991.
Banfield, Ann. *The Phantom Table: Woolf, Fry, Russell and the Epistemology of Modernism*. Cambridge: Cambridge UP, 2000.
Benveniste, Emile. *Problems in General Linguistics*. Trans. Mary Elizabeth Meek. Coral Gables, FL: U of Miami P, 1971.
Blanchot, Maurice. *The Gaze of Orpheus*. Trans. Lydia Davis. Ed. Adams Sitney. Barrytown, NY: Station Hill P, 1981.
de Man, Paul. *Allegories of Reading: Figural Language in Rousseau, Nietzsche, Rilke, and Proust*. New Haven: Yale UP, 1979.
Derrida, Jacques. *Writing and Difference*. Trans. Alan Bass. Chicago: U of Chicago P, 1978.
Foucault, Michel. "Maurice Blanchot: The Thought from the Outside." *Foucault / Blanchot*. New York: Zone, 1984.
Froula, Christine. *Virginia Woolf and the Bloomsbury Avant-Garde: War, Civilization, Modernity*. New York: Columbia UP, 2005.
Gallagher, Shaun. *The Inordinance of Time*. Evanston: Northwestern UP, 1998.
Goldman, Jane. *The Feminist Aesthetics of Virginia Woolf: Modernism, Post-Impressionism and the Politics of the Visual*. Cambridge: Cambridge UP, 1998.
Grosz, Elizabeth. "Thinking the New: Of Futures Yet Unthought." *symplokē* 6.1 (1998) 38-55.
Harvey, David. *The Condition of Postmodernity: An Enquiry into the Origins of Cultural Change*. Oxford: Blackwell, 1989.
Heidegger, Martin. *Being and Time*. Trans. Joan Stambaugh. Albany, NY: State University of New York, 1996.
Levinas, Emmanuel. *Entre-nous: Thinking-of-the-Other*. Trans. Michael B. Smith and Barbara Harshav. New York: Columbia UP, 1998.
——. *God, Death, and Time*. Trans. Bettina Bergo. Stanford: Stanford UP, 2000.
——. *Otherwise Than Being or Beyond Essence*. Trans. Alfonso Lingis. Pittsburgh, PA: Duquesne UP, 1981.

——. *Time and the Other*. Trans. Richard A. Cohen. Pittsburgh: Duquesne UP, 1987.
——. "The Servant and Her Master." *The Levinas Reader*. Ed. Seán Hand. Oxford: Blackwell, 1989.
Lukacher, Ned. *Time-Fetishes: The Secret History of Eternal Recurrence*. Durham: Duke UP, 1998.
Mann, Thomas. *The Magic Mountain*. Trans. H. T. Lowe-Porter. NY: Vintage International, 1992.
Miller, J. Hillis. "The Rhythm of Creativity in *To the Lighthouse*." *Modernism Reconsidered*. Ed. Robert Kiely. Cambridge, MA: Harvard UP, 1983.
Schleifer, Ronald. *Modernism and Time: The Logic of Abundance in Literature, Science, and Culture, 1880-1930*. Cambridge: Cambridge UP, 2000.
Silbergleid, Robin Paula. "'We perished, each alone': Loss and Lyricism in Woolf, Maso, and Young." *Virginia Woolf and Communities: Selected Papers from the Eighth Annual Conference on Virginia Woolf*. Ed. Jeanette McVicker and Laura Davis. New York: Pace UP, 1999. 57-64.
Strauss, Jonathan. "After Death." *diacritics* 30.3 (Fall 2000): 90-104.
Suglia, Joseph. "The Communication of the Impossible." *diacritics* 31.2 (Summer 2001): 49-69.
van Buren Kelley, Alice. To the Lighthouse*: The Marriage of Life and Art*. Boston: Twayne Publishers, 1987.
Woolf, Virginia. *Diary*, vol. 3. Ed. Anne Oliver Bell. New York: Harcourt Brace Jovanovich, 1980.
——. *Jacob's Room*. New York: Penguin, 1992.
——. *Mrs. Dalloway*. New York: Harcourt Brace, 1953.
——. *A Room of One's Own*. New York: Harcourt Brace, 1957.
——. *To the Lighthouse*. New York: Harcourt Brace, 1955.
Wörringer, Wilhelm. *Abstraction and Empathy: A Contribution to the Psychology of Style*

Letters from Readers to Virginia Woolf

Corrections

"Mea culpa," writes Beth Rigel Daugherty. "Mistakes certainly do happen!" Since publication of her transcription of letters from readers to Virginia Woolf in *Woolf Studies Annual* 12 (2006), a number of errors have come to light which we would now like to correct. Thank you to Helen Southworth, relatives of correspondents, and sharp-eyed readers for catching these errors.

In the list below, the first number, in bold, is the letter number as published in volume 12. The corrected text is followed by the error, then the relevant page and line numbers.

19 Aurez vous *not* Avez vous (44, line 11)

58 ont suscitée *not* out suscitée (91, line 3)
  sonnent *not* sonnet (92, line 1)
  m'imagine *not* n'imagine (92, line 3)
  pas *not* par (92, line 6)

71 W. S. Weedon *not* W. G. Weedon (22, in list; 109, signature and foot note)

95 chargée *not* charger (142, line 1)
  vieille *not* vielle (142, line 1)
  ne *not* re (142, line 2)
  des *not* du (142, line 5)
  phénomène *not* phenomène (142, lines 9-10)
  des *not* de (142, line 13)
  Mondes *not* Monde (142, line 13))
  que *not* qui (142, line 19)
  pense à elle . . . *not* pense à elle – (142, line 23)
  aurez *not* avez (142, line 24)
  tant *not* tout (142, line 27)
  cette même revue *not* cette revue (142, line 29)
  préférerais *not* préférais (142, line 30)
  moi *not* mois (143, line 3)

elle songe à votre prochain livre, à ceux qui suivront *not* elle songe à ceux qui suivront (143, lines 5-6)
ce que me sont *not* ce que sont (143, line 9)
on *not* ou (143, line 12)

101   Lyn Newman's papers, and those of her husband, were donated to St. John's College, Cambridge, by her son, William Newman (155)

112   une *not* un (168, line 24)
d'art= *not* d'art – (168, line 28)
chéris *not* ceris (168, line 30)
dans *not* dan (168, line 33)
directement *not* directment (168, line 37)
adresser *not* addresser (169, line 1)

123   David Cecil was the youngest child of James Cecil, 4th Marquess of Salisbury, and Lady Cicely Alice Gore, 4th Marchioness, *not* the son of Robert and Eleanor Cecil (190).

Guide to Library Special Collections
This guide updates the information in volume 12.

Name of Collection: The Beinecke Rare Book and Manuscript Library

Contact: Kevin Repp, Curator of Modern Books and Manuscripts
Patricia Willis, Curator of American Literature

Address: Yale University Library
P.O. Box 208240
New Haven, CT 06520-8240

URL: www.library.yale.edu/beinecke/brblhome.html

Hours: Mon.-Thurs. 8:30AM-8PM
Fri. 8:30AM-5PM

Access Requirements: Register at the circulation desk on each visit.

Holdings Relevant To Woolf: General Collection includes autograph manuscript of "Notes on Oliver Goldsmith." Comments on Edward Gibbon, William Beckford Collection. Letters from Virginia Woolf in the Bryher Papers, the Louise Morgan and Otto Theis Papers, and the Rebecca West Papers. Related material: 41 letters from Vita Sackville-West to Violet Trefusis; files relating to Robert Manson Myers's *From Beowulf to Virginia Woolf* in the Edmond Pauker Papers.

Yale Collection of American Literature includes typewritten manuscripts of "The Art of Walter Sickert," "Augustine Birrell," "Aurora Leigh," "How Should One Read a Book?" "Letter to a Young Poet," "The Novels of Turgenev," "Street Haunting." Dial/Scofield Thayer Papers: manuscripts of "The Lives of the Obscure," "Miss Ormerod," and "Mrs. Dalloway in Bond Street." Letters from Virginia Woolf in the William Rose Benet Papers, the Benet Family Correspondence, the Henry Seidel Canby Papers, the Seward

Collins Papers, the Dial/Scofield Thayer Papers, and the *Yale Review* archive. Material relating to translat-ions of Woolf in the Thornton Wilder papers. Related material: Clive Bell, "Virginia Woolf" (Dial/Scofield Thayer Papers); 43 letters from Leonard Woolf to Helen McAfee (*Yale Review*); 11 letters from Leonard Woolf to Gertrude Stein.

Name of Collection: The Henry W. and Albert A. Berg Collection of English and American Literature

Contact: Isaac Gewirtz, Curator

Address: New York Public Library, Room 320
Fifth Avenue & 42nd Street
New York, NY 10018

Telephone: 212-930-0802
Fax: 212-930-0079
E-mail: igewirtz@nypl.org

Hours: Tues./Wed. 11AM -6:00PM
Thurs.-Sat. 10AM-6:00PM
Closed Sun., Mon. and legal holidays

Access Requirements: Apply for card of admission at Office of Special Collections, Room 316 after first acquiring ACCESS card in room 315. (online form may be printed). Traceable identification required. Undergraduates working on honors theses need letter from faculty advisor.

Restrictions: Virginia Woolf's MSS are now made available on microfilm and CD. N.B. *All the Berg's Woolf MSS are on microfilm and CD published by Research Publications and available at many research libraries.*

GUIDE TO LIBRARY SPECIAL COLLECTIONS 185

Holdings Relevant To Woolf: Manuscripts/typescripts of all of the novels except *Orlando*, including: *Between the Acts*, *Flush*, *Jacob's Room*, *Mrs. Dalloway* (notes and fragments), *Night and Day*, *To the Lighthouse*, *The Voyage Out*, *The Waves*, *The Years*; 12 notebooks of articles, essays, fiction and reviews, 1924-1940; 36 volumes of diaries; 26 volumes of reading notes; correspondence with Vanessa Bell, Ethel Smyth, Vita Sackville-West and others. Su Hua Ling Chen's Bloomsbury correspondence.

Name of Collection: The British Library Manuscript Collections

Contact: Manuscripts Enquiries

Address: 96 Euston Road
London NW1 2DB
England

Telephone: 0207-412-7513
Fax: 0207-412-7745
E-mail: mss@bl.uk

Hours: Mon 10:00-5:00PM
Tue-Sat: 9:30-5:00PM

Access Requirements: British Library Reader Pass (signed I.D. required and usually proof of post-graduate academic status, or other demonstrable need to use the collections—see www.bl.uk). In addition, access to most literary autograph material only available with letter of recommendation.

Restrictions: Paper Copies, Microfilms, and Photography of selected items available upon receipt of written authorization for photo duplication from the copyright holder.

Holdings Relevant
to Woolf: Diaries 1930-1931 (microfilm); Mrs. Dalloway and other writings (1923-1925) three volumes; letter from Leonard Woolf to H. G. Wells (1941); two letters from Virginia Woolf and three letters from Leonard Woolf to John Lehmann (1941); letter written on behalf of Leonard Woolf to S. S. Koteliansky (1946); notebook in Italian kept by Virginia Woolf; notebook of Virginia Stephen (1906-1909); A sketch of the past revised ts (1940); letters from Virginia Woolf in the correspondence files of Lytton and James Strachey; letter from Virginia Woolf to Mildred Massingberd; letter from Virginia Woolf to Harriet Shaw Weaver (1918); letters from Virginia Woolf to S. S. Koteliansky (1923-27); letter from Virginia Woolf to Frances Cornford (1929); letter from Virginia Woolf to Ernest Rhys (1930); correspondence of Virginia Woolf in the Society of Authors archive (1934-37); letter and postcard from Virginia Woolf to Bernard Shaw (1940); three letters (suicide notes) from Virginia Woolf (1941); two letters from Virginia Woolf and three from Leonard Woolf to John Lehmann (1941).
"Hyde Park Gate News" 1891-92, 1895 (add. MSS 70725, 70726). Letters of Virginia and Leonard Woolf to Lady Aberconway, 1927-1941. Letter from Virginia Woolf to Frances Cornford. Letters from Virginia Woolf to Macmillan Co. 1903, 1908. Collection of RPs ("reserved photo copies"–copies of manuscrips exported, some subject to restrictions).

Name of Collection: Harry Ransom Humanities Research Center

Contact: Research Librarian

Address: The University of Texas at Austin
P.O. Box 7219
Austin, TX 78713-7219

GUIDE TO LIBRARY SPECIAL COLLECTIONS 187

Telephone: 512-471-9119
Fax: 512-471-2899

E-mail reference@hrc.utexas.edu

Hours: Mon.-Fri. 9AM-5PM
Sat. 9AM-NOON
Closed holidays; intersession Saturdays; one week each in late May and late August.

Access Requirements: Completed manuscript reader's application; current photo identification.

Holdings Relevant To Woolf: The manuscript collection includes the typed manuscript with autograph revisions of *Kew Gardens,* and the typed manuscript and autograph revisions of "Thoughts on Peace in an Air Raid." The Center holds 571 of Woolf's letters, including correspondence to Elizabeth Bowen, Lady Ottoline Morrell, Mary Hutchinson, William Plomer, Hugh Walpole and others. Further mss. relating to Virginia Woolf include letters to her from T. S. Eliot and reviews of her work. A substantial collection of the first British and American editions of Woolf's published works, as well as 130 volumes from Leonard and Virginia Woolf's library and a collection of books published by the Hogarth Press, is also housed. An art collection holds a landscape painting of Virginia's garden and a series of Cockney cartoons in a sketch book, signed "V.W." The center also has extensive holdings of materials related to Leonard Woolf, Ottoline Morrell, Mary Hutchinson, Lytton Strachey, Dora Carrington, E. M. Forster, Clive Bell, Roger Fry, Vanessa Bell, Bertrand Russell, Elizabeth Bowen, William Plomer, Stephen Spender and Hugh Walpole.

Name of Collection:	King's College Archive Centre
Contact:	Patricia McGuire, Archivist King's College
Address:	Cambridge CB2 1ST
Telephone:	01223-331444
Fax:	01223-331891
E-mail:	archivist@kings.cam.ac.uk
Hours:	Mon.-Thurs. 9:30AM-12:30PM and 1:30PM-5:15PM. *Closed during public holidays and the College's annual periods of closure.*
Access Requirements:	Proof of ID, letter of introduction, appointment in advance.
Holdings Relevant To Woolf:	Woolf MSS and letters: Minute book, written up by Clive Bell, of the meetings of a play-reading society, with cast lists and comments on performances by CB. Dec. 1907-Jan. 1909, Oct. 1914-Feb. 1915. Players included variously Clive & Vanessa Bell, Roger & Margery Fry, Duncan Grant, Walter Lamb, Molly MacCarthy, Adrian & Virginia Stephen, Saxon Sydney-Turner. *Freshwater, A Comedy*—photocopy of editorial typescript prepared from the MSS at Sussex University and Monk's House; photcopy of covering letter from the publisher to "Robert Silvers," 1.29.1976. Papers relating to the Virginia Woolf Centenary Conference held at Fitzwilliam College, Cambridge, 9.20-22.1982. TS with corrections of "Nurse Lugton's Curtain." Typed transcript of R. Fry's memoir of his schooldays. Correspondence with Clive Bell, Julian Bell, Vanessa Bell, Richard Braithwaite, Rupert Brooke, Mrs. Brooke, Katharine Cox, Julian Fry, Roger Fry, John Davy Hayward, J. M. Keynes, Lydia Keynes, Rosamond Lehmann, Charles Mauron, Raymond Mortimer, G. H. W. Rylands,

GUIDE TO LIBRARY SPECIAL COLLECTIONS 189

J. T. Sheppard, W. J. H. Sprott, Thoby Stephen, Madge Vaughan. Woolf-related archival collections held: Charleston Papers; Rupert Brooke Papers; E. M. Forster Papers; Roger Fry Papers; J. M. Keynes Papers;George Humphrey Wolferstan ('Dadie') Rylands Papers.

J. T. Sheppard Papers; W. J. H. Sprott Papers. Various works of art by Vanessa Bell, Duncan Grant, and Roger Fry, held in various locations around King's College. Access via Domus Bursar's secretary.

Name of Collection: The Lilly Library

Contact: Breon Mitchell, Director
Saundra Taylor, Curator of Manuscripts

Address: The Lilly Library, Indiana University
1200 East Seventh Street
Bloomington, IN 47405-5500

Telephone: 812-855-2452
Fax: 812-855-3143
E-mail: liblilly@indiana.edu, mitchell@indiana.edu
taylors@indiana.edu

Hours: M-F 9-6; Sat. 9-1;
Closed Sundays and Major Holidays

Access Requirements: Valid photo-identification; brief registration procedure.

Restrictions: Closed stacks; material use confined to reading room; wheelchair accessible reading room and exhibitions (but no wheelchair-accessible restroom)

Holdings Relevant
To Woolf: Corrected page proofs for the British edition of *Mrs Dalloway*; letters to Woolf from Desmond and Mary (Molly) MacCarthy; 77 letters (published in *Letters*) from Woolf to correspondents including Donald Clifford Brace, Robert Gathorne-Hardy, Barbara (Strachey) Halpern, Richard Arthur Warren Hughes, Desmond MacCarthy and Molly MacCarthy; "Preliminary Scheme for the formation of a Partnership between Mr Leonard Sidney Woolf and Mr John Lehmann to take over The Hogarth Press" (includes contract signed by Lehmann, LW, and VW, and receipt for Lehmann's payment to VW to purchase VW's share in the Hogarth Press); photographs of VW, LW, Lytton Strachey, Strachey family, Roger Fry, and Vanessa Bell (Hannah Whitall Smith mss.); (Richard) Kennedy mss. (four hand-colored lithographs of VW: artist's proofs for RK's portfolio, VIRGINIA WOOLF: "AS I KNEW HER"; Sackville-West, V. mss. (10,529 items: includes the correspondence of Vita Sackville-West, and Harold Nicolson); MacCarthy mss. (ca. 10,000 items: papers of Desmond and Molly MacCarthy); correspondence between LW and Mary Gaither regarding publication of *A Checklist of the Hogarth Press* (1976, repr. 1986); Todd Avery, *Close and Affectionate Friends: Desmond and Molly MacCarthy and the Bloomsbury Group* (The Lilly Library / Indiana University Libraries, 1999).

Name of Collection: Archives and Manuscripts, University of Maryland, College Park, Libraries

Contact: Beth Alvarez, Curator of Literary Manuscripts

Address: University of Maryland Libraries
College Park, MD 20742

GUIDE TO LIBRARY SPECIAL COLLECTIONS 191

Telephone:	310-405-9298
Fax:	301-314-2709
E-mail:	alvarez@umd.edu
Hours:	Mon.-Fri. 10AM-5PM, Sat. Noon-5PM.
Access Requirements:	Photo ID.
Holdings Relevant To Woolf:	Papers of Hope Mirrlees contain five autograph letters and postcards (1919-28) from Virginia Woolf to Mirrlees. Also in the collection are 113 letters from T. S. Eliot to Mirrlees, and three letters from Lady Ottoline Morrell to Mirrlees.
Name of Collection:	Monks House Papers/Leonard Woolf Papers/Charleston Papers/Nicolson Papers
Contact:	Fiona Courage, Special Collections Manager
Address:	University of Sussex Library Brighton Sussex BN1 9QL England
Telephone:	01273-678157
Fax:	01273-678441
E-mail:	Library.Specialcoll@sussex.ac.uk
URL:	www.sussex.ac.uk/library/speccoll
Hours:	By appointment
Access Requirements:	Identification to be presented on arrival. Application for access (including contact details of referee) to be completed on arrival. Photocopying strictly controlled.
Holdings Relevant To Woolf:	The University of Sussex holds two large archives relating to Leonard and Virginia Woolf: The

Monks House Papers, primarily correspondence and MSS of Virginia Woolf, including the three scrapbooks relating to *Three Guineas*; and The Leonard Woolf Papers, primarily correspondence and other papers of Leonard Woolf. (Monks House Papers are available on microfilm in many research libraries.) The Charleston Papers consist in the main of letters written to or by Clive and Vanessa Bell and Duncan Grant which had accumulated in their home; the library houses Quentin Bell's photocopied set. Also included are c. 900 letters from Maria Jackson to Julia and Leslie Stephen (Charleston Papers Ad. 1); letters from Roger Fry, Maynard Keynes, Lytton Stachey, Virginia Woolf, Vita Sackville-West, E. M. Forster, T. S. Eliot, Frances Partridge and others. The Nicolson Papers complement these three Sussex archives relating to the Bloomsbury Group, and consist of Nigel Nicolson's correspondence relating to his editorial work as principal editor of the six-volume *Letters of Virginia Woolf*, published between 1975 and 1980.

The Bell Papers. A. O. Bell's correspondence relating to her editorial work on Virginia Woolf's Diaries. A parallel collection to Nicolson Papers.

Colection level description may be accessed at www.archiveshub.ac.uk

Name of Collection: The Morgan Library & Museum

Contact: Reading Room

Address: 225 Madison Ave.
New York, NY 10016

Telephone: 212-590-0315
E-mail: readingroom@themorgan.org
URL: www.themorgan.org

GUIDE TO LIBRARY SPECIAL COLLECTIONS 193

Access Requirements: Admission to the Reading Room is by application and by appointment.

Holdings Relevant To Woolf: Virginia Woolf. Autograph manuscript notebook, 1931 Sept. 24. 1 item (52 p.) ; 265 x 208 mm. Contains drafts of "A Letter to a Young Poet," a brief letter to the press entitled "The Villa Jones" [ff. 3-5] and a monologue by a working-class woman [ff. 44-46]. MA 3333. Purchased on the Fellows Fund with the special assistance of Anne S. Dayton, Enid A. Haupt, Mrs. James H. Ripley, Mr. and Mrs. August H. Schilling, and John S. Thacher, 1979.

Virginia Woolf. Autograph letters signed (2) and typed letter signed, dated London [etc.], to E. McKnight Kauffer, 1931 Apr. 4-23, and undated. 3 items (4 p.). Concerning a drawing of her and a bibliography of her works. MA 1679. Purchased in 1959.

Vanessa Bell. Autograph letters (83) and postcards (3), signed mainly with initials, and a telegram, dated Gordon Square (London), to John Maynard Keynes, 1907-1936. 87 items (147 p.) Concerning Duncan Grant, Roger Fry, Clive Bell, the Bell children, Virginia Woolf, Lytton Strachey, the Keyneses, & David Garnett. MA 3448. Purchased on the Fellows Fund; a Gramercy Park Foundation (Mrs. Michael Tucker), 1980.

Name of Collection: Archives & Manuscripts

Contact: Michael Bott, The Archivist

Address: The University of Reading, The Library,
Whiteknights
P.O. Box 223
Reading RG6 6AE
England

Telephone: 0118-931-8776
Fax: 0118-931-6636
E-mail: g.m.c.bott@reading.ac.uk

Access Requirements: Appointment needed to consult material. Permission required to consult or copy material in the Hogarth Press and Chatto & Windus collections from Random House, 20 Vauxhall Bridge Road, London SW1V 2SA, UK. (Jean Rose, Library Mgr. JRose@Randomhouse.co.uk)

Holdings Relevant To Woolf: Hogarth Press (MS2750): editorial and production correspondence relating to publications of the Press including Woolf's own titles. Production ledgers 1920s-1950s. Correspondence between Leonard Woolf and Stanley Unwin about progress with his collected edition of the works of Freud.
Chatto & Windus (MS2444): small number of letters 1915-25; 1929-31.
George Bell & Sons (MS1640): 5 letters from Leonard Woolf 1930-66.
Routledge (MS1489): Reader's report by Leonard Woolf on George Padmore's "Britannia rules the blacks" (1935); "How Britain rules Africa."
Megroz (MS1979/68): 2 letters from LW, 1926.
Allen & Unwin (MS3282): Correspondence with LW 1923-24; 1939-40; 1943; 1946; 1950-51, including letters concerning a reprint of *Empire and Commerce in Africa*, and concerning ill-founded rumors about the Hogarth press.

Name of Collection: Frances Hooper Collection of Virginia Woolf Books and Manuscripts/Elizabeth Power Richardson Bloomsbury Iconography Collection.

Contact: Karen V. Kukil, Associate Curator of Rare Books

GUIDE TO LIBRARY SPECIAL COLLECTIONS

Address: Mortimer Rare Book Room
William Allan Neilson Library
Smith College
Northampton, MA 01063

Telephone: 413-585-2906
Fax 413-585-4486
E-mail: kkukil@email.smith.edu
URL: www.smith.edu/libraries/libs/rarebook
Hours: Mon.-Fri. 9AM-5PM

Access Requirements: Appointment to be made with the Curator.

Holdings Relevant To Woolf: The Hooper Collection emphasizes Woolf as an essayist but also includes many Hogarth Press first editions, limited editions of Woolf's works, and translations. The collection includes page proofs of *Orlando*, *To the Lighthouse*, and *The Common Reader*, corrected by Woolf for the first American editions, a proof copy of *The Waves* that Woolf inscribed to Hugh Walpole, and the proof copies of *The Years* and of *Flush*. The Collection also has one of the deluxe editions of *Orlando* that was printed on green paper. Other items include twenty-two pages of reading notes from 1926, three pages of notes on D. H. Lawrence's *Sons and Lovers*, thirty-three pages of notes for *Roger Fry*, a six-page ms. "As to criticism," a five-page ms. of "The Searchlight," and a fourteen-page ms. of "The Patron and The Crocus." The Hooper Collection also owns 140 letters between Woolf and Lytton Strachey as well as other correspondence, including a 13 February [1921] letter to Katherine Mansfield and ten letters to Mela and Robert Spira.

The Richardson Collection is a working collection of books and materials used by Richardson in preparing her *Bloomsbury Iconography*. It includes Leslie Stephen's photograph album, ninety-eight original exhibition catalogs dating back to 1929, clippings and photcopies of such items as reviews of early Woolf works, and Bloomsbury material from British *Vogue* of the 1920s. The Collection also has three preliminary pencil drawings by Vanessa Bell for *Flush*.

The Mortimer Rare Book Room also owns Woolf's 1916 Italian ms. notebook and her corrected typescripts of "Reviewing" and "The Searchlight." In addition, there is a 1923 photograph of Woolf at Garsington. Original cover designs for Hogarth Press publications include *The Common Reader*, *On Being Ill*, and *Duncan Grant*. The Mortimer Rare Book Room also has a Sylvia Plath Collection that includes eight of Woolf's books from Plath's library, several of which are underlined and annotated, as well as Plath's notes from her undergraduate English 211 class at Smith (1951-2) in which she studied *To the Lighthouse*.

Recent Acquisitions: Virginia Woolf's 26 February 1939 letter to Vita Sackville-West, a 1931 bronze bust of Virginia Woolf by Stephen Tomlin, a 1923 Hogarth Press edition of T.S. Eliot's *The Waste Land*, a 1919 Hogarth Press edition of *Paris* by Hope Mirrlees and first editions of Vita Sackville-West publications. Online exhibitions are available on the Mortimer Rare Book Room's web site.

Name of Collection: Woolf/Hogarth Press/Bloomsbury

Contact: Robert C. Brandeis

Address: Victoria University Library
71 Queens Park Crescent E.
Toronto M5S 1K7
Ontario Canada

GUIDE TO LIBRARY SPECIAL COLLECTIONS

Hours:	Mon.-Fri. 9AM-5PM
URL:	http://library.vicu.utoronto.ca/special/bloomsbury.htm
E-mail:	vic.library@utoronto.ca
Access Requirements:	Prior notification; identification.
Restrictions:	Limited photocopying.
Holdings Relevant To Woolf:	This collection, the most comprehensive of its kind in Canada, contains all the work of Virginia and Leonard Woolf in various editions, issues, variants and translations; all the books hand printed by Leonard and Virginia Woolf at the Hogarth Press, including many variant issues and bindings, association copies and page proofs; a nearly comprehensive collection of Hogarth Press machine printed books to 1946 (the year Leonard Woolf and the Press joined Chatto & Windus) including presentation copies, signed limited editions, page proofs, variants as well as substantial amounts of ephemera. The collection is also very strong in Bloomsbury art, especially the decorative arts, and contains important examples of Omega Workshops publications and exhibition catalogues. Vanessa Bell correspondence/MSS; Leonard Woolf correspondence; Ritchie family materials and correspondence re: Anne Thackeray Ritchie/Stephen family. Vanessa Bell dustwrapper designs for Woolf novels; Quentin Bell correspondence; S. P. Rosenbaum mss. 97 additional items: Ephemera Collection.
Recent Acquisitions:	Bronze bust of Lytton Strachey by Stephen Tomlin (1901-37). A companion piece to Tomlin's bronze of Virginia Woolf. More than 150 additional items including Hogarth Press variant bindings and proof copies; translations of Virginia Woolf and Leonard Woolf; ephemera; including

Hogarth Press: Complete Catalogue of Publications to 1939 with annotations by Leonard Woolf; materials relating to Bloomsbury Art and Artists including the catalogue of the second post impressionist exhibition, 1912, and catalogues relating to Vanessa Bell and Duncan Grant exhibitions.

228 items, including Hogarth Press proof copies; Hogarth Press publication catalogues; bronze medal of Virginia Woolf by Marta Firlet; oil on canvas portrait of Amaryllis Garnett by Vanessa Bell (c.1958); Duncan Grant and Vanessa Bell designed Clarice Cliff dinner plates.

Name of Collection: Library of Leonard and Virginia Woolf (Washington S U)

Contact: Laila Miletic-Vejzovic, Head Manuscripts, Archives and Special Collections

E-mail: vejzovic@wsu.edu

or Trevor Bond, tjbond@wsu.edu

Address: Washington State University Libraries
Pullman, WA 99164-5610

URL: www.wsulibs.wsu.edu/holland/masc/masc.htm

Hours: Mon.-Fri. 8:30AM-5PM

Access Requirements: Letter stating nature of research preferred; student or other identification.

Restrictions: Materials must be used in the MASC area under supervision. Photocopying or photographing is permitted only when it will not harm the materials and is permitted by copyright.

Holdings Relevant To Woolf: WSU has the Woolfs' basic working library including many works which belonged to

Virginia's father, Sir Leslie Stephen, and other family members. Over 800 titles came from their Sussex home, Monks House, including some works bought at auction soon after Leonard Woolf died in 1969. Later additions include: 1,875 titles from his house in Victoria Square, London; 400 titles from his nephew Cecil Woolf; and over 60 titles from Quentin and Anne Olivier Bell. WSU has been actively collecting: all works in all editions by Virginia; all titles by Leonard; works published by the Woolfs at the Hogarth Press through 1946; books by their friends and associates, especcially those by Bloomsbury authors and about Bloomsbury artists; relevant correspondence and original works of art. Original artwork by Vanessa Bell; scattered letters by Vanessa Bell, E. M. Forster, Roger Fry, Leslie Stephen, Lytton Strachey, and Leonard Woolf. Original artwork by Richard Kennedy for illustrations in his book *A Boy at the Hogarth Press*; scattered letters by Roger Fry, Leslie Stephen, Ethel Smyth, and Leonard Woolf. Virginia Woolf's initialed copy of *Cornishiana*; Leonard Woolf's annotated copy of *An Anatomy of Poetry* by A. William-Ellis; Leslie Stephen's copy of *Lapsus Calami and Other Verses*, inscribed by James Kenneth Stephen. Several letters from Virginia Woolf, including two written in 1939 to Ronald Heffer, and a letter to Edward McKnight Kauffer. New in the Hogarth Press Collection are a copy of E. M. Forster's *Anonymity, an Enquiry*, bound in cream paper boards, and what Woolmer calls the third label state of Forster's *The Story of the Siren*.

Name of Collection: Yale Center for British Art

Contact: Elisabeth Fairman, Curator of Rare Books and Manuscripts

Address:	1080 Chapel Street P.O. Box 208280 New Haven, CT 06520-8280
Telephone:	203-432-2814
Fax:	203-432-9613
E-mail:	elisabeth.fairman@yale.edu
Hours:	Tues.-Fri. 10AM-4:30PM
Access Requirements:	Call for e-mail for appointment. Permission needed in order to reproduce.
Holdings Relevant To Woolf:	Rare Books & Mss Department: 94 letters from Vanessa Bell and Duncan Grant to Sir Kenneth Clark; Prints & Drawings Department: 4 drawings by Vanessa Bell; 4 drawings by Duncan Grant; 6 drawings by Wyndham Lewis; 1 drawing by Frederick Etchells; Paintings Department: 1 painting by Vanessa Bell, 4 paintings by Duncan Grant (including portrait of Vanessa Bell); 3 paintings by Roger Fry.

Reviews

Virginia Woolf and the Bloomsbury Avant-Garde: War, Civilization, Modernity. Christine Froula (New York: Columbia University Press, 2005) xx + 428 pp.

Christine Froula's fascinating new book, *Virginia Woolf and the Bloomsbury Avant-Garde: War, Civilization, Modernity*, examines Bloomsbury's internationalist stance during a period when virulent nationalism prevailed in Europe. Situating her argument against Raymond Williams's contention that Bloomsbury's supreme value was the civilized individual, Froula maintains that the group's internationalist vision, its critique of violence and belief in the assertion of human agency invites us to read these artists and thinkers—among them Leonard and Virginia Woolf, Clive and Vanessa Bell, Roger Fry, John Maynard Keynes, Duncan Grant—as radical proponents of a democratic, economically egalitarian society. The preface and first chapter help us to rethink European modernity's Enlightenment project by highlighting Virginia Woolf's critical and creative opposition to imperialist exploitation and interwar nationalism. *Virginia Woolf and the Bloomsbury Avant-Garde* acknowledges Woolf's (and Bloomsbury's) class privilege and implication in "racialized imperialism" (31) but argues that she (and they) actively struggled to combat "barbarity *within* Europe and the West" while helping to advance Europe toward " a civilization that had never existed" (xii)—one based upon freedom, peace, and democratic self-governance. This is not a book that self-consciously idealizes Woolf and Bloomsbury as "incontestable heroes, paragons of Enlightenment modernity" (xiii), but it nonetheless argues that they were "as powerfully analytic, critical, and imaginative a proponent as the Enlightenment project has had in the last century" (xii). Froula's book follows a roughly chronological sequence from *The Voyage Out* to *Between the Acts* with admirable dexterity and incorporates a valuable range of sources that include Woolf's letters, diaries, and unpublished manuscripts. The first chapter moves at sometimes breakneck speed, touching upon a dizzying array of critics from Immanuel Kant to Clive Bell in order to demonstrate Bloomsbury's deep aesthetic and political involvement with avant-garde modernity. This chapter contains a wealth of information yet covers so much conceptual ground that by the end, when Froula makes a brief foray into the debates surrounding Woolf's "very fine negress" in *A Room of One's Own*, one wonders precisely how this racialized and ethnographic thread connects to the earlier discussion of Bloomsbury's internationalism. Despite the one hundred footnotes for this chapter alone, one is left a little muddled as to the larger conceptual stakes.

Froula's study is divided into eight chapters, each one focusing upon a different Woolf text that attempts to showcase how her works embody the convergence of aesthetics and politics in relation to important currents in British intellectual thought. Chapter Four interprets *Mrs. Dalloway* as "a communal postwar elegy" (88), situating the novel alongside John Maynard Keynes' and Sigmund Freud's postwar debates about Europe's future. This chapter analyzes the Oedipal dimension of mourning, seeking to demonstrate how civilization is founded "on the sacrifice of female desire" (88) in order to explore the "great crisis of loss, grief, and anger facing post-war Europe" (89). Froula innovatively reads the conflict between the upper-class, English Clarissa Dalloway and the working-class, German-identified Doris Kilman (Kiehlman) as a microcosm of "the competition, envy, hatred, and aggression between classes and nations that had already engulfed Europe in war and would slowly rise to a boil again in the 1920s and 1930s (104). For Froula, Miss Kilman embodies Keynes's warning that the economic sanctions imposed by the Peace would only provoke another war. Deprived of her livelihood—Miss Kilman has lost her teaching post because of her German ancestry—she is a "walking allegory of the aggressively aggrieved postwar Germany Keynes tried to forestall" (105). This historicized reading is both compelling and persuasive—to a point. While one may be willing to read Miss Kilman as a case study of the dynamics of nationalism and class-based aggression in action, it is still difficult to see Woolf's depiction of her envious and tyrannical personality in a wholly benevolent light. Froula wants us to read her thwarted appetites, envy, self-pity, and self-reproach as markers of what Keynes in effect predicted would be the result of Germany's "humiliated and downtrodden" (109) state. This reading positions Woolf as a kind of radical internationalist, sympathetically identifying with the odious Miss Kilman even as the text repeatedly patronizes and denigrates her.

Even if one is happy to accept Froula's inventive reading that Miss Kilman is "a small, ominous emblem of the economic ruin of [Germany]" (109), when we foreground the topic of sexuality, it problematizes the issue of Woolf's internationalism. What we arguably see through Miss Kilman's obsession with Elizabeth are signs of Woolf's xenophobia. The text represents the German Miss Kilman as a predatory lesbian tutor whom the English Clarissa denounces as "some prehistoric monster, armoured for primeval warfare" (*MD* 126). While the novel arguably denigrates Miss Kilman's homoerotic desire for Clarissa's daughter Elizabeth, it redeems Clarissa's homoerotic desire for Sally for reasons that are inflected not only by class but by nationality. Clarissa's same-sex desire is neither tyrannical nor parasitical, as Kilman's is (in keeping with British stereotypes of Germans); nor is she linked like Kilman to prevalent sexological perceptions of the lesbian as a degenerate man-hater. Instead, Clarissa's lesbianism is couched in the language of romantic friendship and largely escapes prevailing sexological condemnations of female inversion and lesbian perversion (see Barrett). This asymmetry betrays not only historical changes in understandings of lesbianism but, more particularly, Woolf's nationalistic bias that the monstrous and vampiric lesbian simply is not English. Froula does not address the intersections between Miss Kilman's nationality and sexuality, but she does argue that *Mrs. Dalloway* depicts a social system in which women's transgressive sexual desire is often incompatible with the laws of culture.

Chapter six, on *Orlando*, *A Room of One's Own*, and *The Waves*, considers the question of autobiography; it loosely reads these texts as a series of self-portraits by foregrounding two key concepts: woman and freedom. In a somewhat puzzling move, given her book's investment in reconciling the tensions between politics and aesthetics, Froula questions recent attempts to assimilate *The Waves* to "political concerns" (177). Instead, she invites us to see how Kant's aesthetic theory helps elucidate the alliance of the terms woman, freedom, and genius; following Kant, for whom "the imagination's freedom exists in the noumenal realm" (178), Froula wants to extricate Woolf's representation of the imagination from its association with economics, politics, empire, and a socially constructed identity. She reads *The Waves* as Woolf's examination "of whether, and how far, a woman can represent...being as such; how far a woman...can aspire to represent the universal" (179). Froula here is talking about the "abstract, nameless, autobiographical 'She'" (200)—the narrator of *The Waves* who "ventriloquizes a [woman]'s vision through six lyric voices that tell a 'life of anybody'" (177). On the one hand Froula eschews a political reading of *The Waves*, but on the other she simultaneously maintains that aesthetics and politics converge in the figure of the woman—a vanishing figure whom Froula nonetheless reads as wholly disconnected from "identity and its politics" (177). I found this chapter's discussion of politics confusing and would have welcomed more incorporation of what Froula, in her first chapter, argues is the centrality of "the geopolitical scope" (31) of Woolf's work.

Ultimately, Froula seeks to extricate the concept of civilization from its association with England's legacy of empire, reading Woolf's fascination with Richard Hakluyt's *Voyages*, for example, as evidence of the author's interest in foreign travel rather than a sign of her Anglocentrism. Although Froula acknowledges Woolf's blindness to her own "complicity with imperial domination" (32), this is not something that she retains as a central focus of her study. Instead, Froula wants us to regard Bloomsbury's Enlightenment struggle for the rights and freedoms of all in opposition to Woolf's and others' susceptibility to the lures of imperial domination. This line of argument does not always command assent, despite Froula's skillful examination of some of the most trenchant instances of the Group's anti-imperial, internationalist vision. Moreover, I wonder to what extent it is even possible for early twentieth century English men and women to invoke the idea of "new lands, new civilizations" (xiii), as Woolf does, without imaginatively recapitulating the notion of colonial worlds? How, in other words, can we read Woolf's fascination with the Elizabethan conquest of "undiscovered land" (17) without interpreting her rapture as a form of cultural imperialism? *Virginia Woolf and the Bloomsbury Avant-Garde* posits that this objective is not only desirable but possible, even likely. Readers may disagree with this premise, but they will agree that this uneven yet wide-ranging book makes a timely contribution to modernist scholarship by inviting us to rethink the aesthetic, historical, and political basis for Woolf's still relevant query, posed in *Three Guineas*: "what is this 'civilization' in which we find ourselves?"

—Jane Garrity *University of Colorado, Boulder*

Works Cited

Barrett, Eileen. "Unmasking Lesbian Passion: The Inverted World of *Mrs. Dalloway*." *Virginia Woolf: Lesbian Readings*, eds. Eileen Barrett and Patricia Cramer. New York: New York University Press, 1997.

Woolf, Virginia. *Mrs. Dalloway.* New York: Harcourt Brace, 1981.

Virginia Woolf's Novels and the Literary Past. Jane de Gay (Edinburgh: Edinburgh UP, 2006) viii + 231 pp.

This is a book about the allusions in Woolf's novels to British writers, mainly the Romantic poets and Shakespeare, but including as well Dante and Greek myth. The underlying theme of the study is Woolf's response to the work of Leslie Stephen, as she moved from the familiar view of her father as an obstacle to her writing, to a realization that she was empowered by his ideas. Woolf's text, as de Gay explains, is not simply "a palimpsest of earlier writings, but a physical space in which past writers are present and active" (10). Woolf emerges from this study a conservative writer, who differs from her contemporaries, Eliot and Joyce, by her deep attraction to the literature that she associated with her father.

De Gay argues that *The Voyage Out* juxtaposes the marriage plot of an Austen novel with allusions to "Comus." Woolf satirizes the patriarchal approval of Jane Austen as a woman writer who remained, in Stephen's phrase "within her own sphere," while at the same time imitating Austen's ability to veil her criticism within the prescribed limits of the woman writer. In her discussion of the echoes of "Comus" in the chapters on Rachel's illness, de Gay argues that Woolf shifts the focus to loss and desolation. The novel sets the pattern of Woolf's later fiction as "a tension between a desire to break and reform and a temptation to restore and reclaim" (41).

The chapter on *Jacob's Room* and *Mrs. Dalloway* opens with an appreciation of Woolf's diverse aims, "to wrest literature from the control of educated men; to embrace it for herself; and to use it for elegiac purposes" (78). But although some aspects of the argument are persuasive, de Gay's concentration on characters to the exclusion of the narrator ignores the very structure that made these novels experimental. She reads the parable of the cave from *The Republic* to demonstrate how illusory is Jacob's education in the Greek classics, and the *Phaedrus* to reveal the elegiac quality of that education. Jacob is paired with his mother Betty Flanders, who "has similar skills of animation" (82). That is, when Betty recalls her husband, Seabrook, dead for many years, lying under the earth, de Gay argues that Seabrook's name suggests a sea-change, and an allusion to Ariel's song from *The Tempest*: "Full fathom five thy father lies;/Of his bones are coral made." It might be a plausible reading, consistent with the elegiac theme, were it not that Woolf's narrator seizes the occasion to query the tombstone inscription, "Merchant of this city," which ascribes a commercial identity to a man who for most of his life had farmed, and to raise a larger question about the identity of the dead. De Gay's discussion takes no account of the shift in tone as

Betty Flanders makes her own kind of appropriation, under the skeptical eye of the narrator. Similarly in *Mrs. Dalloway* de Gay associates Septimus with Hamlet and Shelley's Prometheus, without noting that the narrator recognizes the destructive potential of Septimus' Romantic identification with Keats. Nevertheless the chapter ends with the acute perception that Woolf differed from Eliot and Joyce in that she "did not seek to appropriate that literature for herself but rather to absorb it into her own voice, and to give up her voice into a communal one" (93).

The chapter "*To the Lighthouse* and the Ghost of Leslie Stephen" is a rich discussion of elegy and the problem of presence and absence. De Gay argues that Woolf reconciles empiricist philosophy with Romantic images of the mind in a manner similar to Stephen's. The chapter begins with a comparison of the image of Julia Stephen as Madonna in passages from *The Mausoleum Book* and *To the Lighthouse*. Overtones of the work of August Comte and Wordsworth are apparent in both works as Woolf "grappled with the problem of how to establish female characters within discourses which cast them as border figures" (107). The problem of a woman's existence when no one can see her is connected with both patriarchal discourse and elegy. The discussion of "Time Passes" builds on Gillian Beer's study of Hume and elegy, as de Gay compares Woolf's image of the visionaries who walk the beach to Stephen's Gnostics, and both to Wordsworth's solitary wanderers. Lily Briscoe's painting images the reconciliation of the empiricist and Romantic images of Mrs. Ramsay. While negotiating her position in relationship to both the empiricist idea of perception and the Romantic image of the mind as open to other worlds, Woolf "achieved a balance between two important influences, but she has done so through engaging with her father's texts and has reached remarkably similar conclusions to his" (121-2).

Perhaps owing to its strengths, this chapter raises large questions about history and language. By focusing so steadily on Gnostics and Visionaries, the structure of the argument permits only a brief allusion to "the shadow of war," which seems to me an important omission in the discussion of "Time Passes." The assumption that "language has an ability to represent truth," does not resolve the problematic use of the word "truth" in the language of the writer as well as that of Stephen and Woolf. If Mrs. McNab is an instance of "the thinking subject," the idea requires more explanation. Overall this otherwise suggestive chapter isolates Woolf from her contemporaries, for whom World War I reordered assumptions about time, truth, and language.

Orlando is read as a companion to *A Room of One's Own*: Woolf sought the elements of a feminist/lesbian world in the literature of the past. Defoe's strong female characters were her model. Woolf's reference to the *Dictionary of*

National Biography challenges Stephen's idea of "the spirit of the age," and his ideas of periodization. Ambivalent sexuality and a sense that the renaissance might happen any time are attributed to her reading of Shakespeare.

Woolf's use of quotation often shifts to paraphrase in *The Waves,* a sign that her repeated quotation of Byron, Shelley, Wordsworth, and Dante helped to define her own creativity. Whereas Byron is treated in a playful manner, and Rhoda is associated with Shelley, Woolf's "moments of being" and the six characters' sense of identity are derived from *The Prelude.* The draft version of the novel reveals that the image of the wave as planetary origin echoes the "Immortality Ode." Echoes of Woolf's reading of Dante's *Inferno* mark passages devoted to Neville, Jinny, and Bernard. (Why not Susan, Louis, and Rhoda?) The labor of identifying so many echoes of previous allusions, as the text folds back on itself, leads to the important questions about language and authorial identity which are central to this novel. They are briefly mentioned in the conclusion.

In her discussion of *Between the Acts* de Gay acknowledges the effect of the imminent war on reading, drawing mainly on Coleridge for a model of the social role of the poet in time of war. On the basis of similar themes, she attributes Woolf's image of a child looking at a flower, and the Reverend Streatfield's speech after the pageant to a passage from "The Aeolian Harp." Miss La Trobe's aesthetic is derived from a passage in the *Biographia Literaria.* Other passages echo the myth of Philomela, and Keats' "Ode to a Nightingale." One wonders, why the Romantic poets in particular, since some of the most amusing portions of the pageant parody Restoration comedy. A continued emphasis on thematic similarities which rarely refer to Woolf's language blurs the critical focus.

The book is within its limits carefully researched and clearly written. It presents Woolf as a writer comfortable within domestic and national boundaries; even the references to Homer and the Greek Anthology refer to a Greece that had become a part of English culture. But beyond references to Leslie Stephen the critical argument does not seek to justify what has been excluded from the literary past. If the *Diaries* were a guide to Woolf's reading, then it is significant that as she was working on *Mrs. Dalloway* she was engaged not only with the Romantics, but with her translation of *Agamemnon* and her reading of Proust. Woolf's *Diary* mentions, but de Gay does not, Woolf's reading of Russian writers, Dostoyevsky, Tolstoy, and Turgenev, to whom she was introduced not by her father but by Lytton Strachey. In addition Woolf's holograph reading notes receive virtually no attention, although some of the most suggestive material may be found in the notebooks that Brenda Silver has made accessible and usable. Reading microfilm is tedious and Woolf's handwriting can be a nightmare, but she made copious notes on Austen, Defoe, and Wordsworth, among others. In fact the range of reading that the notes demonstrate is both astonishingly broad, and curiously aligned, with a few exceptions, with the canon of Classical, British, and European literature. Nor has de Gay sought to balance the figure of Leslie Stephen by consulting the *Selected Letters* (1998), which contain some insights that surprised me ("the same book is different to different generations," Stephen, 127), and would have enriched her discussion.

—Emily Dalgarno, *Boston University*

Work Cited

Stephen, Leslie. *Selected Letters*. Eds. John W. Bicknell and Mark A. Reger. Columbus: Ohio State University Press, 1996.

"My Madness Saved Me": *The Madness and Marriage of Virginia Woolf*. Thomas Szasz (New Brunswick: Transaction, 2006) xvi + 154
Our Culture, What's Left of It: The Mandarins and the Masses. Theodore Dalrymple (Chicago: Ivan R. Dee, 2005) xi + 341

I admit to something of a quandary over whether to write about the two books under review here. In *Three Guineas*, Woolf refers to "the small boy [who] struts and trumpets outside the window: implore him to stop; he goes on; say nothing; he stops" (*TG* 167). Much as I would like to believe that people like Theodore Dalrymple and Thomas Szasz would stop writing nonsense about Virginia Woolf were they simply ignored, I worry that left unchallenged, the errors, falsehoods, and just plain barmy opinions of such writers might find their way into, say, undergraduate essays or Wikipedia entries. Another difficulty lies in finding a way to engage in argument with writers who make only assertions. Both these books display the features of a common contemporary public discourse that depends on battering its audience into submission by repeating its opinions over and over without pausing to listen or to entertain the possibility that there might be another and informed point of view (is this "bloviation"?).

The more surprising—given his previous work—of the two is Szasz, who presents his book as a study of Virginia Woolf. Szasz is, justly, celebrated for his radical critique, documented in many books and articles over the past four decades, of the mental illness industry. Given the range of works addressing Woolf's mental state and the arguments these have generated, a contribution from Thomas Szasz might, *prima facie*, have been welcome. This farrago, unfortunately, adds nothing to those arguments because Woolf is merely a pretext for Szasz's real target, which is the cultural influence of Kay Redfield Jamison (author of *Touched With Fire: Manic-Depressive Illness and the Artistic Temperament*). This concern is foreshadowed on the first page where Szasz describes Woolf as a "woman writer 'touched by fire'" (1), but the attack on Jamison is isolated in an Appendix, thus emphasizing the pretextual role Woolf has to play in this screed. Woolf's name does, after all, attract attention.

An alert publisher's reader would have listed every error of fact that appears in this book, but that cannot be the function of a review. Presumably Transaction sent the manuscript to someone qualified to assess it before they agreed to publish it . . . or might they have considered that someone of Szasz's reputation could be trusted implicitly to present them with a sound piece of work? For most of its information, *My Madness Saved Me* relies on websites in the manner of a sloppy undergraduate research paper: to find gradesaver.com cited in a book is quite startling. Quotations from Woolf's own writings are rarely from primary sources, coming instead from the works of other critics and biographers. Many of the arguments rehashed herein can be found in more nuanced and informed expression elsewhere (for example, on the Woolfs' marriage and Virginia's anti-Semitism, in Cynthia Ozick's 1973 piece in *Commentary*, "Mrs. Virginia Woolf").

The caricature named "Virginia Woolf" that Szasz presents led "a largely joyless life" (88), was not interested "in much of the external world" (33), and (my favorite) killed herself "to enhance her fame" (88). Vita Sackville-West (to whom Szasz refers as "the proprietor of Knole" [93], thus restoring to her the house she so famously lost because she was a woman) was "Virginia's supposed lesbian lover" (or, as he puts it in the hilarious "Dramatis Personae" that precedes the text, her "presumed lover"): does Mr. Szasz perhaps have a problem with female sexuality? When Julia Duckworth married Leslie Stephen, apparently she had only two sons—Stella has disappeared. On Leslie's side, there is no mention of Laura Stephen. All kinds of people are included in Szasz's version of the Bloomsbury group, including Rupert Brooke and Gwen Raverat. The notoriously ascetic Leonard Woolf, who used galley pages as toilet paper, "loved money and the comforts it could buy" (18); he was rejected from military service in World War I because he was "mentally unfit" (19). But pointing out such errors and omissions is unfair because it is so easy. *"My Madness Saved Me"* is worth no one's time; to quote its author, "This is gibberish" (37).

Theodore Dalrymple (the pompous pseudonym of an English prison doctor and psychiatrist named Anthony Daniels) reminds me a little of Professor von X, and a lot of Sir William Bradshaw. Most of the essays in this collection first appeared in *City Journal*, a publication of The Manhattan Institute, a conservative think tank. The cover of the book is adorned with a photograph of a pierced punk guaranteed to evoke the deepest distaste in the clubby men who are Dalrymple's audience.

Opening with an account of his work among the poor and violent, Dalrymple dwells at some length on the moral roots of the pathologies he describes. He is particularly concerned with the bad choices of partner made by women who come to him for treatment, and castigates "intellectuals" for their refusal to acknowledge what to him is so clear: that these women "are in large part responsible for their own downfall at the hands of evil men" (11). Like Szasz, Dalrymple's preferred rhetorical mode is assertion. To this, he adds the ploy of positing of imagined "intellectuals," straw persons with whom he can joust. For example, in describing one of his "cases," he writes:

> What better phrase than the frivolity of evil describes the conduct of a mother who turns her own fourteen-year-old child out of doors because her latest boyfriend does not want him or her in the house? And what better phrase describes the attitude of those intellectuals who see in this conduct nothing but an extension of human freedom and choice, another thread in life's rich tapestry? (12)

Oh, those "intellectuals," up to their wickedness again! But might we know who they are? Could he name *anyone* who believes turning a fourteen-year-old into the street is "an extension of human freedom"?

When patients are brought to Dr. Dalrymple, they can, he tells us, "with few exceptions . . . be brought to see the truth . . . they are not depressed; they are unhappy—and they are unhappy because they have chosen to live in a way that they ought not to live, and in which it is impossible to be happy" (15). Does this ring a bell? "Equanimity, practise equanimity Mrs Woolf" (*D2* 189). Perhaps Mr. Dalrymple also has "a friend in Surrey" who teaches that "difficult art" of "Proportion" (*MD* 102). He does, after all, say that Woolf suffered from "a self-pitying lack of proportion" (67). Somebody, I think, must have laughed at Mr. Dalrymple in his cradle (*AROO* 31).

Is it, though, unfair to review work intended so obviously only for the circle in which the writer moves, where for argument is substituted the knowing phrase "of course" ("Virginia Woolf's name is not normally associated with great affairs of state, of course" [62])? Where to engage with the writing of others is really just too tiresome to bother with? If Dalrymple thinks that D. H. Lawrence was "an earnest, but not a serious, writer" (60), "a bad writer and worse thinker," but does not deign to tell us *why* he thinks this, then how can we disagree? We are put in the position of a child whose parent tells us that shrimp, in fact, *does* taste good, despite what we are experiencing; the child says "Yuck." It is not really an argument.

One of his chapters, "The Rage of Virginia Woolf," offers an account of the argument of *Three Guineas* that might be a useful example of the *reductio ad absurdum* for budding writers. The reading of Woolf's "burn the college to the ground" passage is as hilarious as Swift's *Modest Proposal*, but I think Dalrymple actually is serious in his accusing Woolf of inciting arson. The bluntness of his readings is astounding in a mature writer with claims to literary sensibility (it is on the level of the student who once told me, sincerely, that Oedipus should have sought a second opinion after receiving that of the oracle).

As with Szasz's portrait, here again we have a caricature that will cause only bewilderment to anyone who has actually read Woolf's work. This wide-ranging and perceptive critic whose reverence for the tradition of English literature is embodied in hundreds of reviews and essays is "nothing if not a great hater of all that had gone before her" (66) according to Dalrymple: "Her lack of recognition that anything had ever been achieved or created before her advent that was worthy of protection and preservation is all but absolute" (70).

Dalrymple is, however, nothing new on the scene. He is in direct line of descent from misogynist Bloomsbury-bashers like Wyndham Lewis and Prince Mirsky. When Woolf published *Three Guineas* she knew it would arouse the ire of the patriarchs. Maynard Keynes dismissed it ("We all put up with you Virginia"), and her official biographer expressed amazement that his aunt could have such thoughts on the eve of World War II. What is particularly galling for Dalrymple is the coincidence of *Three Guineas*' publication in 1938 and his own mother's fleeing Nazi Germany that year. He invokes his mother at the close of his essay as a contrast with a Virginia Woolf who spent her life in "languorous contemplation of the exquisite" (70). Dalrymple's mother, "with her wrench by day and helmet by night, did more for civilization . . . than Mrs. Woolf had ever done, with her jeweled prose disguising her narcissistic rage" (76). Although we might think we know what Woolf's fate would have been at the hands of the Nazis—she and Leonard were on an SS list of those to be arrested after invasion—Dalrymple believes that had Britain been invaded, Woolf "would have found common cause" with them (74).

It is instructive to place Dalrymple's contrast of his mother's heroic flight and Virginia Woolf's effete fascism alongside another account of "Mrs. Woolf" (that honorific is always a giveaway). Ruth Gruber, who brought one thousand refugees to the USA in 1944, told Woolf in 1935 that her "writing gives me the will to write as a woman" (Gruber 5). Woolf, writes Gruber, "was on the side of the creators, the dreamers, the poets, the women. On the other side were the critics, the predators, the destroyers, the angry, hostile, women-loathing men" (14). Woolf was clear-eyed about the likely reception of *Three Guineas* (an early working-title for which was "On Being Despised"): "I'm going to beaten, I'm going to be laughed at, I'm going to be held up to scorn and ridicule" (*D5* 64). Dalrymple's sneering account of her work and life does not have the weight of knowledge to ground it. Like Queenie Leavis's sneering review of *Three Guineas*—which Woolf put down to her having been snubbed—"The Rage of Virginia Woolf" is an exercise in shallow misogyny. Like that scourge of the fin-de-siècle Max Nordau, whom George Bernard Shaw described as "a vigorous and capable journalist, shrewd enough to see that there is a good opening for a big reactionary book," Dalrymple expresses opinions that are "at bottom, nothing but the familiar delusion of the used-up man that the world is going to the dogs" (Shaw 20).

—Mark Hussey, *Pace University*

Works Cited

Gruber, Ruth. 1935. *Virginia Woolf: The Will to Create as A Woman*. NY: Carroll & Graff, 2005.

Shaw, George Bernard. "*The Sanity of Art: An Exposure of the Current Nonsense About Artists Being Degenerate.*" *The Fin de Siècle: A Reader in Cultural History c. 1880-1900*, ed. Sally Ledger and Roger Luckhurst. Oxford: Oxford UP, 2000. 20-22.

Woolf, Virginia. *A Room of One's Own*. San Diego: Harcourt Brace, 1981.

———. *Three Guineas*. New York: Harcourt Brace, 1938

British Modernism and Censorship. Celia Marshik (New York: Cambridge UP, 2006) xii + 257 pp. Illus.

Let me begin with the ending because Celia Marshik's "Afterword: Forgotten Evils" sums up the exceptional relevance of her study. As Marshik observes:

> In the place of a vague (and historically inaccurate) notion that prudishness or preoccupation with "virtue" ended with the closing of the Victorian era, we should substitute recognition of a multifaceted morality movement that remained active through the first three decades of the twentieth century. (203)

Marshik's work rescues from cultural amnesia a significant amount of what has been lost. Her highly integrated and historically contextual argument details the conflict between societal constraints and British literary creative expression from the 1860s to the 1930s. Marshik crosses genres as she examines in an evenhanded and lucid fashion the key issues at stake in what she terms the "censorship dialectic," demonstrating that censorship, by its very attempts to silence expression, actually fosters rich and complex imaginative resistance. In her reading of selected works by five representative literary figures—Dante Gabriel Rossetti, Bernard Shaw, Virginia Woolf, James Joyce and Jean Rhys—Marshik creates a persuasive and densely interwoven, sequential narrative rather than offering isolated instances of resistance. Her argument regarding literary censorship documents specific authorial responses to censorship, and her thematic study of the texts focuses specifically on the way these particular authors depict women working in the sex trade. Thus, Marshik shows her readers how the very shape of literature in the 20th century was determined by the authors' ever-present awareness of a culture of censorship initiated in the 19th century. The volume also includes illustrations from the period that visually reinforce Marshik's argument.

Marshik specifically positions these authors' literary work in relation to the Social Purity movement, which vigorously sought to ban not only prostitution and sexual exploitation, but also to classify and suppress as obscene all literary depiction of such transgressive sexuality whether such representation was prurient or aesthetic, degrading or inspired. The social purity movement:

> rejected modernism almost wholesale and raised concerns about the motorcar, birth-control accessories, films and the cinemas that showed them, single individuals living in flats, the theatre, 'indecent' books, train stations, employment agencies, ice-cream parlors, and many other modern commodities, spaces, and behaviors. (204)

Marshik examines in depth the risks faced by writers who challenged the social purity constraints and aggravated the moralists. Such consequences ranged from public condemnation to financial losses incurred when circulating libraries refused to stock the books to punitive legal action through obscenity prosecution. As she documents, the legal basis for an obscenity charge was the broadly defined Hicklin Rule authorized under Lord Campbell's Act of 1857. Although there were reassurances that "the law would not apply to serious literature, the vagueness of the Act's language all but ensured that literature would fall under its purview" (22). Quite simply, the Hincklin Rule did not distinguish between the sordid and the artistic or between pornography and social commentary.

Marshik's "Introduction: The Ethics of Indecency," begins with the account of William T. Stead's 1885 journalistic foray into sexual exploitation. In the "Maiden Tribute of Modern Babylon" series, he reported vividly on "white slavery," the exploitation of working class young girls sold or tricked into the sex trade, often by their own parents. Stead's systematic exposure of the Maiden Tribute ultimately resulted in legislation raising the age of consent for girls from 13 to 16. Ironically, Stead himself was tried, convicted and jailed for having purchased a girl for £5 to illustrate his claim that girls were routinely sold to brothel recruiters. Stead's influence continued in a spooky fashion even after his death in the sinking of the *Titanic*. Marshik points out that Stead, like Arthur Conan Doyle, was very interested in spiritualism and the paranormal and that after his death mediums of the period continued to communicate his ideas as if coming from him.

As Marshik indicates, Stead's personal effort to end the traffic in girls continued Josephine Butler's work. Butler, an activist whom Virginia Woolf held in high regard (as is indicated by her references to Butler in *Three Guineas*), was a key player in an earlier campaign to defend women and girls from the outrages perpetrated under the auspices of government-regulated prostitution, a provision authorized by the Contagious Diseases Acts which Butler fought to repeal. Butler's success, as Marshik points out, was reversed during the Great War "when Parliament passed one provision of the Defense of the Realm Act [DORA 40d] effectively putting the Victorian Contagious Diseases Acts back into effect to protect military personnel from venereal disease" by "mak[ing] it possible for a woman to be compulsorily subjected to medical examination on the accusation by a member of H. M. Forces that he had been infected with a venereal disease" (105).

By beginning her argument with the issue of the Maiden Tribute and white slave traffic, Marshik exposes the conflicted territory between the sex trade and literary obscenity that continued into the 20th and remains an issue in the 21st century. Both prostitution and pornography were then, are now and will no doubt continue to remain entangled with the global issues of policing sexuality[1]—an activity that necessarily includes both the identification of obscenity and the subsequent decision to censor it.

In the first chapter—"Dante Gabriel Rossetti and the Censorship Dialectic"—Marshik closely examines Rossetti's anxieties about censorship as he crafted the revisions of two particularly incendiary poems—"Jenny" and "Nuptial Sleep," works that he included in *The House of Life*. "Jenny" is the more obviously problematic poem because of the male speaker's commentary on the charming and lovely prostitute whom he addresses directly. Yet, it was the other poem, "Nuptial Sleep," a sonnet depicting post-coital caresses between a married couple, that triggered the attack on Rossetti. A minor contemporary writer, Robert Buchanan, writing as Thomas Maitland, launched the assault in his review. Coining the term the "Fleshly School of Poetry" to describe the degenerate nature of such work, Buchanan accused Rossetti of coarsely displaying the private intimacies of marriage in public. Marshik points the reader to Ezra Pound's 1920 belated but stinging counter-attack deriding the prudery of "foetid Buchanan" in his poetic manifesto "Hugh Selwyn Mauberly." Such continuity reminds us that, although most of the modernists and many subsequent scholars have attempted to sequester modernism from the Victorian era, such a distinction is an historical impossibility.

In the second chapter, "Bernard Shaw's Defensive Laughter," Marshik examines *Mrs. Warren's Profession* and *Pygmalion* as prime sites of Shaw's battle with the censors. Shaw, who initially had supported Stead's efforts, soon discovered that Stead—like other social purity advocates—viewed theater as a threat to virtue while Shaw himself saw the genre as a didactic vehicle for social reform. Marshik dedicates much of the chapter to the history of Shaw's efforts to produce *Mrs. Warren's Profession* on the stage. Shaw countered the "precensoring" of the production in England by publishing the work in print—with an extensive preface, of course. Although the play was produced in America, there

---

[1] See, for example, articles by op-ed contributors Bob Herbert and Nicholas D. Kristof of *The New York Times*. Kristof relatively recently did something very similar to what W. T. Stead had done to make his point. As Kristof recounts:
> Three years ago, I purchased two teenage girls from the Cambodian brothels that enslaved them and returned them to their families. Plenty of readers promptly wrote to say: "Buy one for me, too."
> Those readers had honorable intentions (I think) and simply wanted to do something concrete to confront global poverty and sex trafficking. But buying enslaved girls isn't a general solution — partly because it raises the market price and increases the incentive to kidnap other girls and sell them to brothels.

were immediate consequences. The play opened first in New Haven, where the mayor shut it down after the first performance. After the performance, in New York City, Police Commissioner William McAdoo "obtained arrest warrants, on charges of 'disorderly conduct'" for many of those associated with the production (54).

In the face of this kind of aggressive resistance to his work, Shaw decided that his strategy would have to change. While Rossetti had raged at his critics, Shaw, as Marshik notes, chose to fight back with humor. Thus, in *Pygmalion,* Shaw avoided explicit references to prostitution. However, as Marshik points out, the theme of sexual exploitation is still evident, though it is mitigated by comedy. Marshik's discussion of Eliza is particularly important. For example, Eliza protests in the first act that she has done nothing by speaking to a gentleman—she was just selling flowers, not her virginity. Not only is the character's first name identical to the real name of Eliza Armstrong (a.k.a. "Lily"), the young girl whom Stead purchased for £5, but there is specific reference to this very same purchase price for Eliza Doolittle's father actually demands that Henry Higgins pay him for £5 for his daughter—and Henry Higgins complies.

Marshik's chapter "Virginia Woolf and the Gender of Censorship" reinforces the existing scholarship showing that Woolf engaged in self-censorship while relying heavily on irony and humor as her primary defenses against external censorship. Marshik begins with commentary on one of Woolf's earliest instances of frustrated self-silencing. The young Virginia Stephen, as Marshik notes, "wanted to write an article on Louise de la Vallière, mistress of King Louis XIV of France" for the *Cornhill Magazine.* But, in a letter to her sister Vanessa, Virginia worries somewhat sarcastically about phrasing, asking: "will the Cornhill call a prostitute a prostitute, or a mistress a mistress?" (88). Of course, most contemporary readers would have known just from the context the nature of the relationship whether it was named or not—as was certainly the case with Oscar Wilde's "the love that dares not speak its name." Thus, the crux of the matter is not that a given illicit practice exists but that its existence has been articulated. Woolf hints at this silencing in her description of an encounter in *Jacob's Room.* As Jacob leaves a prostitute's place of business, he cringes inwardly: "Madame herself seeing Jacob out had about her that leer, that lewdness, that quake of the surface (visible in the eyes chiefly), which spills the whole bag of ordure, with difficulty held together, over the pavement" (*JR* 105). Thus, like a homosexual man, Woolf—as Marshik indicates (and as the passage quoted above suggests)—was able to speak openly only in private and was forced to speak obliquely in public to avoid censure as well as censorship, a conundrum that keenly "illustrates the divided world into which Stephen was born and which she had to navigate in order to become the successful novelist Virginia Woolf" (89).

Marshik follows a chronological sequence in her discussion of Woolf's major works, beginning with the calculated silences and omissions in *The Voyage Out*. As Marshik argues: "Throughout the novel, Rachel continues to encounter the 'things people don't say'" (98). Such deliberate silences in *The Voyage Out* include oblique references, ellipses and dashes, (a technique that Katherine Mansfield also used to allude to the forbidden). For example, the character Mrs. Thornbury murmurs to her friend: "'And I have heard young women talk quite openly of—,'" and Mrs. Elliot responds "Dreadful, dreadful!," an exchange that Marshik interprets as an implicit reference to the "surplus" of British women who, unable to find either a husband or a job, turn to prostitution for a livelihood (99). There is also Mrs. Lola Mendoza, a woman "who trips in and out of the hotel's rooms 'with paint in the hollows of her cheeks'" and is "evicted from the hotel right before Rachel's illness" but is never given a voice. When St. John Hirst tells Rachel: "'They've hoofed out the prostitute'" and wants to initiate "'a full enquiry'" into the incident, Terence, Rachel's fiancé, displays indifference to the situation: "'it's a great shame, poor woman; only I don't see what's to be done—'" (101).

Marshik accurately situates *Jacob's Room* as more audacious, "reveal[ing] a deep interest in the sexually marginal, particularly in prostitutes. Unlike *Voyage*, the book represents the history, thoughts and speech of whores such as Florinda and Laurette" (104). As Marshik points out, ironically, at the moment Woolf was writing this more intrepid novel (and rejoicing in her independence from editorial interference from her previous publisher, her half-brother, Gerald Duckworth), she was also exercising prudence in her role as a publisher facing the likelihood of obscenity prosecution. She and Leonard had initially agreed to publish *Ulysses*. However, since they would have had to outsource the project to a printer (and the printers they approached flatly refused to take on the liability in the face of inevitable legal action), they ultimately had to back out of the agreement.

Differentiating between the women depicted in Rossetti and Shaw and the female characters in Woolf's novel, Marshik argues the male authors had a greater degree of freedom in their discussion of the prostitute and that Woolf had to be more circumspect because of her sex. For example, specific reference to a character as a prostitute is scarce. Instead, Woolf uses a coded technique, or as Marshik remarks, "a script that allows for little individual expression," in which a woman, by sitting on a man's knee, is identified for the reader as loose. Early on in the novel, Florinda sits on Jacob's knee; in the manuscript version of the novel (but not in the published version), Fanny Elmer, "an artist's model," also sits on Jacob's knee; later in the novel, an actress aptly named Magdalen sits on the knee of a man named Mangin. Marshik notes that "Mangin" is not an accidental name but rather has "a specific historical reference" to "a Parisian prefect of police who brought regulation of prostitutes to its highest degree of efficiency in the 1830s" (109).

Marshik also contends that in the novel all the young women who loved Jacob are depicted as the victims of societal constraints. For example, when the uneducated prostitute, Florinda, becomes pregnant, she "faces an uncertain future: abortion or unchosen motherhood, perhaps venereal disease" (105). By contrast, Clara Durrant enjoys a degree of privilege. But, although Clara "maintains the gracious life of her family and class," she nonetheless "lacks access to education and employment and is also prohibited from voicing or acting on desire" in "a public sphere and social movement increasingly suspicious of women's morals" (106).

Marshik links her discussion of *Orlando* to the obscenity trial of Radclyffe Hall's *Well of Loneliness* and, in the larger context, in relation to other works such as *Sleeveless Errand* by Norah James (another book that the Hogarth Press declined to publish that provoked an obscenity prosecution). As Marshik argues, Woolf's *Orlando* openly mocks the social purity rhetoric especially when Orlando is transformed into a woman. There, the narrator (whom Marshik regards as somewhat prudish) states that "'whole edifice of female government is based on that foundation stone; chastity is their jewel, their centre piece which they run mad to protect, and die when they are ravished of'" (114). While scholars have long thought that *Orlando* survived unscathed in the censorship wars despite its suggestive references to prostitution and its hints of Sapphism, Marshik discovered in her research at the Home Office that *Orlando* actually did provoke a reaction regarding its salacious qualities; however, despite the annotation on the document "Considers shd be suppressed" (118) no action was ever taken, Woolf was never apprised of the complaint, and the file disappeared, perhaps destroyed during the Blitz.

The subsequent section of the chapter on Woolf focuses on *A Room of One's Own*. Here Marshik (in a less radical reading of the text than that offered by Jane Marcus in "Sapphistry: Narration as Lesbian Seduction in *A Room of One's Own*") discusses in depth Woolf's specific references to Sir William Joynson-Hicks, Sir Archibald Bodkin, and Sir Chartres Biron, "the government officials responsible for suppressing literary works" (121), including the *Well of Loneliness*. Marshik also integrates the passage from "Professions for Women" in which Woolf describes the harsh self-censorship imposed on women writers who wished to speak of what Marshik terms the "sexed body" (125).

Key highlights in the chapter "James Joyce and the Necessary Scandal of Art" include Marshik's compelling argument that Joyce was consciously engaged in defying the prim and prude values of the censorship advocates in his work—and that he deliberately ignored the legal risks that the printers who refused to publish his work would have faced if they had agreed to bring out works such as *Dubliners*. Marshik notes that the social purity movement in Ireland created an elaborate rhetorical argument that "mapped" corrupt values onto England and the Continent, and that Joyce actively sought to expose the absurdity of this sham by foregrounding the ever-present fact of prostitution in Dublin. Thus, in *Portrait*, Joyce "subtly depicts the prostitute as a kind of artist and prostitution becomes a trope that offers Stephen distance from, as well as accord with, the Irish people" (146). Marshik also offers a thorough discussion of *Ulysses*, printed in France—a safe zone for creative expression at the time— and its categorization as a "Continental" (and therefore degenerate) publication as well as its impact on the censorship debates.

The chapter "Jean Rhys and the Downward Path" examines the aftermath of this literary culture war. As Marshik contends, Rhys's work "suffered" "from a kind of repressive tolerance that points to the role of censorship in, paradoxically, *helping* other modernists to find audiences" (170). The lives of the fallen women Jean Rhys portrays correspond all too closely to the warnings of social purity activists. As Marshik notes, "an anonymous 1916 book[,] *Downward Paths: An Inquiry into the Causes which Contribute to the Making of a Prostitute*" (170), instructing women how to avoid this fate, is a blueprint of the lives of Rhys's characters. But, rather than endorsing these dire admonitions, "Rhys's novels [. . .] direct irony at government censors and the social purity movement" by "encourag[ing] readers to sympathize with [her] protagonists" and "condemn moralists for their lack of sympathy" (169-70). This final chapter begins with a discussion of a new female sexual role that emerged in the 1930s —the "amateur prostitute" (167). This development in the sex trade resulted from the greater economic independence and sexual freedom of single women. The amateur prostitute typically exchanged sexual services for gifts, jewelry, attractive clothing and the like, a lifestyle that Rhys understood first-hand. Rhys's characters work in seedy jobs (just as she did) as chorus girls or at manicure and massage businesses, forms of employment that the social purity pamphlets of the period warned were closely associated with prostitution. Marshik pays particular attention to this strange intersection in Rhys's work where the rhetoric of the morality discourse merges with the dire realities that lonely, desperate women confront. As Marshik observes, Rhys counters the judgmental condemnation of the fallen woman "by depicting those in power from the perspective of the powerless" (180).

Brilliant and thoroughly grounded in archival material and historical context, this book is essential reading for scholars of Victorian and Modernist literature. Marshik's study is unquestionably a landmark contribution British literary studies and offers a perspective that no previous book-length scholarly work has addressed.

—Vara Neverow, *Southern Connecticut State University*

Works Cited

Kristof, Nicholas D. "Fighting Brothels with Books." *The New York Times.* 24 December 2006.

Marcus, Jane. "Sapphistry: Narration as Lesbian Seduction in *A Room of One's Own.*" *Virginia Woolf and the Languages of Patriarchy.* Bloomington: Indiana UP, 1987. 163-87.

Woolf, Virginia. *Jacob's Room.* 1922. New York: Harcourt Brace Jovanovich, 1950.

Virginia Woolf: Feminism and the Reader. Anne E. Fernald (NY: Palgrave Macmillan, 2006) xii + 223

Anne E. Fernald's *Virginia Woolf: Feminism and the Reader* is composed of an "eclectic historicism" (14). Elegantly written and meticulously researched, her study looks at a diverse and divergent group of writers—Sappho, Hakluyt, Addison, and Byron—to establish the relationship between Woolf's feminism and her reading habits. In order to do this, we are called to reconsider literary history in general, its construction, and its impact on our understanding of Woolf. With her own sensitivity to literary history, Fernald has successfully merged Woolf the feminist with Woolf the literary historian, showing that it is unnecessary to separate the two.

In developing a new method for literary history Fernald attempts to move beyond the metaphors of family and apprenticeship (advocated by critics like Harold Bloom) and instead proposes a feminist theory of tradition based on Wai Chee Dimock's notion of "resonance." Resonance embraces and celebrates literary adaptation rather than viewing it as part of an Oedipal struggle, and Fernald asks her readers to consider the implications of developing a theory of literary history that is free from family metaphors. In order to put historical context ahead of family romance, she creates three contexts for reading Woolf's work: the original context of the source text's literary production; the context in which Woolf received, read, and wrote; and the context of Fernald's study itself (4). Each chapter traces a single aspect of Woolf's feminism as it develops from the beginning of her career to the end, "looking at her feminism in the contexts of nation, the imagination and memory, the public sphere, and fame" (9). The chapters then move through Woolf's writing life, but each chapter contains a different context, thereby allowing different conclusions to emerge. By using this approach, Fernald avoids a reductive determinism that the family romance structure inevitably leads to.

Taking Woolf's commitment to feminism as her starting point, Fernald examines the "shifting nuances of her feminism in response to the central political questions of her art" (10). Sappho, Hakluyt, Addison, and Byron function as synecdoches for literary history, and Fernald illustrates how Woolf uses each to refine her attitude toward particular aspects of feminist thought. In doing so, *Virginia Woolf: Feminism and the Reader* echoes other modernist methodologies, such as Strachey's *Eminent Victorians*, that hypothesize figures who are not necessarily viewed as icons of their age's greatness. In letting these figures stand synecdochally for Woolf's reading, the book demonstrates how Woolf "creates resonances and [how] feminist possibilities for her are far beyond what other critics . . . have recognized" (12).

The first chapter, titled "Sapphic Fragments as English Literature," is full of implications for Woolf's notion of literary history, particularly her notion of modernist criticism. The chapter gives a fine overview of Woolf's relationship to Greece and Greek literature, starting with her early juvenilia through three major texts from the mid-1920s: *Mrs. Dalloway*, *To the Lighthouse*, and *The Common Reader*. It also explores Woolf's complex relation with her own Englishness, particularly her engagement with Greek culture and her rejection of nationalist English Hellenism.

As Fernald asserts, Britain, as an aspiring Imperial power, had long developed an identification and obsession with ancient Greece. Woolf too attaches herself to Greek culture, represented for her by Sappho, and looks to it for insight into the role of women as well as other aesthetic possibilities. Her essay "On Not Knowing Greek" quotes passages from Greek literature on grief and mourning. Woolf shows us that we do not just experience grief and mourning with the Greeks when we read them, but we also grieve "our distance from them." The fragmentary nature of our knowledge of Greek language and culture adds another layer of sadness. But an even more provocative insight is that Woolf, rather than grieve the fragmentary nature of our knowledge of Greek, celebrates and embraces it. The Victorian archaeological discoveries that preceded Woolf's essay had the unintended result of heightening awareness of the fragmentariness of knowledge about ancient Greece. For Woolf, as well as other modernist writers, this developed into a greater appreciation for the "aesthetic of the fragment" (32). Fragments offer "a rich array of intertextual resonances" (37), and Sappho's fragments of poetry in particular emphasize the poem's aesthetic. The fragments "nicely illustrate the emerging modernist sense of reality as wholly constructed by language" (38). But for Fernald this also holds political implications: Sappho's combination of pacifism, sublime poetry, love of women, and mystery make her the ideal Greek ancestor of Woolf (38). Sappho's poems may represent the greatness of the Greek language, but "they cannot be pressed into the service of official state nationalism, Greek or English" (39).

The idea of nation in English culture is continued in the second chapter, "The Memory Palace and the Lumber Room." Through careful analysis of "The Elizabethan Lumber Room," Fernald argues that Woolf "documents the transformation of the English language from the humble, pragmatic language of ordinary people into the language of Shakespeare" and that her "originality lies in her claim that the agent of that transformation was Hakluyt's *Trafficks and Discoveries*[,] a huge collection of narratives of voyages, mostly English, mostly by sea" (51). The chapter discusses Hakluyt's influence on Woolf from her very earliest essays to her later novels. Virginia Stephen's first publication on Hakluyt was a 1906 review of Professor Walter Raleigh's *The English Voyages of the Sixteenth Century*. From there Woolf went on to write *The Voyage Out* (1915), where references to *Trafficks and Discoveries* are most literal.

It is not until Woolf's middle phase that we see the more substantial references and allusions. Fernald creatively traces Woolf's transformation of Hakluyt in four ways. The first is by way of further comparison to Raleigh, whose thesis on the impact of voyages on poetry Woolf extends; second, there is a reading of "The Mark on the Wall," wherein she shows her antipathy to system and her desire for imaginative openness. The third approach to Hakluyt is found in a reading of "The Elizabethan Lumber Room," where Fernald emphasizes comparisons between voyaging, collecting travel narratives, and richly imagined texts. Finally, we start to see Woolf address the question of gender, travel, and imagination in *Mrs. Dalloway*. The chapter ends with a discussion of *Between the Acts* as Woolf's retreat from internationalism and women's travel, concluding with the suggestion that Woolf's anti-imperialism was, at the end of her life, "more isolationist than cosmopolitan" (84).

Though isolationist in her anti-imperial views, Woolf was always interested in the "public sphere," and it is her engagement with the public sphere that

Chapter Three—"A Feminist Public Sphere? Virginia Woolf's Revisions of the Eighteenth Century"—addresses. Fernald first traces Woolf and Bloomsbury's intellectual admiration for the eighteenth century and then focuses on Addison's resonance in Woolf's work. It is not, Fernald argues, in the eighteenth-century coffee houses and salons that Woolf finds her public voice, but in the essays of the eighteenth-century newspaper, the *Spectator* particularly. In those essays, Woolf finds the tools for entering public discourse, along with her identification with the outsider, the "spectator." This chapter follows Woolf's development from an anonymous review writer for the *Times Literary Supplement*, to the optimistic depiction of same-sex public discourse in *Night and Day* (1919), to the essays "A Society" and "Eccentrics," through the 1920s, where Woolf develops a satirical view of masculinist public discourse in *Mrs. Dalloway* (1925), *Orlando* (1928), and her 1938 treatise, *Three Guineas*.

As Fernald points out, "Woolf sought to participate in public debate and make a living as a respected mainstream cultural authority without giving up her feminism" (86). Woolf began her career as a public intellectual writing for the *TLS*. Well placed to appreciate the importance of rational critical thought, Woolf began to be skeptical of the public sphere represented by the eighteenth century. For Woolf, "society's compromises and exclusions of women's talk [are linked] directly to an eighteenth-century legacy of exclusion" (93). But this exclusion is a product of the coffee house, the thousands of coffee houses, from which women were barred. Male conversation was translated for eighteenth-century women through Addison's *Spectator* essays, and it is his periodical essays, not his conversation, that Woolf venerates.

Fernald further illustrates Woolf's ambivalent relation with Addison in *Mrs. Dalloway* and *Orlando*, which emerge as biting satires of the public sphere. *Mrs. Dalloway* investigates "the significance of women's influence on the male-dominated world of politics with a jaded eye" (102); *Orlando*, in comparison, "exposes the eighteenth-century's reputation for intellectually stimulating and politically influential conversation as myth" (105). The chapter concludes with *Three Guineas*, where Woolf not only defines herself as an outsider, but moves into an exploration of "the moral ambiguity of detachment" (112). The model of Addison's "spectator" finds a "substantial and modern object." Woolf's spectator, her outsider and observer, is feminized and is used to criticize patriarchy itself (113).

In the final chapter, "A Very Sincere Performance: Woolf, Byron, and Fame," Fernald draws an immediate comparison between Woolf and Byron by stating that they were both "famous in their own lifetimes and they worried about how to control the dissemination and commodification of their image, works, and ideas" (119). In order to make this comparison Fernald looks at two extensive diary entries Woolf wrote on Byron, one in 1918 when she read him for the first time and the other in 1930 when she returned to him while writing *The Waves* (1931). In that novel she "uses Bernard's impersonation of Byron as a vehicle through which to explore the linked themes of promise, fame, death, and writing" (120). Fernald ends her discussion of Woolf and Byron by examining Woolf's last years, in which the Spanish Civil War "causes her to intensify her opposition to political martyrdom and, thus, her suspicion of what Byron, a martyr himself, signifies for his admirers" (120). The Byronic figure in Woolf crosses gender, age, and even (in the case of *Flush*) species. The chapter moves through Woolf's attitude toward fame and its consequences, "its effect on one's financial and intellectual independence, its intrusions into one's privacy, and the political clout and responsibility that comes with cultural capital" (120).

The epilogue to Fernald's study, "Woolf in Africa: Doris Lessing, Nawal El Saadawi, and Ama Ata Aidoo," contains interesting readings of Woolf's "resonance" in other women writers. As Fernald acknowledges, writing about Woolf in Africa is an "unusual choice" (162). She does this to remind us of the overarching method of her study, to show that just as Woolf read her precursors closely so do the women writers who follow Woolf. The epilogue is not so much a conclusion, but a reiteration of how to look at and discuss literary history.

Though the epilogue is appropriate for this kind of study, it does leave one wondering what to do next. The method of *Virginia Woolf: Feminism and the Reader* takes us beyond the family romance structure of literary history, and it focuses on context and resonances in Woolf's work. It also has a specifically Woolfian tone, looking at "moments" of literary history and their contributions to feminist thinking. Though Fernald clearly states the advantages of looking at Woolf's work through its resonances and that the analysis of Sappho, Hakluyt, Addison, and Byron reveals different things, we never receive a fully articulated vision of the impact of this approach. Beyond the introduction, there is little reference to the problems of building the infrastructure of an alternative history. Nor does Fernald articulate a means for using this method to discuss other writers, male or female.

What Fernald does open up for us is an understanding of how Woolf uses literary history as a source for much of her feminism. There are still many resonances in Woolf's work to be uncovered and further connections to be made. Fernald's study has gracefully taken that first difficult and provocative step through careful attention to history and how it intersects with political and cultural discourse.

—Beth C. Rosenberg, *University of Nevada, LV*

Virginia Woolf's Nose: Essays on Biography. Hermione Lee (Princeton: Princeton University Press, 2005) 141 pp.
Bombay to Bloomsbury: A Biography of the Strachey Family. Barbara Caine (Oxford: Oxford University Press, 2005) xvii + 488pp. illus.

The art of biography, its practitioners always tell us, is a remarkably difficult one. The biographer must simultaneously provide what Virginia Woolf, in a famous essay, termed the solid granite of specific facts and the evanescent rainbow of personality in bringing the biographical subject to life. The mismatch of Woolf's natural metaphors was intentional, given how near impossible she felt it was to blend substantive historical documentation with the freeing spirit of the biographical subject's inner being. Woolf herself experimented in the genre in her 1928 *Orlando* and her 1933 *Flush* (both of which were subtitled "A Biography"), and both of these works ultimately document her awareness of the absurdities and impossibilities inherent to the genre. How can one ever fully apprehend the biographical subject's personality and re-present it textually, both works ask, while simultaneously being faithful to the spectacular or mundane facts of his or her life?

This impossible conjunction in the writing of biography between historical facts and animating spirit underlies *Virginia Woolf's Nose*, a new collection of essays inquiring into the genre's inherent traps and problems from Hermione Lee, herself the author of the current gold standard among Woolf biographies. Although Lee has also written a life of Willa Cather (and will bring forth a new biography of Edith Wharton in 2007), it is clear throughout this new collection that her work on Woolf has particularly animated her particular line of inquiry here. Lee's ambulatory and anecdotal tone in this collection, which can charmingly distract the reader momentarily from her key and persuasive points of argumentation, ultimately owes much to Woolf's own distinctive essayistic style, and the motivating ideas behind the pieces seem motivated by Woolf's own fascination with biographical genre. The central concern in Lee's essays are what she calls the inevitable "gaps and absences and unprovable stories" in the biographical subject's record—the holes in the granite, as it were—that so often form intriguing and telling stumbling points for biographers in their attempts to portray the inner lives of their subjects. Manipulating the presentation of what exists in the biographical record (as in the five differing biographical accounts Lee dazzlingly retells of Jane Austen's famous faint in 1800 after being told her family was moving to Bath) can allow biographers to cast their subjects as they see fit:

in Austen's case, as everything from a frail and wilting violet to an independent and brave proto-feminist. In the extremely amusing title essay, Lee demonstrates how the bizarre concrete detail of the shape of Virginia Woolf's nose (or more precisely, of the spoonbill-like prosthesis Nicole Kidman wore in her Oscar-winning turn in Stephen Daldry's 2002 film *The Hours*) became the crucial point of contention in a brouhaha among the filmmaker, the novelist Michael Cunningham (on whose novel the film was based), and various professional Woolf scholars, all of whom contended over the "ownership" of Woolf. Lee repeatedly argues that no scholar or writer ever can lay final claim to the core meaning of a writer's life, although the biographer's and scholar's imperative to do so become demonstrably and uncannily repeated. For example, the argument waged among Percy Bysshe Shelley's widow and surviving friends over who should possess the drowned poet's heart became reiterated, Lee shows, in the contesting versions of this debate among Shelley's various biographers (including Edward Trelawney, André Maurois, and Richard Holmes), each of whom staked a claim to owning "the heart," or true meaning, of Shelley's life. While this awareness of the extreme and problematic subjectivity of the biographical process is of course not original here to Lee's collection (and has been written about in recent years by, among others, Holmes and Janet Malcolm, both of whose biographical writings form fodder for Lee's analysis), her argument is made with style and conviction, and her choices of anecdotal examples are both fresh and engaging. Her essays demonstrate with real verve how, in attempting to present fresh takes on the inner world of their subjects, a biographer can unconsciously manipulate her available data in order to shape a Woolf (or a Shelley, or a Chekhov) of one's own.

While such manipulation, as Lee demonstrates, is almost necessary in recounting the life of a subject like Jane Austen, so many of the original important documents of whose life were burned or are otherwise missing or non-existent, it is not a serious problem for Barbara Caine in *Bombay to Bloomsbury,* her thorough and learned new family biography of Sir Richard and Lady Jane Strachey and their ten children. As Caine readily admits in her introduction, her work of documenting the story of this great intellectual family was eased considerably by the sheer amount of materials available to her because of the Stracheys' characteristic sense of "their own history, tradition, and importance." As Caine explains it, "[The Stracheys] were inveterate and in some cases immensely talented letter-writers and, as a significant family with a long tradition of imperial administration, they tended to keep the letters and documents which came into the household." It is almost miraculous that Caine should even have been able to shape, out of such a prodigious amount of documentary granite, such a comprehensive and comprehensible sculptural likeness of the Strachey family.

Such a family biography has been strongly needed for years by scholars of Bloomsbury, psychoanalysis, feminism, and Victorian imperialism alike; indeed, Caine's biography should be invaluable to anyone interested in Victorian and Edwardian British history given the importance of the Strachey family, who were both the inheritors and the continuations of what Noel Annan famously termed "the intellectual aristocracy" of nineteenth-century Britain. Leonard Woolf, who was taken into the family fold as a young man by dint of his undergraduate friendship with Lytton Strachey, noted, "The atmosphere of the dining-room [of the Strachey home] at Lancaster Gate was that of British history and of that comparatively small ruling class which for the last one hundred years had been the principal makers of British history." Sir Richard Strachey, the dynasty's patriarch, was from a prominent family of Anglo-Indian administrators, and himself was crucial to the public works administration of the Raj as either acting or permanent secretary to the government of India, and also an important geographer, engineer, and scientist. His wife, Julia Grant, the daughter of the Indian Chief Justice, shared her husband's intellectual aspirations, and studied under his tutelage the writings of Tyndall, Huxley, Comte, and Mill; later in life she became a successful writer and suffrage rights organizer. Together they had an impressive brood of thirteen children, and the ten who survived into adulthood were all expected to follow in their parents' footsteps in the disparate fields of scholarship, suffrage, Indian administration, or military service. Most of the Strachey siblings in fact became important figures in these areas in their own right, as were sometimes their spouses as well. Ralph Strachey, for example, became Chief Surveyor of India, while his younger brother Oliver became an important figure in military code-breaking during the two world wars. Their sister Dorothy authored the important lesbian novel *Olivia* and was André Gide's English translator, while their younger brother Lytton became, of course, the most important and famous British biographer of the first half of the twentieth century. The youngest Strachey son, James, and his wife, Alix, were the English translators of Freud, and as such were key figures in the early history of psychoanalysis. Pernel Strachey became the principal of Newnham College at Cambridge, while her sister Pippa, like their mother, worked as an important organizer in the battle for suffrage (as did also Oliver's second wife Rachel Costelloe).

With such a vast amount of material of family achievement available to her, it is exceptionally impressive that Barbara Caine can shape it so cohesively and sharply in this biography: she presents her central thesis, that the Stracheys were important figures in the British encounter with modernity, with conviction, and also shows persuasively the ways in which the family's earlier efforts for the imperial British mission became echoed and evoked in their other and later scholarly and social endeavors. A professor of history at Monash University in Australia with several studies of Victorian and Edwardian feminism to her name, Caine is especially strong in her analyses of the Stracheys' revolt against typical Victorian and early twentieth-century gender and sexual roles, and she amply delineates the contributions of Lady Jane, Pippa, and Rae (and to some extent Pernel) to the causes of women's rights. She also tellingly demonstrates how the non-traditional single lives and sexual experimentations of the younger Strachey children were in marked protest against the dynastic pretensions of the Lancaster Gate household. Perhaps owing to her historian's training, Caine organizes her vast stores of information about the Stracheys not by chronology or by particular family member, but rather by theme: thus her chapters bear such titles as "School Days," "Modern Marriages," "Single Life," "Gender Transformation and the Question of Sexuality," and so on.

This organization is ideal for contemporary scholars interested in Victorian and Edwardian social history; it is, however, perhaps less successful for idler common readers heretofore unfamiliar with the Strachey family history or their times. The narrative within the chapters hopscotches so much from Strachey to Strachey that it becomes difficult, at times, to remember just who is who; all their deaths, from that of Sir Richard in 1908 to that of his last surviving child, Pippa, sixty years later, are postponed until the biography's final chapter. And, almost inevitably, Caine repeats key details too often from one chapter to another. More grievously, Caine's scholarly approach to detailing the family's many achievements (and failures) seems to occur a bit at the expense of conveying the famous Strachey family character. The Stracheys were much remarked, by themselves and by others, for their peculiar consummate love not only of intellectual conversation but also, intermingled with it, of hilarity: as Leonard Woolf notes in his first volume of autobiography, "When six or seven Stracheys became involved in an argument over the dinner table, as almost always happened, the roar and rumble, the shrill shrieks, the bursts of laughter, the sound and fury of excitement was deafening and to an unprepared stranger paralysing." As Caine herself often tells us, the family delighted in making one another laugh as well as think through their animated discussions and lengthy letters; but she reproduces little of the substance of the latter, leaving the reader bereft of the Stracheys' pleasures in one another's sense of humor. Even on those rare occasions when Caine does directly reproduce the Stracheys' constant efforts at amusing one another, she seems baffled into silence. For example, a typically delightful letter from Pernel's early years at Cambridge describes to her elder sister Pippa a typical Newnham College nightly ritual:

> I have got to go to a hideous entertainment called a cocoa; you are given one spoonful of powdery cocoa and one spoonful of 'cow' that is condensed milk. These you mix together in a cup of milk till they look like mud; boiling water is then poured on, the next process being to try and drink it. Weird cakes are also passed around. At 10 o'clock at night this depresses me somewhat.

This and other similarly droll passages from Pernel's letters to Pippa occasion little comment from Caine other than to detail Pernel's characteristically Stracheyan exaggerated language, particularly the word "weird" (a family favorite, much like the word "portentous"). After a while, one begins to wish Caine could stop poring over all of her considerable stores of historical granite so as instead to admire, if only briefly, the fleeting wonder of rainbows dancing among them. The overall accomplishment of this monumental and long-needed family biography, however, allays such casual regrets. So much is here for future scholars to use and appreciate from this tremendous and substantive quarry of Stracheyan biographical material that it seems finally petty to bemoan the slightings of more ephemeral and colorful pleasures—even concerning a biography bearing the name of Strachey.

—Jay Dickson, Reed College

Radio Modernism: Literature, Ethics, and the BBC, 1922-1938. Todd Avery (Hampshire: Ashgate Publishing Limited, 2006) v +158 pp.

Was early twentieth-century Britain a proto-postmodern society, balancing ruling class and populist interests as it remade itself into a *technoculture*? Did technological innovation in artistic production and dissemination, and the conveniences of social practice—the cinema, the underground, the telegraph and telephone, and especially the radio—change the relations of the listener, reader, and citizen to time and space, to subjectivity, and to the state? At once a culture industry history, an assertion of literary modernism's good character, and a presentation of varying perspectives of the newly intensified focus of humanities disciplines on ethical philosophy, Todd Avery's *Radio Modernism,* while disavowing any desire to revolutionize the fields on which it draws, nevertheless has much to teach us.

In this compact but meticulously sourced and argued volume, Avery's objectives are to advance and fortify the field of Radio Studies and participate in the ongoing retooling of literary modernism that is making a period once too susceptible to claims of aesthetic elitism suddenly reveal rich veins of ethical insight and engagement. The arguments and archives at the author's disposal are varied and well searched. At the base of the book is BBC Radio, an ideological apparatus of the democratic, monarchical, socialistic, class-structured, ancient, cutting-edge state. Avery has combed transcripts of the BBC's on-air offerings and its print archives in order to provide examples of both conflict and cooperation between BBC administrators and the modern writers whose relations to radio general readers will be anxious to discover.

Virginia Woolf aficionados may be pleased that Avery has chosen the long-lived Orlando's astonishment over radio itself having turned "the fabric of life now" to "magic" as emblem of a receptive artistic community's response to the "supernaturally transforming" properties of the new form (30). That radio offers unprecedented access to large numbers of people (a history of what we mean when we say 'the masses' or 'mass media' is one of the many fascinating riffs in the book) excites the collectivist impulses of collectivists, especially Bloomsbury, and puts them, somewhat ironically, in sympathy with those who view the BBC as a means to reinvigorate and amplify high-Victorian artistic standards, national culture, and Christian social practice. As Avery's evidence demonstrates, in the early years of the BBC, the mission of its executive director and the contribution to its content by London's in-crowd aesthetes explicitly recalls the swerve from prescriptive to impressionistic literary production and criticism. This swerve is what gives modernism its reputation for repudiating the Victorian. In other words, before radio has a chance to magically remake the culture of early twentieth-century Britain, it internalizes and replicates literary history. Does this make radio a merely reflective entity, or has Avery managed to capture the postmodern daemon *recontainment* in one of its earliest manifestations? Did once-primitive voice swallow and make profit of once-sophisticated writing?

The return of logocentrism, a belief in the possibility and importance of expressions of transcendent truth, comes to the BBC and Avery's account in the form of British radio's first director. Avery introduces this central figure of the drama of radio's destiny in his beginning chapter "Arnold over Britain? John Reith and Broadcasting Morality" (11).

> It would be difficult to overstate the impact that Sir John Charles Waltham Reith (later Lord Reith) had on twentieth-century British culture. And yet, like Philo T. Farnsworth, the almost forgotten American technical prodigy who invented television in his early teens, Reith is probably still, outside the various fields in media studies but certainly within modernist studies, one of the most influential unknown cultural figures of the past century. (12)

Showing that Reith admired, quoted, and palely imitated Matthew Arnold, Avery concludes that the BBC's noble-minded executive "set himself the simultaneously spiritual and utilitarian goal of creating an institution whose political, social, cultural and moral purpose would be to place the largest possible population into instantaneous contact with a carefully governed version of the best expression of British and international thought" (13). The implications of the term "careful governance" are confirmed when Avery plucks from the biographies of Reith a snippet of dialog in which the director of British radio and Marconi himself celebrate the achievements of Mussolini. Thus *Radio Modernism* provides timely encouragement to its readers that we might consider the complicity of the popular and the convenient with the goals of a thought-policed culture. Pressing this point, Avery brings into the fascist-friendly frame of Lord Reith's BBC the modern writers, Bloomsbury, Wells and Eliot principally, to play their parts in determining "the sonic architecture of twentieth century ethical thought" (31).

The first question to be asked about literary modernism's participation in BBC radio is one that allows Avery to join the chorus of voices seeking to redeem the textual practices of Bloomsbury writers from claims of insular, trivial and elitist aestheticism. Whether or not the modern writers are appalled by the low-culture of radio is a litmus test. If they disdain radio and therefore its hordes of listeners, the Bloomsburyites are caught in yet another act of snobbery and modernism's elitist and pretentious nature is proved again. But Avery finds the professional writers, the culture warriors, and the budding ethicists of Bloomsbury, grumble though they do, to be fascinated by radio and anxious to make use of and influence the intention of its broadcast capacity.

"Common Talkers: The Bloomsbury Group and the Aestheticist Ethics of Broadcasting" (33) is *Radio Modernism*'s second and most satisfying chapter. That critical claims of effete elitism still stain accounts of Bloomsbury, at least as recently as 1992, Avery can demonstrate, but 1992 is a long time ago given the rapid pace of change in the value of the currency of modernism. Yet, the easy claim of intellectual snobbery is never just a straw man or a relic of distant reception theory. Cheapening of modernist influence is one of postmodernism's prime movements. Tastes in art and even national elections can be warped by claims that innovative and dissenting thinkers are merely narcissists at play, mocking the average and the good. *Radio Modernism*'s careful discussion of the ethical perspectives developed within Bloomsbury constitutes a significant contribution to current discussions of ethics being conducted in philosophy, literary studies, and cultural studies.

Beginning with an epigraph taken from *Three Guineas* that, not without a touch of the snide, advises Woolf's manifesto's politically and ethically minded addressee to tune in and find out the judgment of "the public psychometer," Avery presents a war of wills between Reith's intention to reify assumptions about British nationalism in the years between the wars and the efforts of writers and some collaborating producers to use radio for just the opposite purpose. Arguing that Bloomsbury's response to radio comes right from the heart of G.E. Moore's *Principia Ethica* (1903), particularly its claim that illuminating conversation is the highest ethical activity, Avery is unrestrained in his attribution of right and revolutionary motives to the moderns' attempts to influence the nature of radio broadcast. "The Bloomsbury writers saw radio as a potential partner in the advancement of a utopian internationalism in the tenets of their ethical aestheticism. . . .They hoped also, through their talks on culture, economics, and politics, to rewrite the public, or mass psychography and align it with their deeply held aesthetic and ethical beliefs" (36), Avery writes, and then provides many nice illustrations of his proposition. One example of Leonard and Virginia Woolf's contributions to the cause (one of the three broadcasts that are the sum of Virginia's on-air career) is a conversation between the two on the topic of what is wrong with the publishing industry. Virginia, in socialist-feminist mode, claims that the problem is the glutting up of the market with the books of writers already too well known and the corresponding crowding out of new ideas and voices. Leonard, resolutely Marxist, accuses all writers of pandering to a culture industry that works them for slave wages and determines the content of their writing to boot. The account satisfies our great desire to witness previously unexamined topics and attitudes passing between the Woolfs, as do the descriptions of Lytton Strachey's clumsy and wistful attempts to take to the microphone please our notion of Strachey as a brilliant bundle of nerves. But while these peeks at the Bloomsbury all-stars are exciting, it is with the microphone in the hands of Desmond MacCarthy that the group makes its most passionate defense of media new and old.

Avery connects MacCarthy's residency as BBC literary critic to the theoretico-ethical discussions of the past two decades that focus on the relation of self and other, particularly those that draw on the writing of philosophers Jacques Derrida and Emmanuel Levinas. MacCarthy's ethics of readership may have privileged impressionistic response, the ear of the other, as Derrida might have termed it in one of his roundtables, but it is the stylistic virtuosity with which MacCarthy brought imaginative literature and its criticism to the listening public, thereby calling for their response, that overshadows the equally earnest and ethical but far less audiogenic contributions of E.M. Forster to the modern writers' success in pushing radio "by the early 1930s. . .in fundamental ways beyond John Reith's control" and making it "eminently congruous with Bloomsbury's modernist ethics" (41).

But, as Avery shows, things do fall apart. In 1932 Harold Nicolson is forbidden by Reith to praise *Ulysses* or *Lady Chatterley's Lover*, and as the decade lengthens and political realities grow stark again, the fun and funky Bloomsbury set cede the airwaves, and the stage of *Radio Modernism,* to H.G. Wells and T.S. Eliot. Discussions of ethical communications in the age of social Darwinism and Christian imperatives in a fallen world recovering from one war and bracing for another take up central positions on the BBC soundstage. "A Natural Selection: H.G. Wells and a Huxleyan Ethics of Communication" (73) discusses utopian efforts to unite the community of mankind and the presumption that the great reach of the wireless could so easily be made good use of. But it is not so clear, Avery discovers, which species of broadcast, internationalist philosophy or nationalist propaganda of both democratic and fascistic timbre, is destined to be selected the fittest. As if to move the entire question of fascism vs. socialism aside, Avery concludes his discussion of modernism and radio with the BBC's and one modern giant's return to a Christian mission and a version of ethics that departs from the Deleuzean separation of the ethical from the moral.

To help us understand this final chapter, *Radio Modernism*'s brief conclusion might be consulted. There Avery suggests that one potential use of his scholarship is to read the moderns' interface with radio as an allegory of current cultural and technocultural (there is after all still a difference) conflicts. Is it to be prophetic or cautionary, or both, then, that the book's final juxtaposition of modern thought and writing with the presence of the radio is in the chapter "Talks Toward a Definition of Morality: T.S. Eliot and the Consecration of Broadcasting"?

In this grim but fascinating discussion, Avery presents an Eliot most relevant to himself and to the radio after his conversion to Catholicism has given him the calling of pressing Christian values (ethical or moral?) on the world. For example, Eliot is ambivalent about the well-received radio broadcast of *The Waste Land* and insists for most of his career on confining his talks to defiantly staid topics such as six episodes on Tudor prose. But, toward the end of his run, the Victorian sage of modernism seems to look upon the nearly complete saturation of the population with wireless access (see how the terms have always already been in place?) the way that Mel Gibson must imagine the potential of crowded movie theaters. Eliot broadcasts to convert.

"It is no less important," Avery writes, "to look at the content of Eliot's broadcasts than it is to foreground the formal means by which he expressed a cultural *cum* moral agenda that in many ways very closely resembles Reith's own" (115). Ending with the natural collaboration between the faintly fascist Reith and the ultra-Christian Eliot recapitulates the terms of literary history's efforts to reconcile Eliot's exclusive and austere beliefs with the beauty of his poetry. This is the same formation Avery uses by beginning the book with the figure of Matthew Arnold, an ultimate touchstone for literary historians. *Radio Modernism*'s great strategic achievement, and the key to its unusual readability, is this identification of compelling relay stations—Bloomsbury, Wells, Eliot—that send its signal bouncing between the familiar surfaces of literary history and technoculturalism, locating a wealth of material to which readers of modernism may well wish—and need—to become attuned.

—Nick Smart, *The College of New Rochelle*

Women's Vision in Western Literature: The Empathic Community. Laurence M. Porter (Westport CT, Praeger, 2005) vii + 256.

Reading Laurence Porter's book gives one the effect of homing in on debates about gender difference from a great distance: like zooming in on one's home town from a picture of the world as seen from outer space. Porter's introduction eschews familiar debates about literature and gender to start by setting out a model of gender difference drawn from sociology, biology, neurological research, and an engaged observer's reading of current affairs, to posit the theory that men think and act competitively while women place greater value on co-operation and empathy. The male competitive ethos, Porter argues, gives rise not only to the omnipresence of war throughout human history, but also underlies the traditional narrative pattern of order disrupted and order restored, with revenge as an ever-popular theme. By contrast, Porter identifies a different tradition, that of the "women writers of the empathic community" who "urge collaboration based on a tolerant understanding of the Other" (11). Such an approach leads to different perspectives and more complex or diffuse narrative structures. Porter accords Woolf a place in this tradition, along with Sappho, Marie de France, Madame de Staël, Mary Shelley, Marguerite Yourcenar, and Christa Wolf.

Porter's premise makes provocative reading and readers will no doubt wish to question many of his assertions. It is disconcerting that Porter makes no use of feminist scholarship—and, indeed that he rules out feminist criticism as unhelpful on these issues. Feminists, he argues, have two tactics. One tactic is "autonomy (glorifying difference)," represented by "separatists, eco-feminists and practitioners of *l'écriture féminine*"—the latter point yoking together the separatist position of Luce Irigaray with the more inclusive approach of Hélène Cixous. The second tactic, he writes, is "assimilation" or "minimizing" difference. He argues that both of these approaches risk "unwittingly collaborating with the patriarchy" (12-13), thus ignoring the fact that feminist scholarship has long been exercised by this problem.

The individual chapters home in on their subjects from a similarly long range, generally beginning with a sketch of the life and works of each individual author. Such an approach is necessary in a book that covers writers from such a wide historical and cultural range, although it means that the individual chapters will be of greater value to students and to researchers of women writers in general, than to specialists on the chosen authors. Some students will be helped by the schematic structuralist outlines of some of the texts, such as the summary of key points in the plot of *Mrs. Dalloway*, the list of narrative layers in Shelley's *Frankenstein*, a guide to themes in Yourcenar's *Memoires d'Hadrien*, and narrative patterns in Christa Wolf's *Patterns of Childhood*.

The chapter on *Mrs. Dalloway* is interesting as a study of how Woolf appears from outside the Woolfian community. After the synopsis of Woolf's life and work, Porter offers an account of her changing reputation that includes a debate on questions raised by Elaine Showalter's 1971 attack on Woolf's feminist credentials in *A Literature of their Own*. We had hoped that this debate had been resolved, following refutations of Showalter such as Toril Moi's in *Sexual/Textual Politics,* and now that many feminist debates since the 1970s have tended to move closer to Woolf's position on androgyny. It is disappointing, then, that Porter returns to it here, for it suggests that Showalter's attack is difficult to overturn.

On the other hand, the chapter helps us view *Mrs. Dalloway* afresh by presenting a close, detailed reading of how the different characters experience community in different ways: Porter's study ranges from considering national and imperial sentiments, through social consciousness to the sort of imaginary community which enables Clarissa to empathise not only with Septimus but also with Peter. Porter is even-handed in showing how Woolf questions the value of community, showing how the novel is a study in alienation (and characters' recognition of another's sense of alienation) as much as it is a study of communities. As a result the novel, crystallized in the image of the party, enables difference, including the freedom to distance oneself from the oppressions of society and the political system, for example when we see the Prime Minister through Peter Walsh's cynical eyes.

The book's subtitle, "The Empathic Community," implies a project of drawing female writers from several stages of history into one tradition, but the chapters are self-contained studies of each author, with no cross-referencing between them. Comparisons are left until the conclusion, and, whilst remaining sceptical of providing a system to link all of the subjects, Porter suggests two fruitful lines of comparison among the seven writers. First, all his chosen writers lived during times of political unrest, tension, or full-blown war: Sappho at a time of tension between Greek city-states; Marie de France during the Crusades;

Madame de Staël during the French Revolution and reign of Napoleon; Mary Shelley in the aftermath of these movements; Woolf between the World Wars; Marguerite Yourcenar after Hitler's defeat; and Christa Wolf during the time of the Holocaust. His chosen writers therefore all offer case-studies of how women writers can question the predominant values of their time. His suggestion that all these writers tended to retreat into dealing with issues within the worlds of their writing (sometimes after initial confrontations with the system), is reasonable, although his account that they all "regress to a retreat in pastoral or ancient legend and express a melancholy resignation in which anger at the frustrating, obdurate other has been partially turned against the self" (187) seems overly prescriptive. Applied to Woolf, this statement appears to dismiss the considerable scholarship on her "political" engagement (by Alex Zwerdling, Mark Hussey, Anna Snaith and others), and threatens to leave us with the suicidal Bloomsbury recluse of recent legend.

Second, Porter detects similar techniques in the work of all seven: "Their creative efforts . . . share a tendency toward polyvocalism, toward the dramatization of conflicting and often clashing voices. They do not close off debate to seek to impose a uniform, ideological message" (187). So, Sappho parodied and readapted Homeric phrases and motifs, subverting these to glorify love not war. Marie de France challenged the medieval Catholic cultural hegemony by drawing on non-Arthurian Celtic tales and translating animal stories from the Indo-European tradition. Madame de Staël sought to blend different European national cultures, including angering Napoleon by advocating a "cultural union of German sensibility with French logic" (189). Mary Shelley uses five different layers of narrative in Frankenstein and Woolf articulates different views (including those of members of the establishment and the disenfranchised) in *Mrs. Dalloway*. Christa Wolf's adoption of modernist techniques reflected her attempt to develop a more complex world-view after moving away from a hard-line Socialist perspective (with its attendant emphasis on social realism), and she came to use the literary past as a source of allegory. Porter adds a further author to his conclusion, by mentioning Francophone Guadaloupean author Maryse Condé, whose polyphonic techniques, he suggests, help her articulate her African roots. These interconnections merit further investigation by scholars, although the thesis needs to be developed to reflect on the different kinds of polyphony in evidence across the different writers, and to distinguish dialogues with other literary works and cultures from stylistic techniques for handling different narrative voices and perspectives.

The book leaves us with an open question about what conclusions to draw from the similarities observed:

> At this point, the reader may feel that seven scattered examples from nearly three thousand years of cultural history in the West owe their affinities to coincidence.... What empirical proof have I offered that (some) women's literature is really so distinctive? (193)

In answer to this question, Porter goes on briefly to discuss Condé, to show a similarity in approach between her work and that of the seven main authors covered, and to suggest differences between her work and that of contemporary male Francophone writers in "masculine" Martinique (ibid.). This brief sojourn raises a plethora of new questions for the reader, not least the issue of how to make direct comparisons between a postcolonial author and a set of writers selected as representatives of "western literature." Such a comparison might be enabled through a framework of seeing women as the colonized other, but this needed to be articulated more thoroughly. As it stands, we are left with an essentialist view that women, regardless of their cultural position, write in different ways from men.

As a Woolfian, I could not help noting many points in Porter's argument where he would have done well to have drawn on Woolf's essays. *Three Guineas* only merits one, passing reference (as evidence of Woolf's opposition to World War II), whereas that essay is strongly relevant to his argument that war is the result of the male competitive ethos. Woolf's argument that "as a woman I have no country ... as a woman my country is the whole world" would have been a useful focal point for Porter's discussion of how Marie de France, Madame de Staël and Maryse Condé broke the bounds of their own particular national cultures. *A Room of One's Own* is only mentioned in passing, but Woolf's suggestion that "we think back through our mothers" would have been useful for thinking about literary tradition. Intriguingly, Woolf is occluded in the closing salvo of Porter's introduction, where he overlooks her essay "Anon" by noting that "there is an axiom in feminist art history: 'anonymous' was a woman" (16).

A harsh view of this book would be to say that Porter tries to reinvent the wheel, by engaging in gender debates whilst overlooking the contributions of Woolf and feminist scholarship more generally. On the other hand, it is refreshing to see Woolf's work discussed in a wider context, and to be reminded that while she articulated ideas about the female tradition and feminist-pacifism very beautifully, these concepts are not her sole preserve. Porter's book would be useful for anyone wanting to research or teach his chosen writers, but his methodology needs to be approached with caution.

—Jane de Gay, *Leeds Trinity and All Saints*

Recovering Your Story: Proust, Joyce, Woolf, Faulkner, Morrison. Arnold Weinstein (New York: Random House, 2006) xii + 496 pp.

"I used to love to read, but not anymore." Where I teach, these words, or ones like them, have begun to haunt reading autobiographies and attitude surveys in general education classes and even reflective essays submitted in senior English major portfolios. Something happens to these students, usually in junior high, sometimes in high school, but most damning for us, occasionally in college: once avid or eager or willing, they turn into resistant or hostile or reluctant readers. They develop what the NEA Report on "Reading at Risk" calls "aliteracy," an ability to read accompanied by an unwillingness to do so.

When I became curious about why this resistance to reading was developing in young people who used to read, I was also wondering why our profession has developed increasingly stringent standards for tenure at a time when publication is increasingly difficult. The resulting anxiety has seeped down into graduate school where we have incorporated more and more professional-level practices and goals (teaching beyond the introductory level, presentations and publications, service on committees, community outreach), which then seeps down into undergraduate education where we have incorporated more and more graduate-level practices and goals (research methods, application of theory, publication). We may then neglect English majors who do not want to become graduate students or professors. What are we doing?

Arnold Weinstein, it turns out, has had similar concerns. My late-career doubts about my real purpose as a teacher have led me to try to match my pedagogy to a very basic goal, at least in my general education classes—to create reading experiences that will lead alumni to pick up books rather than shun them. His late-career doubts about the academy's direction have led him to reach out to the general reader rather than to the expert. In courses on literature and medicine, in an NEH-funded partnership among professors, high school English teachers, and their respective students, in numerous tapes produced for The Teaching Company, and in books such as *A Scream Goes Through the House: What Literature Teaches Us About Life* and the one under review here, *Recovering Your Story: Proust, Joyce, Woolf, Faulkner, Morrison*, Weinstein wants to persuade readers that literature is worthy of their time, attention, and effort.

Weinstein could have subtitled his book "How Should One Read the Moderns?" The Edna and Richard Salomon Distinguished Professor of Comparative Literature at Brown University, he has thought long and hard about reading both inside and outside the academy. He knows common readers still exist—he sees them everywhere, recognizes their hunger, and believes in their abilities. It saddens him that readers, whether college-educated or not, often avoid the moderns, perceiving them as difficult, as belonging only to intellectuals and academics, as unrelated to ordinary lives. He refuses to accept the (highbrow) assumption that only initiates can read and enjoy Proust's *The Remembrance of Things Past*, Joyce's *Ulysses*, Woolf's *Mrs. Dalloway* and *To the Lighthouse*, Faulkner's *The Sound and the Fury* and *Absalom, Absalom!*, and Morrison's *Beloved*. His pedagogical moves, in other words, are similar to the ones Woolf makes in her essays. Weinstein never downplays the formidable skills these books ask of readers (the reader of Joyce must be like Odysseus, for example, cunning, resourceful, and confident [110]); Woolf respects readers, understands that reading a novel is a "difficult and complex art," and notes that reading requires "the rarest qualities of imagination, insight, and judgment" ("How Should One Read a Book?" *CR2* 260, 269). Weinstein insists readers do not need literary training to glean what Proust, Joyce, Woolf, Faulkner, and Morrison have to offer; Woolf points out that Aeschylus, Shakespeare, Virgil, and Dante would say to anyone without a university education, "Don't leave me to the wigged and gowned. Read me, read me for yourselves." Woolf believed we should not "shy away from the kings because we are commoners," that great writers do not care "if we get our accents wrong, or have to read with a crib in front of us" ("The Leaning Tower," *CE2* 181). Weinstein agrees, and provides the common reader with a crib to the moderns.

Weinstein works to allay general readers' fears and frustrations by becoming a guide; he leads readers through these great twentieth-century works one by one. And his guidance stimulates curiosity, creates confidence, and engenders competence. Although informed by great learning and wide reading in both primary and secondary sources, his discussions do not include footnotes, and he generally succeeds in writing as a reader addressing other readers rather than as a scholar addressing other scholars. Having read these novels (well, all but the later volumes of Proust), I do not know how a novice would react to Weinstein's guidance. But I believe some readers will, in fact, be tempted, persuaded, even provoked by Weinstein to give the moderns a try (and yes, I've dug out those remaining Proust volumes). Even if Weinstein's readers do not turn to the moderns, they will have come to understand the "double gift" of the literature of consciousness: "It makes our own days and nights keener and larger, but it also teaches us about the depths and integrity of others" (475).

So how does Weinstein lower barriers between the common reader and the modernist author? How does an academic insider help the hesitant outsider feel welcome?

To invite readers into the modernists' worlds, Weinstein does many things right. For one thing, he takes seriously the common reader's questions, "Why should I read these books? Especially when I will have to work? What is the payoff?" His book directly confronts and answers those questions, exploring what the reader can learn, enjoy, and take away from these authors. In each chapter, he acknowledges the difficulties a particular author presents, gives voice to common reader and student complaints and frustrations, and cheerfully admits to having had similar reactions. But he then explains why the reader should read the author anyway ("[Faulkner] makes us see the stature as well as the depths of our moral and national life" [294]). He also enacts the reading process, frequently verbalizing a reader's specific questions when they might occur ("Where, we wonder, is the plot?") and then proceeding to answer them ("Well, it's everywhere you look [. . .] At the level where Joyce is taking his data, it would seem there is nothing but plot" [126]). Throughout each chapter, he reinforces readers by reminding them why they read and by articulating reading's rewards, variations on his theme that "great art discovers for us who we are" (xii). Although he is aware of aesthetic, critical, and theoretical concerns and occasionally explains or comments on them (see his excellent discussion of Barthes, for example, in his Conclusion), he usually focuses on some of the most basic reasons for reading, the most personal of rewards. We read for guidance. We read to find ourselves. We read "to recover our story" because "our felt life is what most eludes us" (x). We read to learn "literature's golden rule: Everyone has a story" (476).

Second, he writes a clear introduction that summarizes how realistic fiction works, why the moderns choose another path, why they use the techniques they do, and what they add to our understanding of literature and humanity. Logical and compelling, this introduction could well become the first reading assignment on many modern literature syllabi. He introduces his thesis early—that the moderns, better than anyone else, help us to access, understand, and tell our own stories. Difficult they may be, but they help us understand our selves, attend to our inner lives, feel life in all its chaos.

Third, Weinstein's book is a pleasure to read. He uses descriptive and often witty headings to organize his chapters into short sections ("How to Write Sexual Otherness," "Bloom the Artful Dodger," "Party Girl," "Faulkner's Sins," "Lethal Love"), thus making his book easy to read in fits and starts, and he has a friendly and conversational tone. He does not so much present conclusions as take readers along on an exploratory ride that includes many twists and turns. He uses language and metaphors and stories that people can understand to confront difficult concepts and issues head-on. Although a couple of verbal tics (he loves the words "pulsion" and "notation") and his use of the colon can be irritating, his prose is generally accessible, interesting, and down-to-earth. With a sense of humor about himself, the academy, and life, Weinstein enjoys making the "special conversation" between book and reader "audible" (xii), and his enthusiasm is contagious.

Then, too, Weinstein's book participates in the cultural move toward the personal essay, a form that combines memoir with interpretation. He gives the reader a glimpse into his own heart and mind and soul as he wrestles with the ideas and emotions brought up by these books, and in doing so, he reminds us how deeply realistic the moderns are no matter how rebellious they were against realism. In some of the most moving parts of the book, Weinstein reveals himself—his life, his teaching, his reading—to show how these books tap into the pains and joys and confusions at the center of existence. Sharing his own passions and uncertainties, he is not above criticizing himself as a professor, acknowledging he may be wrong as a reader, or questioning his own motives as a person. By embodying his search for illumination in the intersections between books and life on page after page after page, his journey becomes a powerful testimony for reading modern literature.

In addition, Weinstein's courage inspires the reader. He is open about his own biases and the reasons for them (his young man's love for Mrs. Ramsay, for example, and his realization that the novel was "also about my mother" [244]). He fearlessly presents earlier readings he now thinks are mistaken and juxtaposes them with current readings (implying or stating they too could be mistaken). He is honest about how readers actually read (about how he actually reads): not knowing, struggling to put pieces of information together, not "getting" it until you are almost finished or until you talk about it with someone or until you read it again. He is not afraid to make his own position clear (a white male who grew up in the South); not afraid to mark a digression onto a soapbox ("But let me now go on the offensive" [305]); not afraid to admit that "All of this huffing and puffing on my part doubtless makes it quite clear that Faulkner is special to me" (306); not afraid to distinguish between his practice, that of engaging with and promoting feminist, ethnic, and cultural questions throughout his book, and some departments' practice, that of assessing novels only "in terms of their views on race and gender" in order to remove those novels from course lists (305). He courageously chooses to end his book with Toni Morrison because her work "radically calls into question what [the great modernists] achieved" (409), because "one's story might just be a luxury item beyond reach [. . .] or the door that opens onto the unbearable" (410), because she threatens his own earlier statements about literature. Weinstein courageously says these five writers are great, uses the word "truth," and talks about literature's ethical dimension; he claims that literature gives us something, something we desperately need, something that other art forms, disciplines, and modes of thought cannot; and he confesses that he loves these books more than any others he has ever read and that he is trying, "at some gut level," to "pass that love on" to us (16). It is refreshing to read a teacher and critic so unabashedly enthusiastic about literature's beautiful, strange, and troubling qualities, so emotional and hopeful about its power, and so eloquent about its potential to speak across barriers of all kinds.

Finally, Weinstein uses comparison between and among the five authors effectively. Within each chapter, he keeps his focus on the author and book in front of him, linking each author to a particular concept or word or metaphor (the umbilical cord in Morrison or music in Joyce, for example), describing each author's distinctive contribution to literature, and providing some thoughts about what each author reaches in the reader, but he also recursively looks ahead to later chapters and back to earlier ones: "[Woolf's] grasp of time and memory (and their pathos) rivals Proust's, her sense of social comedy and of city-art [. . .] is as saucy and bold as Joyce's, and her depiction of the outsider's despair and the scapegoat's execution matches anything Faulkner wrote" (199). Readers thus gain a clear sense of five individual writers, but they also gain a cumulative sense of the similarities and contrasts between and among them. By the time readers get to the end of his book, they are very well prepared for his brief but satisfying comparative conclusion.

Although basically convinced by the arc of Weinstein's discussion and frequently stunned by Weinstein's insights into how modern literature captures us body and soul, I did not always agree with a particular interpretation. For example, he, like many of my romantic students, gives too much credence to Peter Walsh's assessment of Clarissa. And yet . . . And yet he uses Clarissa's sense that she has turned her back on gaiety by refusing Peter and our sense that she has turned her back on passion by resisting her attraction to women to set up a brilliant discussion of how "the death of the soul" is "the nightmare that threatens all Woolf's players" (220). "To [Woolf's] enormous credit," he writes, "and to older readers' delight, I suspect—Woolf suggests that age has its virtues, that the passing of time confers as well as removes, that life consists of more than heat, passion, and romance. The soul doesn't die all that easily" (220). I was also sometimes puzzled by seeming contradictions, such as when he says the "final pages of community support" in *Beloved* "seem forced" (462) at the same time he understands that Morrison believes "connection precedes individuation" (464). More worrisome, perhaps, are mistakes of fact: Richard Dalloway is in Parliament; what he has not achieved is a seat in the Cabinet (219); it is James, not Jasper, who is part of the scene with Cam and the green shawl (278); and Toni Morrison's master's thesis is on both Faulkner and Woolf, not just on Faulkner

(427). The ongoing force and integrity of Weinstein's interactions with the moderns, however, make any such flaws seem minor indeed.

Weinstein works to create readers for the moderns; he, like Woolf, tells them to trespass. Of course, the same sneer used against Woolf when she aligned herself with her working class audience in "The Leaning Tower" could be used against him as well: "easy for you to say; you're already an insider." He, like her, sometimes struggles with pronouns. The "we" that generally refers to readers can occasionally (and disconcertingly) shift into a "we" that refers to critics: "We know that Joyce loved music . . ." (152). He, like Woolf, sometimes uses allusions that only the most well-read general reader could be expected to know. Yet allusions to Dante or Homer or Nietzsche or Rimbaud also communicate a respect for the common reader, a belief that common readers desire a wider frame of reference. Refusing to patronize or heap scorn, Weinstein simply relies on the common reader's interest, on the creative act of reading.

Weinstein believes the risk of being sneered at or misunderstood is worth taking: helping readers trespass and giving them the tools to join (maybe even transform) the conversation is preferable to erecting barriers and insisting that certain authors are off-limits for certain readers. He fights the tendency to divide readers into huge mass vs. tiny elite. His discussion of Proust, Joyce, Woolf, Faulkner, and Morrison grows out of a democratic belief in people's ability to grapple with difficult writing if given enough reasons to do so, enough preparation for the struggle, and enough framework or context for the work.

Why then should Woolf scholars read Weinstein's memoir about reading the moderns? Because we teach the moderns. Translating his classroom practices into written prose, Weinstein gives us the opportunity to translate his prose back into classroom practices. Frequently making connections between these novels and life that might engage our students, he helps us remember what baffled us when we first read these books, and more wonderfully, what took our breath away. Just as he gives common readers permission to feel frustration in the face of modernist complexity, he gives teachers and scholars permission to feel awe again in the face of the modernists' audacity, authenticity, and achievement.

Ultimately, Weinstein's discussion implies that in our attempt to become a discipline, we may have divorced ourselves and our students from reading for enlightenment and pleasure. Have we, in our rush to move students into that discipline, put up barriers between them and reading? Have we inadvertently implied that as they gain critical and theoretical sophistication, they must lose their visceral identification with characters and stories? Weinstein fervently hopes his book will make those unfamiliar with modernist authors feel emboldened enough to read them. I fervently hope his book will make those familiar with modernist authors feel comfortable enough to have open conversations with students about why "we"—people, teachers, students, common readers—read. A call for restoring balance (not for banishing criticism or theory) and for rethinking how we teach literature, Weinstein's book asks faculty and students to recall their roots, the time when they used to love to read.

—Beth Rigel Daugherty, *Otterbein College*

To the Boathouse: A Memoir. Mary Ann Caws (Tuscaloosa: Alabama UP, 2004) 204 pp.
Letters to Virginia Woolf. Lisa Williams (Lanham: Hamilton Books, 2005) 78 pp.

In Mary Ann Caws's *To the Boathouse: A Memoir* and in Lisa Williams's *Letters to Virginia Woolf,* Virginia Woolf functions as both a catalyst and measure for each author's journey to confront the legacy of their own internalized Mrs. Ramsays. Similar to Woolf's personal struggle with identity and her efforts to dispel "the angel in the house" through her writing ("Professions" 241), Caws's memoir discloses the internal conflicts that she has faced as a woman and renowned academic who had learned from an early age the "tradition of daughters not talking, not telling, not speaking up" (xi), lessons that reverberated throughout most of her personal and professional development. Williams's work, by contrast, engages with Woolf in more liminal ways, linking Woolf to cultural and personal traumas that do not extend beyond Williams's own internalization of them. Despite their differing approaches to Woolf and her legacy as a woman and as a writer, both Caws and Williams follow Woolf's belief that women should tell the truths about their lives. Thus, both books provide readers with meditations on the role of the female intellectual/artist and her responsibility to self and society.

In many ways, Caws's *To the Boathouse* can be seen as following upon the trajectory of the Memoir Club to which Woolf belonged, but unlike the limited number of participants in Woolf's circle, Caws deliberately opens her inner world for scrutiny to a boundless audience. Woolf considered the memoir a useful writing venue, believing that at age fifty she should be able to turn the "diamonds of the dustheap" from her diaries into memoirs as they "should be made" (D1 234). Using this same analogy, Caws's memoir is a veritable diamond mine. Beginning with her reminiscences of growing up as a young woman from a privileged and notable family in North Carolina, Caws describes in lyrical prose her deeply formative and complex familial relationships, especially the one with her grandmother, who "always knew what was more important and what was less so" (26), and the one with her father, a man who was as "difficult and silent as he was upstanding and scrupulous" (33). While Caws admired her father in many ways, she internalized his critical side which in turn shaped her view of herself. Whether it was her appearance, her scholarship, or her relationships with men, Caws long assumed that she was never quite measuring up to the occasion. Her self-doubt, especially around men who were as accomplished and critical as her father (like her former husband Peter), was intensified from having learned at a young age not to speak up for herself and from also witnessing how her mother, in Mrs. Ramsay fashion, constantly assuaged her father. And the one prevalent motif that runs throughout her recollections, linking such memories together, is that of dining.

Caws's association of food memories with certain people and events in her life is similar to Woolf's use of food as metaphor in her work. One need only to recollect references to food in Woolf's diaries or letters, or in such works as *Mrs. Dalloway*, *To the Lighthouse*, or *A Room of One's Own* to see the connection. For example, Caws's anger at both her father and husband regarding the way their authority over her sometimes manifested itself around food recalls Woolf's rage at her doctors and Leonard for being coerced by them to eat during her manic bouts. Caws's father not only demanded that he not be questioned, particularly at dinner (4), but once exclaimed "how fat" she was after she had returned from summer camp, compelling Caws to apologize to him for the weight gain (27). This incident was the start of a lifetime of Caws not feeling comfortable in her own body. Likewise, although her husband Peter had proposed to her "in a bargain diner" (61), this low-rent setting did not apply to domestic arrangements. In a chapter Caws entitles "Peter and I, and the Egg," she describes how once, early in their marriage, Peter chastised her because the egg that she had cooked for him was "not a three-minute egg" and he expected that she would properly cook him another one as he read his paper (64). This incident sets up the contentious relations that would continue throughout their marriage, relations that were often predicated upon what Peter expected of Caws as a wife, scholar and mother, and what Caws expected of herself.

Not all of Caws's food memories are with problematic people or events. There are many moments in her memoir, such as those with her grandmother and friends, that are celebratory. Thus Caws envisions herself at one point as "Mrs. Ramsay doing her boeuf en daube, knitting people together by candlelight" (190). Caws also includes recipes in her memoir such as the ones for her grandmother's cheese soufflé and Boston Cookies (22-23) and that for Cathedral

Pudding, a favorite dessert she enjoyed as a student at the National Cathedral School (48-49). The inclusion of recipes is effective in both revealing her personality and creating a sense of intimacy with the reader, suggesting that secrets, familial or culinary, are only shared with a select few.

One incident reflects on Caws's own development as a woman and scholar. Caws was on the orals committee for a young woman whose tentative thesis was on philosophy and Beckett. Considering the young woman not very bright, and ill-informed at best, Caws became more and more frustrated with the student's inability to answer what Caws thought reasonable questions (179). What agitated Caws further was that the three other members of the committee, all men, responded approvingly to the young woman's open flirtations with them during the exam. It was not until the young woman connected with a text and shared her passion for the piece, discussing it in ways Caws herself had never thought of, that Caws began to see both the young woman and herself in a different light and realized that "what was happening here, in my own place, with my own colleagues, with myself, was what had happened to me all those years before" (181). After the exam she invited the young woman to have a cup of coffee with her, again linking a significant event with food.

While Caws may be specifically referencing her own exam at Yale years earlier, her recap of the orals resonates with the exam-like conditions that she has lived with for the greater part of her life. By the end of her memoir, the doubts about how she is measuring up as a woman, daughter, wife, and scholar no longer trouble her. Like the young woman who connects with something that is true for her, momentarily disregarding the judgment of others, *To the Boathouse* is ultimately the journey of a woman who has learned to trust in herself and make peace with her past.

Although *Letters to Virginia Woolf* may fall into the category of a memoir, Williams fashions it more as a diary. Like novelist Michael Cunningham, Lisa Williams feels a deep connection to Woolf that has been personally and creatively empowering. Instead of reimagining one of Woolf's novels as Cunningham did, however, Williams connects to Woolf through her own poetry and epistolary self-discoveries. Williams begins *Letters to Virginia Woolf* with an immediate reference to *Three Guineas*. She addresses Woolf about her "vision of a world without war. . . waft[ing] up [to Williams] now from layers and layers of sorrow" (2). Williams then recollects playing with her son Max in a park the morning of 9/11, oblivious to the magnitude of the unfolding tragedy. After her husband (who worked five blocks from where the Twin Towers stood) phoned her to reassure her of his safety, he walked for hours and arrived home covered in grime and white soot. Williams states that when she saw him, she "knew that he had been to a remote place, a place where [she] could never enter" (5). To combat her husband's descent into trauma, she suggested that they all go to the park, so he could be with her and Max as they played. She observes that it was "the children that day who took a defiant stance against terror. While the rest of us waded through a vague and undetermined sense of dread, the children played on, refusing for now, to give up their short-lived innocence" (6).

While Williams's initial thoughts on 9/11 are about Woolf's epistolary response to war and the hegemonic infrastructure that perpetuates it, Williams's own reflection of war is clearly rooted in the private and the familial. There is no questioning of the "whys" behind the violence, the motives for the attacks and the deadly repercussions that would soon follow. Indeed, in a subsequent letter that again begins with a notable quotation from *Three Guineas*, "As a woman I have no country. . .," Williams recounts a visit to Monk's House and wonders how Woolf dealt "with all those losses," such as that of her mother, her half-sister and her brother (8). In these instances there is a disconnect from the public significance of *Three Guineas* in favor of a correlation to the private. One wonders how Woolf may have responded to the 7/7 terrorist attacks in London, particularly those bombings that occurred in the immediate Bloomsbury area, the bus that exploded very near to where 52 Tavistock once stood, and close to the Tavistock Square park where sculptures of both Woolf and Gandhi can be found. Would she think back to her youth (as Williams has) or that of her niece and nephews for some insight into this latest tragedy, or look beyond the self to see the global implications? Obviously, this question is purely speculative, but it does function as a reminder that *Letters to Virginia Woolf* is not about What Woolf Would Do in a similar circumstance. *Letters to Virginia Woolf* is about how Lisa Williams interprets her world through a Woolfian lens, one that focuses more upon the private, merely referencing the public as a point of departure.

Williams's quest for personal edification continues throughout *Letters*, linking quotes from Woolf's novels, diaries and essays with her own experience with in vitro fertilization, motherhood, the death of her father, her forays into heterosexuality, her mother's post-divorce dating, and her own anorexia. For instance, in one letter, Williams conflates Septimus' shellshock after witnessing Evans' death with her remembrance of her brother's poster of the My Lai Massacre in relation to her miscarriages and a memory of her father's death: "What did it mean to be a survivor?" she wonders, as she recalls the images of the massacre (42). Interspersed with her anecdotes and Woolf's quotations is Williams's own poetry, primarily about her miscarriages, and poetic utterances such as the one delivered after the birth of Max: "I am no longer just a daughter, reliving the wounds of the past. I wade through those same streets of Queens, this time both mother and daughter simultaneously" (52). What Williams paints through her creative journeys is an internal canvas where Woolf and Max, Lily Briscoe and

Mrs. Ramsay, the massacred of My Lai and the victims of 9/11 are filaments in the fabric of her own life. For readers who view Woolf's life and work in the context of her feminism, *Letters to Virginia Woolf* may seem myopic, not examining the political ramifications of women's lives, especially when Williams translates Woolf's most socially critical works into the register of the apolitical. However, for those readers who are more engaged with Woolf's internal life and a writer's creative process towards self-discovery, *Letters to Virginia Woolf* offers a potential touchstone.

Mary Ann Caws's *To the Boathouse: A Memoir* and Lisa Williams's *Letters to Virginia Woolf* provide readers with disparate narratives of truth-telling about women's lives. Caws's memoir may focus on her personal story, yet it is a narrative that links her to other women and one that holds socio-political significance. Williams's text, on the other hand, initially references the socio-political, but withdraws wholly into the private. In the preface to *To the Boathouse*, Caws refers to her memoir as an "autofiction, as half-true as are all memoirs," and that at the very least it is "a meditation and a wondering" (xi). The best memoirs lure the reader into this place of reflection.

—June Elizabeth Dunn, *Southeastern Louisiana University*

Notes on Contributors

Erica G. Delsandro is a graduate student in English at Washington University in St. Louis where she is studying British modernism. In addition to her work on Woolf, she has published an article on Rainer Maria Rilke and modern poetry in *Soundings: An Interdisciplinary Journal* 88.1-2 (Spring/Summer 2005).

Renée Dickinson is an Assistant Professor of English at Radford University. She is currently working on the life and works of Olive Moore.

Jennie-Rebecca Falcetta is a doctoral candidate at the University of Connecticut and a 2006-2007 fellow of the University's Humanities Institute. Her work on Woolf grew out of a dissertation on modernist literary appropriation of the techniques and theories of avant-garde art. She has published previously on Thomas Mallory, Seamus Heaney, and the Marianne Moore-Joseph Cornell correspondence.

Jane Goldman is Senior Lecturer in English and American literature at the University of Dundee and a General Editor of the Cambridge University Press Edition of the Writings of Virginia Woolf. She is author of *The Cambridge Introduction to Virginia Woolf* (Cambridge UP, 2006), *Modernism, 1910-1945: Image to Apocalypse* (Palgrave, 2004), and *The Feminist Aesthetics of Virginia Woolf: Modernism, Post-Impressionism, and the Politics of the Visual* (Cambridge UP, 1998). She is editing Woolf's *To the Lighthouse* for Cambridge, and writing a book, *Virginia Woolf and the Signifying Dog*. In May 2007, Dr. Goldman will assume the post of Reader in English Literature at the University of Glasgow.

Emily M. Hinnov received her Ph.D. at the University of New Hampshire in 2005 and is now Assistant Professor of English and Women's Studies at Bowling Green State University, Firelands College in Huron, Ohio. She is currently revising a book manuscript based on her dissertation, *Choran Community: The Aesthetics of Encounter in Literary and Photographic Modernism*. Her most recent publication, "A Counter-reading to Conquest: 'Primitivism' and Utopian

Longing in Sylvia Townsend Warner's *Mr. Fortune's Maggot*," is included in *Critical Essays on Sylvia Townsend Warner, English Novelist 1893-1978*, Eds. Gill Davies, David Malcolm, and John Simons (Edwin Mellen Press, 2006). Emily is also writing on narratives of community as an approach to teaching literary modernism, specifically in the work of women writers of the Harlem Renaissance. Emily wishes to thank Freda Hauser for her kind and valuable advice in revising this essay; she is also particularly pleased to share these pages with long time friend and colleague Jennie-Rebecca Falcetta.

David Sherman is a Language Lecturer in the Expository Writing Program at New York University. His academic work focuses on narrative and ethics in Anglo-American modernism. He is currently working on a book manuscript, *Modernism and the Ethics of Time: The Event of the Other in Woolf, Faulkner, and Beckett*, which explores the ways that modernist narrative techniques open new ethical possibilities for the modern subject.

Eve Sorum is an assistant professor of English at the University of Massachusetts-Boston. She has published work on Virginia Woolf, T. S. Eliot, and Ford Madox Ford in the *Journal of Modern Literature* and *Modernism and Mourning*, edited by Patricia Rae. She is currently working on a manuscript that examines modernist literature in relation to twentieth-century cartographic and geographic discourses.

Policy

Woolf Studies Annual invites articles on the work and life of Virginia Woolf and her milieu. The Annual intends to represent the breadth and eclecticism of critical approaches to Woolf, and particularly welcomes new perspectives and contexts of inquiry. Articles discussing relations between Woolf and other writers and artists are also welcome.

Articles are sent for review anonymously to a member of the Editorial Board and at least one other reader. Manuscripts should not be under consideration elsewhere or have been previously published. Final decisions are made by the Editorial Board.

Preparation of Copy

1. Articles are typically between 25 and 30 pages, and do not exceed 8000 words.

2. A separate page should include the article's title, author's name, address, telephone & fax numbers, and e-mail address. The author's name and identifying references should not appear on the manuscript.

3. A photocopy of any illustrations should accompany the manuscript. (Black-and-white photographs or digital files will be required for accepted work.)

4. Manuscripts should be prepared according to most recent MLA style.

5. Three copies of the manuscript and an abstract of up to 150 words should be sent to: Mark Hussey, English Dept., Pace University, One Pace Plaza, New York NY 10038-1598. Only materials accompanied by a self-addressed, stamped envelope (or international reply coupon) will be returned.

6. Authors of accepted manuscripts will be asked to submit one hard copy and an electronic version. Authors are responsible for all necessary permissions fees.

Please address inquiries to: Mark Hussey, English Department, 41 Park Row Rm. 1510, New York, NY 10038. Email: mhussey@pace.edu
Fax: (212) 346-1754.

Introducing a New Title from Pace University Press

Virginia Woolf and Trauma
EMBODIED TEXTS

Edited by Suzette Henke & David Eberly

ISBN 0-944473-79-2 (paper)
March 2007 $30

A timely contribution to one of the most contentious areas in Woolf studies, Virginia Woolf and Trauma extends existing scholarship on both Woolf and narratives of trauma in provocative and challenging ways.

David Eberly & Suzette Henke: Introduction / **Patricia Morgne Cramer:** Trauma and Lesbian Returns in Virginia Woolf's The Voyage Out and The Years / **Toni McNaron**: The Uneasy Solace of Art: The Effect of Sexual Abuse on Virginia Woolf's Aesthetic / **Karen DeMeester**: Trauma, Post-Traumatic Stress Disorder, and Obstacles to Postwar Recovery in Mrs. Dalloway / **Jane Lilienfeld**: "Could They Tell One What They Knew?": Modes of Disclosure in To the Lighthouse / **Suzette Henke**: The Waves as Ontological Trauma Narrative: The Anxiety of a Death (Un)Foreseen / **Clifford E. Wulfman**: Woolf and the Discourse of Trauma: The Little Language of The Waves / **Patricia Moran**: Gunpowder Plots: Sexuality and Censorship in Woolf's Later Works / **David Eberly**: Face-to-Face: Trauma and Audience in Between the Acts / **Claire Kahane**: Of Snakes, Toads, and Duckweed: Traumatic Acts and Historical Actions in Between the Acts / **Holly Laird**: Reading "Virginia's Death": A (Post)Traumatic Narrative of Suicide / **Suzette Henke**: Afterword

To order, or for information about other titles available from Pace University Press, visit www.pace.edu/press, or call (212) 346 1405

"Lee's immensely enjoyable study will energize debate among thoughtful readers and should become essential reading for aficionados of literary biography."—*Publishers Weekly*

New in paperback
Virginia Woolf's Nose
Essays on Biography
HERMIONE LEE

By looking at stories about Percy Bysshe Shelley's shriveled, burnt heart found pressed between the pages of a book, Jane Austen's fainting spell, Samuel Pepys's lobsters, and the varied versions of Virginia Woolf's life and death, preeminent biographer Hermione Lee considers how biographers deal with and often utilize these missing body parts, myths, and contested data to "fill in the gaps" of a life story. *Virginia Woolf's Nose* is a witty, eloquent, and funny text by a renowned biographer whose sensitivity to the art of telling a story about a human life is unparalleled—and in creating it, Lee articulates and redefines the parameters of her craft.

"Lee's tales of the battles of the biographers are gripping and vivid.... The nose is a funny thing anyway; stick it on to 'Virginia Woolf' or any other of the illustrious names Lee discusses, and you are bound to bring them down a peg. All part of the biographer's power to make or unmake, sniff out or sniff at, which Lee so engagingly shows us."
—Rachel Bowlby, *Financial Times*

Paper $12.95 978-0-691-13044-6 Due April

Not available from Princeton in the Commonwealth, except Canada

PRINCETON University Press

800-777-4726
Read excerpts online
press.princeton.edu

www.ingramcontent.com/pod-product-compliance
Lightning Source LLC
Chambersburg PA
CBHW021823300426
44114CB00009BA/293